AF719404

LAW IN DIPLOMACY

OTHER BOOKS FROM
THE CENTER OF INTERNATIONAL STUDIES
PRINCETON UNIVERSITY

Gabriel A. Almond, *The Appeals of Communism*

Bernard C. Cohen, *The Political Process and Foreign Policy: The Making of the Japanese Peace Settlement*

W. W. Kaufmann, editor, *Military Policy and National Security*

Klaus Knorr, *The War Potential of Nations*

Lucian W. Pye, *Guerrilla Communism in Malaya*

Rolf Sannwald and Jacques Stohler, *Economic Integration: Theoretical Conditions and Consequences of European Unification*, translated by Herman F. Karreman

Charles De Visscher, *Theory and Reality in Public International Law*, translated by P. E. Corbett

Myron Weiner, *Party Politics in India*

LAW IN DIPLOMACY

BY PERCY E. CORBETT

PRINCETON, NEW JERSEY
PRINCETON UNIVERSITY PRESS
1959

Copyright © 1959 by Princeton University Press
ALL RIGHTS RESERVED

The Library of Congress catalog entry for
this book appears at the end of the text.

Percy E. Corbett, who has had a long and distinguished career as teacher, administrator, writer, and adviser in the field of international law, was formerly Research Associate at the Center of International Studies, Princeton University. He currently holds an appointment as Visiting Professor in the Indian School of International Studies at New Delhi. His most recent books include *Law and Society in the Relations of States*, 1951; *The Individual and World Society*, 1953; *The Study of International Law*, 1955; *Charles De Visscher, Theory and Reality in Public International Law*, Translation and Introduction, 1957.

Printed in the United States of America by
Princeton University Press, Princeton, New Jersey

ISBN 978-0-691-65265-8

FOREWORD

FROM the beginning of the modern international system, statesmen and diplomats have talked to each other about international legal principles, rights, and obligations as if they were carrying on their business inside a genuine legal order. They confront each other with elaborate juridical arguments and are concerned to justify their actions by frequent reference to universal norms.

Yet it is well known that several of the characteristics of a true legal system, as found at the national level, are missing from the international arena, or are present in very deficient forms. There is still not an effective global community in which all member-states submit to law and to collective monopoly of force. There is not a true legislative mechanism which can override minority opposition. Such judicial apparatus as exists is hemmed in by the need of voluntary submission of the parties and by the absence of specific sanctions. States insist on retaining their full sovereignty and independence in the face of all pleas that such a position makes the establishment of real international legal order virtually impossible. While their public declarations are generally in accord with the traditional rules of law, their actual foreign policies are often at odds with them.

In the face of these obvious deficiencies, what role do legal reasoning and legal rules play in the diplomacy of nations? It is to this question that Professor Corbett addresses his attention in the following pages. He brings to this task the experience and wisdom of a lifetime devoted to the study and practice of international law. His focus is the use of legal language, categories, and procedures in British, American, and Soviet diplomacy. He makes use of an abundance of examples—many of which make engrossing reading—in his efforts to discover the influence that legal notions have had upon foreign policy. All this is presented in a style that is far more luminous and graceful than one normally expects to find in books about international law.

This book is part of a continuing program of research in comparative politics and parties, carried out under the auspices of the Center of International Studies. The Center was established at Princeton University in 1951. Its basic purpose is to bring to bear on the elucidation of foreign policy problems the full resources of available knowledge and modern methods of analysis. To this end it engages in and publishes research directed toward the development of systematic, disciplined, and comprehensive appraisals of the varied aspects of international relations, with special emphasis on the foreign policy of the United States. The members of the Center work at all times in close association, but each member is free to formulate his research project in his own way and each published study represents an individual analysis of a problem.

FREDERICK S. DUNN
Director

Center of International Studies
Princeton University
October 1, 1958

PREFACE

A MOUNTING volume of criticism is being directed against the products of desire, imagination, and learning that have been presented to the world under such titles as *International Law* and *Law of Nations.* This literature has been characterized as generally confused or contradictory in content, remote from reality, and wastefully weak in its influence upon events. There is an insistent demand for new approaches to the role and potentialities of law in international affairs.

Defects in the traditional approaches have been attributed to obsession with system, excessive deference to the verbal communications of governments, and inadequate observation of practice—the whole leading to an intolerable strain between the codes so elaborated and the realities of world politics. It is argued that the high abstraction of these codes accounts in some measure for their failure to control the more serious aspects of policy.

The invocation of legal rules is a commonplace of diplomacy. Logically this practice implies the assertion of a legal system governing both the invoking and the addressed States. But the explicit and implicit reservations by which governments retain for the State the discretion to determine for itself the limits of its submission to law import a subjectivity that seems incompatible with the essential objective properties of a legal system. These reservations do not prevent those making them from dividing the world into law-abiding and law-breaking States and blaming the weaknesses of international law upon the latter.

This book proposes to study and in some degree measure the influence of legal notions on foreign policy without assuming or elaborating a system of international law. Its focus is the use of legal language, categories, and procedures in British, American, and Soviet diplomacy. I have chosen to start with the assumption that the international sphere, not being one where any over-all constitutional authority reigns, is not in principle a realm of law. I try to answer the questions to what purpose, with what implications, within what limits, and with what results the governments of Great Britain, the United States, and the Soviet Union, in such a milieu, invoke legal rules and employ legal procedures. Attention is given to the bearing upon this practice of new problems in world politics and new methods of dealing with them, and some attempt is made to assess factors making for rise or decline in the efficacy of legal modes of settling international disputes and serving common interests.

This is an introductory study, and it was necessary to limit its scope as narrowly as possible without losing an adequate range of interaction. The reasons for devoting special attention to the United States and the Soviet Union are obvious. Great Britain was joined with them partly because there is still more than the average likelihood that positions taken by British Governments in regard to legal procedures of settlement will have world-wide repercussions (witness the Suez imbroglio of 1956), and partly because of the intimate historical connection between British doctrine and practice and the developing views of the United States Government on the function and scope of law in international relations. It is the historical relationship that explains why the study begins with Great Britain. The fact that the Soviet Union occupies less of the text than either Great Britain or the United States is due to the recent date of its peculiar part in international legal intercourse. The difference is no reflection upon the skill or the importance of the Soviet use of legal argument in international relations.

ACKNOWLEDGMENTS

BERNARD COHEN, Gordon Craig, Frederick Dunn, Philip Jessup, and Oliver Lissitzyn all read this book in typescript and made criticisms and suggestions that are reflected in the text. To each of them I offer thanks for friendly interest, attentive labor, and good counsel. Allan Nevins kindly permitted me to quote in Chapter 5 from his *Hamilton Fish.* My obligation to the Center of International Studies and its long-suffering secretarial staff has always been beyond reckoning. Finally, I must record my appreciation of the skilled and tactful assistance of Mrs. Polly Hanford of Princeton University Press.

PERCY E. CORBETT

Center of International Studies
Princeton, New Jersey
September 1958

CONTENTS

ABBREVIATIONS

ADI Rec.—Académie de Droit International, *Recueil des Cours*

AJIL—*American Journal of International Law*

BYBIL—*British Year Book of International Law*

DSB—*Department of State Bulletin*

ESCOR—*Economic and Social Council Official Records*

GAOR—*United Nations General Assembly Official Records*

Hackworth, *Dig.*—Green H. Hackworth, *Digest of International Law*

ICJ—*International Court of Justice*

LNOJ—*League of Nations Official Journal*

Moore, *Dig.*—J. B. Moore, *Digest of International Law*

Opinions of the A. G.—*Official Opinions of the Attorneys General of the United States*

PCIJ—*Permanent Court of International Justice*

RIIA—*Royal Institute of International Affairs*

SCOR—*United Nations Security Council Official Records*

SGIP—*Sovetskoe Gosudarstvo i Pravo*

UNCIO—*United Nations Conference on International Organization*

UNYB—*Year Book of the United Nations*

U.S. and U.N.—*United States Participation in the United Nations*, an annual report by the President to the Congress

Wharton, *Dig.*—Francis Wharton, *Digest of International Law*

LAW IN DIPLOMACY

CHAPTER I

BRITAIN AND ITS LAW OF NATIONS

IT was inevitable that men speaking for groups internally governed by law should formulate relations between their groups in terms of law. Accustomed to dealing with their fellows within a framework of rules and casting their transactions in set forms, they could not easily conceive of human relations in a legal vacuum. Frequently they were lawyers or made their decisions in consultation with lawyers. There need not be in fact any body of rules commonly recognized as binding upon all the participating groups to sustain this legal style of communication. Practice varied. A spokesman might invoke legal principles familiar to him in his own community, with no suggestion of doubt as to their universal validity. He might appeal explicitly to some general system asserted or assumed to govern all parties to the business in hand. In the latter case, the system appealed to might be one municipal in its origin but now, like the Roman, so widely received as to be deemed "written reason," or it might consist of imperatives attributed to nature or to God or, again, of usages said to have become obligatory through long and widespread observance.

The habit, at any rate, seems as old as history. However primitive their institutions, however mingled their notions of law, religion, and magic, political communities in the earliest recorded ages are found assuming some universally valid norms for their external relations and transacting their business with one another in forms attributed to immemorial use and backed by human sanctions or invitations to divine intervention.

Relations between the Greek cities exhibit a measure of conformity with a considerable though loose-knit code of substantive rules and ceremonial procedure. Somewhat less code and less conformity are to be observed in the dealings of the Hellenes with the barbarian peoples.[1] Early Rome conducted its business with non-Roman communities more or less in harmony with rules and rites attributed to supernatural authority or to universal human practice and classified as *jus fetiale* or, later, as *jus gentium.* As time went on, the extension of a centralized imperial authority left little room for any conception of a distinct law governing States as such. But the notions of *jus naturale* and *jus gentium* as law common to all men flourished, and it was chiefly the practical development of these notions by the Roman jurists that was to inspire the scholars of the Renaissance in their elaboration of a law for princes.

In the long interval between the breakup of the Empire and the revival of learning, the potentates of Medieval Europe reached a stage where, like those of earlier centuries, they sought to fortify their mutual arrangements by the use of solemn written forms for truce and treaty, by oaths, by the exchange of hostages and pledge of property, and by the appointment of truce-keepers, treaty guarantors, and arbiters. Though the lore of *jus naturale et gentium* survived in the canonical literature, there are few traces of it in these transactions. References there are to *jus* and *injuria,* to *droit, équité,* and *bona fides,* but less explicit evidence here than in classical times of any image of a general human law to which ruling princes owed obedience.[2] Ernest Nys observed that "*L'exacte notion du droit international ne se rencontre pas dans les écrits des auteurs du moyen age proprement dit. . . enchevetré dans le droit naturel, il demeure confondu en même temps que lui dans le droit canonique et dans le droit romain.*"[3] Certainly we are far, in these royal and ducal docu-

[1] Cf. Coleman Philippson, *The International Law and Custom of Ancient Greece and Rome,* London, 1911, *passim.*

[2] Cf. Fritz Kern, *Kingship and Law in the Middle Ages* (Chrimer translation), Oxford, 1939, pp. 182 seq.

[3] *Les Origines du Droit International,* Brussels and Paris, 1894, p. 7.

ments, from any "exact notion" of international law as that is now understood.

What is more striking is the fact that it was not until late in the fifteenth century that the documents appeal to the *jus naturale* and *jus gentium* that were familiar to the churchmen.[4] Schwarzenberger, in the invaluable article just cited, talks confidently of international law as something operating in the period, yet emphasizes the absence of "generally accepted rules of international customary law," and the state of violent anarchy that obtained between princes and peoples where no treaty stipulated peace. He concedes that even maritime law, distinguished as it was by a long history of elaboration and compilation, was municipal in its basis of authority, though its rules tended to be shared by peoples actively engaged in international trade. What he calls "medieval international law" consisted, then, of treaties; but he is under no illusion that elaborate ritual and securities invested these with much of the stability usually associated with legal institutions. On the contrary, save where, as in the case of economic agreements, retaliation in kind was particularly ready to hand, the medieval treaty was set aside even more lightly than its modern equivalent.[5] The one concept of universal law supporting these transactions seems to have been that of the divine law invoked in the oaths taken by the parties, and, if this concept had ever been operatively present in the minds of the treaty-makers, it had already faded into a ghostly form with little observable influence on action. Only later, and then with no great access of stability to treaty relations, would it be supplemented in diplomatic intercourse by appeals to a general law established by consensus among peoples or deduced by reason from the nature of men and things.

With the revival of learning, the Roman law of the Pandects, called in England the "civil law" to distinguish it from

[4] Georg Schwarzenberger, "International Law in Early English Practice," BYBIL, vol. XXV, 1948, p. 88.

[5] *ibid.*, pp. 61, 87-88, 89-90.

the native common law, was more and more invoked in the foreign business of governments. This had been studied at Oxford and Cambridge, mainly as an essential introduction to the canon law, which was of course basically Roman. Even Henry VIII recognized the need of trained "civilians" in the conduct of diplomacy. In England, as in other Protestant countries, the Reformation brought with it a marked falling off in the teaching of canon law, and this meant neglect also of the civil.[6] It was to counteract this tendency that Henry founded the Regius Chairs of Civil Law at Oxford and Cambridge. But the subject was still in peril in the reign of his minor son, Edward VI. A letter of the Duke of Somerset, Protector, written in 1594 to Bishop Ridley, one of the Visitors to the University of Cambridge, is eloquent testimony to the dependence of governments on the language and forms of law in their mutual intercourse, and of the extent to which Roman law had to be drawn upon for the necessary terminology, principles, and categories. This, after all, was the law most familiar to the largest number of participants in the international relations of the period. "We are sure," wrote the Protector, "you are not ignorant how necessary a study that study of civil law is to all treaties with foreign princes and strangers, and how few there be at present to do the King's Majesty service therein. . . . Marry, necessity compelleth us to maintain the science."[7]

[6] See Robert Phillimore, *Commentaries upon International Law*, London, 1854-1857, preface to the first edition, pp. xxx, seq., and Sir William Searle Holdsworth, *A History of English Law*, London, 1922, vol. IV, pp. 232-233 and vol. V, p. 44.

[7] The letter is quoted in Phillimore, *loc.cit.*, and also in Holdsworth, *op.cit.*, vol. IV, p. 233. James I or a secretary must have perused it before the speech to the Lords and Commons on March 21, 1609, just sixty years later, when James said, "It is trew, that I doe greatly esteem the Civill Law, the profession thereof seeming more for general learning and being most necessary for matters of Treatie with all forreine Nations; but I onely allow it to have course here, according to those limits of Jurisdiction, which the Common Law itself doeth allow it: . . . As the Ecclesiastical Courts, the Court of Admiraltie, Court of Requests, and such like." See *The Political Works of James I*, ed. C. H. McIlwain, Harvard University Press, 1918, p. 310.

None knew better than the Tudors the frailty of this legal framework; but fashion had come to demand that sovereigns formulate their relations as if all were subject to one law, however vaguely conceived. Agreements, patterns of practice, and tentative rules would be broken; but the legal formulas were also useful for stating the resulting complaints and claims. Arguments would indeed descend from the high legal plane and end more frequently in arms than in arbitration. Yet, where the stakes were not high, the advice of counsel or the finding of an *ad hoc* commission might dispose of an issue without recourse to violence. Finally, if war came, it was convenient that there should be rules of the game for the "trial by battle."

The Roman law texts not only furnished a sort of legal *lingua franca* understood throughout Europe,[8] they also contained the lore of *jus naturale* and *jus gentium*, which the Roman jurists themselves had regarded as a fund of principles universal in their acceptance and validity. *Jus gentium* was not law specifically designed for the regulation of business between independent political units. It represented for the Romans the institutions common to different bodies of civil law and so valid for men everywhere without distinction of political allegiance. It was usually identified with *jus naturale*, for common adoption was evidence that it was dictated by the nature of things. Being thought universal, it was adopted by Renaissance scholars as peculiarly suitable for the mutual dealings of princes, since in this context no merely municipal system could be accepted as binding on all parties. The step from this to special applicability to political collectivities as distinct entities was not a long one, and by 1612 we find Suarez, in his *Tractatus de legibus ac Deo legislatore*,[9] distinguishing clearly between the *jus gentium* of common legal

[8] "Celui qui écoute le langage du droit romain entend à vrai dire le langage de toutes les nations." Bynkershoek, quoted in William Senior, *Doctors Commons and the Court of Admiralty*, London, 1922, p. 12n.

[9] Book 2, chaps. vi, xvii, xix, and xx.

institutions and the *jus gentium* governing transactions between peoples.

Before Suarez, however (and before Richard Zouche, the Englishman who adopted his distinction and consolidated the notion of *jus inter gentes*), *jus gentium*, translated as "law of nations," was furnishing a bridge between the *a priori* doctrines of the civilians and the gropings of the common lawyers towards a universally valid body of practice and procedure. This law of nations, as the body of institutions common to civilized peoples, was theoretically a matter of observation, of watching how things were done in various places, in other words, of gathering precedents; and this, for the common lawyer, was the normal way of discovering the law. True, the common lawyer was not above resting his case on principle when precedents proved hard to come by, and the time was not far distant when "law of nature" would come easily off his tongue. But his confident reliance was upon established practice and past decisions. In England even the civilians were inevitably swayed by this tradition. It was the seventeenth-century English civilian Zouche whose emphasis upon practice earned him the title of first of the positivists.

Elizabeth and the law of nations

In Elizabeth's reign, the legal style was becoming prominent in the language of English diplomacy. Matters of high import to the nation were the subject of legal debate and conference with foreign governments, or were referred to jurists for advice and formulation. Among such matters were the validity of treaties, the liberty to navigate, fish, and trade in maritime waters, relations between belligerents and neutrals, the position of princes in foreign territory, and the immunities of diplomatic agents. The time was well before the publication of Huig de Groot's *De jure belli ac pacis*, and a study of actual communications touching these questions in comparison with similar interchanges in the seventeenth century reveals the exaggeration in the traditional estimate of the great Dutchman's work. No doubt Grotius provided the diplomats of the seventeenth century with formidable intellectual authority for claims supported by his writings. Governments pushing opposing claims often felt it necessary to buy counterarguments. This unquestionably stimulated the elaboration of legal principles suitable for invocation in the relations of States. But the same process can be shown in active operation in the time of Elizabeth. Grotius' compendium of precept, myth, and ancient practice was not there to be used; but the jurists did tolerably well with the more scattered pickings from other pundits. Both for domestic and for foreign effect, legitimacy was already a *desideratum* in governmental action and, after as before the appearance of *De jure belli ac pacis*, the "law of nations" was less a code of rules for observation than a supply of materials from which a clothing of legitimacy could be fashioned for State claims.

There was much in the Queen's character to encourage the diplomacy of legal debate. A. L. Rowse's description has the ring of authenticity. "She did not like war. . . . She wanted peace. She was a pacific, humane woman to whom compromise was the essence of her subtle, difficult, precariously poised nature."[10] Her insistence upon discussion, her disputatiousness, the constant, parsimonious care for her own and the nation's resources that made expensively decisive action distasteful to her, have been amply attested by contemporaries and subsequent historians. Raleigh put the matter in a nutshell: ". . . if the late Queen would have believed her men of war as she did her scribes, we had in her time beaten that great empire (Spain) to pieces. . . ."[11] These were qualities disposing her to make the most of any kind of legal case against a foreign opponent. Certainly she and her counsellors were as adept at finding their way out of an embarrassing obligation as in establishing the obligations of others. Her allies, the United Es-

[10] *The Expansion of Elizabethan England*, London, 1955, p. 303.
[11] Quoted Rowse, *op.cit.*, p. 362.

tates of the Netherlands, were among those who found this out to their cost.

In 1585 Elizabeth had agreed to supply the Estates with foot and horse, paid from her treasury, to assist in the war with Spain. Within ten years she was finding the burden troublesome, and asked to be relieved from further payment of the troops and to be repaid immediately, rather than at the end of hostilities, part of what she had laid out. The Dutch were willing to go some way to meet these demands, but, when the Queen asked more, took their stand on the original agreement, which called for reimbursement only after the war.

Richard Zouche tells the story.[12] On the opinions of jurists and statesmen, he recounts, the Queen took the position that every convention, even though sworn, was understood as binding only while things remained in the same condition. England had been exhausted in men and wealth by long war, and princes were not bound by their contracts when performance would mean injury to their own people. This kind of reasoning was evolving in the hard school of practice; it did not have to wait for Pufendorf's teaching[13] that treaties of alliance and guarantee must not be relied upon when observance would run counter to the promissor's interest. The same arguments would be used two hundred years later by Alexander Hamilton to justify American neutrality notwithstanding the 1778 alliance with France,[14] and again—so constant are the mainsprings of national action—by President Franklin D. Roosevelt when, in August 1941, the United States being still a nonbelligerent, the Load Line Convention of 1930 impeded supplies to the Powers allied against Germany.

Elizabeth had propounded with her accustomed sharpness what came much later to be known as the doctrine of *rebus sic stantibus*. Her ambassador, Thomas Bodley, prevailed upon

[12] *Juris et judicii fecialis, sive juris inter gentes et questionum de eodem explicatio*, Oxford, 1650, Brierly translation, Carnegie Institution of Washington, 1911, p. 102.

[13] *De jure naturae et gentium*, book VII, chap. vi, sec. 14.

[14] "Pacificus," no. 3, *The Works of Alexander Hamilton*, Lodge edn., New York, 1904, vol. IV.

the Estates to release her from further expense on the auxiliaries and to pay off their debt in annual instalments of £20,000. Zouche, however, is under no illusion that it was the force of the legal argument that bore down the Dutch resistance. He explains Bodley's success by the Estates' fear of provoking the anger of so puissant a Princess.

Robert Cecil followed his father as Chief Minister. He was probably reflecting two generations of statesmanship when in the Queen's last year he set down his judgment on the covenants of princes. The dictum of this man of great affairs justified that of Pufendorf, scholar and theorist. No solemnity could preserve treaties against shifts in their authors' interests. Always there was the excuse of public duty overriding private conscience.[15] No exception in favor of his own sovereign was needed. The gap between individual morals and reason of State was already a recognized convenience for embarrassed governments.

Law of the sea

Of all topics of legal argumentation between English and other sovereigns in the sixteenth and seventeenth centuries, the most actively debated was the claim to dominion over large areas of sea. The busy controversy over *mare clausum* and *mare liberum* had a unique part in stimulating the formulation of general theory and specific principles for a distinct law defining the rights and duties of States *inter se*. Much of the growing literature on the subject was commissioned writing done at the bidding of governments always anxious to fortify their claims with moral and legal doctrine.

The literary polemic had not got under way when Elizabeth began laying down the law of the matter. Spain was protesting Drake's depredations in the Indies, and the Queen's tart reply insisted that the harassed Spaniards had no one but themselves to blame. They had no title to exclusive navigation, commerce, or colonization. The sea was common by

[15] Cf. Rowse, *op.cit.*, p. 331.

the law of nations, and only effective possession could support prescriptive claims. The pope was not lord of the world and his donation was not a valid grant. Merely touching here and there along a coast and naming a few capes and rivers was no possession. To attempt a monopoly without title was to invite violence.[16]

In 1602 Elizabeth sent commissioners to Bremen to negotiate with Denmark about British fishing. As the Stuarts had been doing in the sea about Scotland and would later do in all the ill-defined "British seas," the King of Denmark claimed dominion, and with it the exclusive right of fishing, not only in the Baltic and its approaches but in all the waters between Norway on the one side and Iceland and Greenland on the other. The instructions that Elizabeth's envoys carried were an essay on the law of nations. Disregarding extravagant assertions of sovereignty in the "sea of England" by a long line of predecessors, Elizabeth would have none of this Danish maritime dominion.

"And you shall further declare," she commanded her commissioners, "that the Lawe of Nations alloweth of fishing in the sea every where; as also of using Ports and Coasts of Princes in Amitie for Traffique and avoiding danger of Tempests; so that if our Men be barred thereof, it should be by some contract. . . .

"And for the asking of Licence, if our Predecessors yelded thereunto, it was more than by Lawe of Nations was due; —yelded, perhaps, upon some special Consideration, yet growing out of use it remained due by the Law of Nations, what was otherwise due before all Contract; . . ."

In this instance, the Queen would not insist upon the full measure of her right. If her "good brother the king" for some special reason desired to renew some licensing or to reserve some special place for his particular use, the commissioners

[16] William Camden, *History of Elizabeth*, 3rd edn., London, 1675, p. 255; and see Edward P. Cheyney, "International Law under Queen Elizabeth," *The English Historical Review*, vol. 20, 1905, pp. 659-672.

might concede this, provided it did not substantially prejudice her subjects' fishing.

As for any property in the sea between Norway and Iceland because Denmark had dominion on both sides, this would have the intolerable consequence that "by like reason, the half of every sea should be appropriated to the next bank, as it hapneth in small rivers, where the banks are proper to divers men; whereby it would follow that noe sea were common, the banks on every side being in the propertie of one or other." Here was a repudiation in no uncertain terms of the middle-line doctrine that had long figured in the jurisprudence of northern Europe and that even English jurists of that and later times would still invoke on occasion.[17]

Elizabeth's own claim to maritime jurisdiction, as set forth in the same document, was much more modest than would satisfy her successors for more than a century to come. It gave some trouble to Selden, who in his *Mare clausum* (1635), 1,2,c.24 tried to explain it away as an archaism or special pleading designed for the Danes. It was in these terms: ". . . though Propertie of Sea, in some small distance from the Coast, maie yeild some Oversight and Jurisdiction, yet use not Princes to forbid Passage or Fishing, as is well seen in our Seas of England, and Ireland, and in the Adriaticke Sea of the Venetians, where We in ours, and they in theirs, have Properite of Command; and yet neither We in ours, nor they in theirs, offer to forbid Fishing, much lesse Passage to Ships of Merchandize; the which, by Law of Nations cannot be forbidden ordinarilie. . . ."[18]

Scotland, an awkward exception, is not mentioned, and it may be noted that this legal brief passes over in silence the Venetian practice of taking tribute for navigation in the Adriatic. The whole truth is not told even of England; for, though no restrictions or tolls had been imposed on navigation or fishing in the "sea of England," naval officers even in Eliza-

[17] A. Raestad, *La Mer Territoriale*, Paris, 1913, pp. 32-36.

[18] Thomas Rymer, *Foedera, Conventiones*, etc., vol. XVI, pp. 433-434.

beth's reign were forcing foreign ships, encountered anywhere between Britain and the continent, to strike their flags and lower topsails—an assertion of sovereignty that often resulted in impediments to navigation, damage to property, and loss of life.

Civil law, so often invoked in international business at this period, is not mentioned in these instructions, despite the fact that one of the commissioners was Daniel Dun, Doctor of Civil Law and Master of Requests.[19] The Queen's advisers well knew that, though Justinian's *Corpus juris* declared the sea common, Italian civilians, led by so great an authority as Bartolus of Sassoferrato, asserted jurisdiction to distances of one hundred miles seaward. Alberico Gentili, Regius Professor of Civil Law at Oxford, was in the tradition when he argued in the High Court of Admiralty that England's jurisdiction and responsibility reached to one hundred miles from her shores.[20] One hundred miles around Iceland and Norway would have given the Danish King far too much of what he wanted. The case for England rested on a law of nations, "growing out of use." As we have seen, it was not too strong at that.

Prize Law

The laws, treaties, and customs invoked in the adjudication of prize can be traced far back beyond the reign of Elizabeth to early recognition of the need to distinguish, however subtly, between privateering and piracy. Until privateering was declared abolished in the Declaration of Paris, 1856, it was not unusual for States to depend more for their strength in sea warfare upon profit-seeking private vessels than upon a formal, State-owned navy. The conditions under which these operated were a matter of municipal law, but by the end of the thirteenth century international treaties had begun to be made limiting their scope in terms of shipping open to attack and

[19] *ibid.*, p. 429.
[20] *Hispanicae advocationis libri duo*, book 1, chap. viii.

cargoes subject to capture.[21] These treaties and the national lists of seizable goods that began to be published under Elizabeth[22] constitute the first stages in the development of the shifting body of practice that now passes under the somewhat euphemistic name "law of contraband."

The chief things distinguishing the privateer from the pirate were an official commission or license, often in the form of letters of marque or reprisal, and the security given not to "spoil" friendly shipping and in general to abide by governmental instructions. Such efforts at control were anything but uniformly successful, and accusations of piracy shuttled back and forth between belligerents and between belligerents and neutrals. Courts of prize had the double function of seeing that municipal laws and instructions (including those fixing the shares of profit due to the sovereign or his deputies, to owners, victuallers, commanders, and crew) were obeyed, and of ordering ships and goods restored where capture violated agreements with foreign States.

Complaints by foreign merchants of unlawful seizure of ships and cargoes by English mariners were being made to the Crown in the fourteenth century. The importance of commercial interchange in general, plus the government's interest in maintaining treaties restricting neutral aid to enemies, won consideration for these pleas. They were referred for examination to the King's Council, to the Chancellor, or to special commissions. The common law and its courts, with their territorial and other limitations, were ill adapted to the adjudication of such cases, though the common-law judges long continued to assert their right to hear them. By 1360 some of them were being referred to the Admiral's court. From that time on, the commissions of admirals included judicial powers, to be exercised *secundum legem maritimam.*[23]

[21] Marsden, "Early Prize Jurisdiction and Prize Law in England," *English Historical Review*, vol. XXIV, 1909, pp. 678-679.

[22] Cheyney, *op.cit.*, p. 663.

[23] Marsden, *op.cit.*, p. 680.

Two hundred years had to pass, however, before the High Court of Admiralty established beyond dispute its jurisdiction in prize. Even under Elizabeth, its place was sometimes taken by special commissions. The struggle with the common law courts was not quite over until 1616; but proclamations of 1589 and 1602 laid down the rule (sometimes overlooked) that no prize should be disposed of until the Judge in Admiralty had decided upon the legality of its capture and given order for its disposition.[24]

According to Sir Julius Caesar, Judge of the High Court of Admiralty under Elizabeth and James I, the law determining the fate of ships and cargoes in his tribunal was "the civil and maritime law, the truest and most indifferent judge between all nations."[25] Gentili, who argued many cases in admiralty at this time, was emphatically of the same opinion, adding a rider very similar to Dr. Caesar's, namely that foreigners readily submitted to this civil law, which was in a way a law of nations.[26] They had not, it seems, begun to think of the rules applied to international causes in admiralty as part of a distinct system, the law of nations, which, though it might draw its content from many sources, including ancient and modern municipal systems, had its own mode of formation and its own authority. That point seems to have been reached only in the following century, when Sir Leoline Jenkins, Judge in Admiralty and subsequently Secretary of State under Charles II, advised the King that to condemn a ship for the carriage of one parcel of enemy goods would not be "agreeable to the law of nations," and added, "by the law of nations I do not mean the Civil Imperial Law, but the generally received customs among the European governments which are most renowned for their justice, valour, and civility."[27] Jen-

[24] Marsden, *op.cit.*, p. 690; C. John Colombos, *The International Law of the Sea*, London, 1954, pp. 652-653.

[25] Marsden, *op.cit.*, p. 693.

[26] Below, p. 19.

[27] Holdsworth, *Some Makers of English Law*, Cambridge, 1938, p. 218, quoting Jenkins MSS, All Souls Library, no. 216.

kins' successor as admiralty judge, Sir Charles Hedges, declared that his Court was "as much obliged to observe the laws of nations as the Judges of the Courts of Westminster are bound to proceed according to the statutes and the common law."[28] The delay in reaching this clear-cut conception is all the more curious in that Elizabeth, in her series of acrimonious diplomatic controversies over captured ships and cargoes, always invoked the law of nations as ruling in such matters. True, she incidentally appealed to the civil law and the law of God, but the weight of her argument rested upon a law of nature and of nations manifested by immemorial practice "in all countries betwixt prynce and prynce, and country and country."[29]

What Elizabeth was asserting in these arguments with France, Denmark, Poland, the Hanse Towns, and the United Provinces was an unlimited right under the law of nations to stop "any kind of provision fitt for the maintenance of the king of Spayne for his wars against this realm, upon pain of confiscation of the same goodes and the shippes upon which they should be laden," and also to seize enemy goods even on neutral ships.[30] Her most constant allies were among the offenders. The Dutch complained that if they had to give up trading with Spain and the carriage of Spanish goods, poverty would compel them to make peace with that country.[31]

Some treaties there were imposing upon the parties a general obligation not to assist each other's enemies. But for the scope and vigor of their operations against trade with the enemy, the English had to rely upon a law of nations which, according to them, permitted a belligerent, independently of special agreement, to seize anything calculated to strengthen his foes. It is quite clear, too, that they intended to do the

[28] Colombos, *op.cit.*, pp. 10-11, quoting State Papers Dom., Nav. 1, October 22, 1689, from Marsden, *Documents relating to the law and custom of the sea*, vol. 2, p. 131.

[29] Cheyney, *op.cit.*, pp. 661-670.

[30] Cheyney, *op.cit.*, p. 662, quoting State Papers Dom. Eliz. ccxxv. 43.

[31] Marsden, *op.cit.*, p. 692.

calculating. For reasons of policy they might make concessions, especially where harshness might drive a neutral over to the enemy. When lenience was politic, they might, following some of the usages recommended in such compilations as the *Consolato del mare*, purchase rather than confiscate cargoes and pay freight on seized enemy goods. They might limit seizures to listed goods. But *they* made the lists. Their law of nations was one over whose content they exercised firm control.

Alberico Gentili

The use of law as a bludgeon for sovereign opponents was thus quite familiar in the English diplomacy of the sixteenth century. But this was not its only role. Elizabeth's government was also capable of shaping policy in deference to legal principle. Alberico Gentili, the Italian religious refugee who was lecturing in civil law at Oxford, became one of the most notable predecessors of Grotius as a result of his consultation in connection with the Mendoza case in 1584. Mendoza, Ambassador of Spain, was implicated in a plot against Elizabeth. Some of the Queen's Council would have imprisoned or even beheaded him. Along with Hotman, the French jurist who was also consulted, Gentili advised that mere expulsion would be more consistent with *jus gentium*, which gave special status and protection to diplomatic envoys. The advice was accepted. A year later, Gentili published a thin little volume under the title *De legationibus libri tres*. In 1588, having meanwhile been appointed Regius Professor of Civil Law at Oxford, he delivered a lecture on the laws of war, which was expanded into his justly famous *De jure belli.* Though a Protestant, he was subsequently thought worthy of employment by Spain as advocate of Spanish claims before the Court of Admiralty, and his work in that capacity provided the material for the posthumous *Hispanicae advocationis libri duo*, notes on problems of maritime law, rights of capture and confiscation, and prize procedure, raised in the course of his advocacy. England's contribution to the literature of international law had begun—in the work of an Italian trained in Roman law at the University of Perugia.

Gentili was irrevocably a civilian, steeped in the "written reason" of the *Corpus juris civilis*. When it was suggested that common lawyers might profitably be included among the judges hearing admiralty appeals, he was outspoken in his assertion of the superiority of the civil law in the business of the High Court of Admiralty. The judge there administered civil law, and anyone appointed to hear appeals from his decisions should be a master of that system. Foreigners would hold it an injustice to have their maritime interests adjudged by the common law, but would be happy to submit to the civil, *which was as it were a law of nations.*[32] An interesting sidelight here is that Gentili compares the quarrels of the common lawyers and civilians with those of the Sabinians and Proculeans at Rome, and warns that such bickerings would not make for the good administration of justice.[33] He goes on to argue that the civil law applicable in this context should not be regarded as foreign law. It had been adopted as part of the law of England and, though its roots were of course in the *Corpus juris* of Justinian, it was, as expounded by Gentili, a system adapted to the needs of a new time not only by the commentary of recent Romanists but by the observation of contemporary practice.

In his *De jure belli*, too, Gentili had proved himself no slavish follower of Justinian's texts. These, he pointed out in his Introduction, had little to offer on the laws of war, and recourse must be had to natural law. But for Gentili in this mood natural law was not to be discovered in the dogmas of moral and political philosophers and theologians. Though a *particula juris divini* and the basis of *jus gentium*, it manifested itself most authentically in the practice established by common consent among the nations. Like Francisco Vitoria

[32] My italics.

[33] *Hispanicae advocationis libri duo*, book I, chap. xxi.

(whose *Relectiones theologicae* he cites frequently in spite of his distrust of theologians), Gentili sought support for these views in the notion of a *societas orbis* where, as in the individual State, law and government lie in the will of the majority (book 1, chap. 1): *Imo ut rectio civitatis, & legis latio est penes civitatis majorem partem: ita orbis rectio est penes congregationem majoris partis orbis.*[34]

It cannot be claimed for Gentili that his works reveal any single, integrated theory of international law. The modern reader will find here much of the familiar confused rhetoric with which other writers of the sixteenth and seventeenth centuries tried to identify and at the same time distinguish *jus naturale*, *jus divinum*, and *jus gentium*. If there are brief glimpses of a world-society with its own law-making consensus, there is also the traditional attribution of at least equal authority to the words and acts of ancient heroes, the pronouncements of Greek and Latin poets and philosophers, and the writings of Roman jurists on matters that had nothing to do with the relations of States. Intimations of a fresh and independent outlook upon the world and a direct grasp of its problems are smothered in the still imperative paraphernalia of classical scholarship. It was not for one man to break from the genetic mold. The exaggerated impression of modernity made upon some of Gentili's admirers[35] is only to be explained by the less relieved scholasticism of some predecessors and followers.

Rights and rules of legation

It was no accident that the two formal treatises of Gentili should be devoted respectively to ambassadors and war. The problem of the justice and legality of war, being connected with the warrior's chance of salvation, had occupied the at-

[34] "Just as the government and legislation of the State belongs to the majority of its citizens, so the government of the world belongs to the congregation of its greater part."

[35] See, e.g., Holdsworth, *A History of English Law*, vol. v, pp. 53-54.

tention of churchmen from St. Augustine to Suarez; and the literature on the subject, starting from Roman-law texts and the philosophical works of Cicero, and concerned not only with the legality of war but with its legal modes and effects, had been swollen by the contributions of legal advisers to military commanders, such as Pierino Belli[36] and Balthazar Ayala.[37] In Gentili's century there had begun a rapid increase in the literature about the rights and rules of legation. For this too there was basic material in Roman law and ancient history; but the special access of interest at the time was undoubtedly due to the spreading institution of resident embassies. This new practice was in turn a response to the mounting tempo and complexity of international life in the age of discoveries, revival of learning, and religious reformation. Thus it came about that of the two main lines of development contributing to a body of general rules regulating the dealings of sovereigns, one was concerned with war, the other with the machinery and incidents of diplomatic intercourse.

Mendoza's case was far from being the only one of its kind that troubled the reign of Elizabeth. Fifteen years earlier, in 1569, the Queen had arrested and sent back to Flanders the emissary of the Duke of Alva on the formal ground that the Duke, not being a ruling prince, had no right of legation. She was detaining money intended for the payment of the Spanish forces in the Low Countries, and in the same year she kept the Spanish Ambassador, Don Guereau de Spes, confined to his house for six months because he had complained of this freezing of Spanish assets and had advised retaliatory measures. When, three years later, his attempts to raise a Catholic rebellion under the Duke of Norfolk and to place Mary Queen of Scots on the throne were checkmated, Elizabeth ordered him home.[38]

[36] *De re militari.*

[37] *De jure et officiis bellicis, et disciplina militari libri III*, 1582.

[38] E. R. Adair, *The Exterritoriality of Ambassadors in the Sixteenth and Seventeenth Centuries*, London, 1929, pp. 46-47.

In 1571 occurred the *cause célèbre* of the Bishop of Ross. This prelate was in London pleading and intriguing for the release of Mary Queen of Scots. Arrested for his part in the Duke of Norfolk's plot, he was brought before the Council, where he stoutly defended his immunity as Mary's ambassador, admitted in that capacity to the Kingdom, and given safe conduct. The five civilians consulted joined in the opinion that "an Embassador procuringe an Insurrection or Rebellion in the Prince's Cowntrey towards whome he is Embassador, ought not, *Jure Gentium et Civili Romanor*, to enjoy the Previleges otherwise dew to an Embassador; but that he may notwithstandinge be ponished for the same." They also advised that the "Sollicitor of a Prince lawfully deposed, and an other being invested in his Place, cannot have the Previlegs of an Embassador; for that none but Prynces, and such other as have Soverayntye, may have Embassadors."[39] The Bishop was sent to the Tower; but eventually, though he had been one of the principals, and though Norfolk and others were executed, he got off with dismissal from the country.[40]

Thus, while the advice of the civilians differed in this case from that given by Gentili and Hotman in regard to Mendoza,[41] the government took the same action in both. Political practice, then as now, followed its own line of expediency. Even now the material of international law is relatively sparse and contradictory. Then, the jurists felt it necessary to draw the meager fragments together from the law, history, poetry, and philosophy of the Greeks, Hebrews, and Romans, up through the literature of the Church, to the decisions of contemporary dynasties. It was certainly, therefore, no less easy

[39] Burghley State Papers, 2, 18, reproduced in Lord McNair, *International Law Opinions, Cambridge University Press*, 1956, vol. 1, pp. 186-187.

[40] Camden, *History of Elizabeth*, vol. 2, p. 62.

[41] The difference may have been due to the length to which the conspiracy had gone. Gentili would not have advised immunity if Mendoza's plot had been carried into action, for, according to his view, it was at this point only that the law of nature and of nations recognized crime. *De legationibus*, book 2, chaps. xviii and xxi.

in that period than it is now for a government to get from its legal advisers any desired statement of the law. This has never meant that the legal formulation is useless. If expediency dictates a measure of severity less than the formulation allows, the government wins the moral advantage of calling attention to its generous leniency.

In regard to immunity from criminal jurisdiction, practice was certainly moving away from the views of the more conservative civilians. Continental writers before Gentili had drawn the most diverse views from the *Corpus juris* and ancient precedents. In 1548 the German Conrad Brunn had published a work which recognized a very general freedom from coercion for the well-behaved envoy, but denied him all privilege if he overstepped his mandate and indulged in conduct unworthy of his office.[42] Pierre Ayrault, writing thirty years later in France, based upon the same materials a thesis of complete extraterritoriality. However an ambassador might behave himself, the ultimate recourse was to send him home to be dealt with as his master saw fit.[43] In England, despite Gentili, the tendency among lawyers was to agree with Brunn.[44] As for civil immunity, the dominant juristic opinion both on the continent and in England allowed proceedings against an envoy on any contract made during his term of office.[45] It was only with Grotius that the thesis of broad civil and criminal immunity became dominant in the literature. Grotius attributed civilian arguments restricting diplomatic privilege to a misinterpretation of the Roman-law texts due to confusing the *legati* who represented Roman provinces with those representing independent peoples. It was the latter who had the chief claim to immunity.[46] Whatever the source of the doctrinal differences, practice was forging its own way.

[42] *De legationibus libri tres*, book IV, chap. i.

[43] *L'Ordre, Formalité et Instruction judiciare*, 1576, book I, part iv, secs. 13-15.

[44] See, e.g., Coke, *Institutes*, vol. 4, p. 153.

[45] Gentili, *op.cit.* book 2, chap. xv.

[46] *De jure belli ac pacis*, book 2, chap. xviii, sec. x.

If it ran ahead of doctrine in the matter of criminal immunity, it lagged behind in civil. Even in the eighteenth century, diplomats were arrested and detained for debt.[47] If this was not so in England, the difference was again due to a bit of special legislation enacted partly as a solatium to Peter the Great, who had been enraged by the arrest of his ambassador at the Court of St. James's and partly as a practical way of avoiding similar embarrassments in the future.[48]

The rules relating to the treatment of diplomatic missions have become one of the most regularly observed divisions of the so-called law of nations—perhaps, indeed, the closest approach to law in the relations of States. The reasons for this prosperous development have never been far to seek. Gentili pointed out[49] that the sovereign who violated the privileges of a foreign ambassador must anticipate quick retaliation in kind. The rules evolved because diplomatic missions, *ad hoc* or resident, were indispensable. They were fully developed before the safety of travel and the security of the foreigner had reached anything like their present level. It is debatable whether the degree of immunity eventually achieved is now either necessary or desirable, and there is a trace of irony in the fact that the law of nations should have reached its highest point of development in institutions which are more decorative than essential. But governments will probably continue to find agreement relatively easy on advantages that redound to the comfort and prestige of their emissaries. At any rate, there is little difference between the justification shrewdly argued by Chief Justice Sir Mathew Hale in the seventeenth century, and that stated by Secretary of State Cordell Hull in the twentieth.

"The truth is," wrote the Chief Justice,[50] "the business of embassadors is rather managed according to rules of prudence,

[47] Cf. Percy E. Corbett, *Law and Society in the Relations of States*, New York, 1951, p. 154.

[48] 7 Anne, c. 12, 1709.

[49] *op.cit.* book 2, chap. xii.

[50] *History of the Pleas of the Crown*, Serjeant Wilson edn., London, 1778, pp. 98-99.

and mutual concerns and temperaments among princes, where possible severe construction of an embassador's actions, and prosecution of them by one prince may at another time return to the like disadvantage of his own agents and embassadors; and therefore they are rather temperaments measured by political prudence and indulgence, than according to the strict rules of reason and justice. . . ."

When the Iranian Minister to the United States was arrested, handcuffed, and brought before a magistrate in Maryland on November 27, 1935, on a charge of violating traffic regulations, Mr. Hull issued the following by way of justifying the punishment of the police officers concerned and the official apology to the Iranian Government: "If we are to be in a position to demand proper treatment of our own representatives abroad, we must accord such treatment to foreign representatives in this country, and this Government has no intention of departing from its obligations under international law in this respect."[51]

The trial of Mary Queen of Scots

One of the great occasions in Elizabeth's reign for invoking such law as there was defining the rights of princes *inter se* was the trial of Mary Queen of Scots. Having abdicated and revoked her abdication, having been deposed, defeated, and replaced by her minor son, James VI, Mary had sought refuge in England. That was in 1568. In 1586, after eighteen years of custody and many intrigues for her liberation, still asserting title to the English Crown, she was brought to trial before a special Commission on charges of having conspired with Babington and others for the destruction of Elizabeth and her realm and the subversion of its religion. Confronting the Commissioners with dignity and courage, she demanded to know by what law she was to be tried, the civil or the canon.

[51] Quoted in Charles Cheney Hyde, *International Law Chiefly as Interpreted and Applied by the United States*, 2nd edn., Boston, 1947, vol. 2, pp. 1267-1268; cf. Hackworth, *Dig.*, vol. 4, pp. 515-516.

The Commission replied that it "would proceed neither by the Civil nor Canon Law, but by the Common Law of England." Neither Mary nor the Commission so much as mentioned a law of nations in this dialogue, and the only time the term appears in Camden's account of the actual proceedings is when Sir Christopher Hatton makes a flourish of it in urging Mary to appear for her trial. "You say you are a Queen: be it so: However in such a Crime as this the Royal Dignity itself is not exempted from Answering, neither by the Civil or Canon Law, nor by the Law of Nations, nor of Nature. For if such kind of Offenses might be committed without Punishment, all Justice would stagger, yea fall to the ground."[52]

In fact, despite her stubborn insistence that as a Queen she was not subject to English law, Mary was tried under the Statute of Elizabeth 27, c. 1, enacted only a year earlier, and aimed especially at conspiracies to overthrow Elizabeth, with the religion which she defended, and to put the Catholic Mary in her place.

In England there were many guilty or troubled consciences, and Mary's execution was the subject of much debate. One condemnatory line of argument was that since the law of nations gave inviolability to ambassadors, it *a fortiori* exempted princes from territorial jurisdiction. But, as we have seen, professional opinion differed on the extent and conditions of the envoy's immunity, and it was easy to answer that, whatever the privileges of ambassadors, there was no such immun-

[52] Camden, *op.cit.*, p. 352. There are, however, briefs, or "discourses" for the prosecution in C. P. vol. xx, *Calendar of Scottish Papers IX*, 112-116 and 127, Elizabeth, October 1586 (reprinted in *Trial of Mary Queen of Scots*, ed. A. Francis Steuart, London, 1951, pp. 104-131), which do rely on the "law of nations." In the first (p. 106) it is said that Princes are by that law "bound to receive distressed Princes into protection" and that, if such refugees were not subject to their protector's jurisdiction he would have by that law no protection against their conspiracies. The writer then, foreseeing the objection that as the *delictum* here was not consummated it was not punishable by death, shifts to "the positive laws" of England and argues that Mary's actions are to be "measured" by those laws, "in respect to her allegiance to the Crown of England."

ity for "Kings that shall attempt Mischief and Disturbance in another King's Dominions."[53]

James interceded for his mother in eloquent letters to Elizabeth. But, so far as Camden's account goes, he invoked only the law of God.[54]

The French King sent a special ambassador, M. Pompon de Bellieure, who "having got access to the Queen in company with L'Aubespine à Chateau-neuf the Ordinary Embassadour," argued that "an absolute Prince was not to be called in Question." Special reasons were also urged for mercy, in view of the fact that Mary had come to England as a suppliant and had been unjustly detained. The plea was fortified, in the style of the time, with a citation of Cicero and a reference to King Porsenna's treatment of Mucius Scaevola. But here again is no mention of law of nature or of nations. Elizabeth answered with a detailed rebuttal, even to the point of rejecting the French interpretation of Cicero's text and the relevance of the legend of Porsenna. She included a sweeping generalization quite out of keeping with the advice she had received and followed two years earlier in the Mendoza affair. "No man," she averred, "was ignorant of that saying of the Lawyers, A man offending in another's Territory, and there found, is punished in the place of his Offence, without regard of his Dignity, Honour or Privilege."[55] Obviously, whatever truth there was in her elaborate expressions of doubt, grief, and reluctance in this terrible business, once she had made up her mind on the political expediences she was able to select with dogmatic certainty the law that they demanded.

Foreign policy and the legal consultant

We have seen Elizabeth taking counsel of individual or grouped civilians—Gentili and Hotman in regard to Mendoza, five advocates at Doctors' Commons when the Bishop

[53] Camden, *op.cit.*, p. 372.
[54] *ibid.*, pp. 373-374.
[55] *ibid.*, p. 376.

of Ross was tried, others again when legal briefs were wanted to justify the trial and conviction of Mary Queen of Scots. The practice continued under Elizabeth's successors. Doctors' Commons, the guild as it were of the civil lawyers, long provided most of the consultants, for here were the specialists in that Roman brand of jurisprudence which was the common heritage of Europe. But practitioners of the common law, barristers and judges, were also called in from time to time to add their weight to a case or to join with civilians on commissions appointed *ad hoc* to decide points at issue. It was by order of Charles I that the common lawyer John Selden published under the title *Mare clausum* the most famous of the counterblasts to Grotius' *Mare liberum.* When Don Pantaleo de Sa, brother of the Portuguese Ambassador, was arrested for murder, the special commission to which Cromwell submitted the debatable question of diplomatic privilege included common-law judges in addition to Richard Zouche and other civilians.

All the Stuarts tapped these sources for arguments to support their outrageous claims to sovereignty in the elastic "English sea," and the jurists rarely failed to meet the royal demand. They were, after all, advocates, and as such ready to make the best even of a bad case. But the other concept of the lawyer's function—that of keeping his client to a course in conformity with what he holds to be the law—was also present. The famous Sir Leoline Jenkins could prepare a brief upholding the Crown's right to compel the whole Dutch fleet to strike to a single British man-of-war met anywhere between the British Isles and the continent. But he could also oppose confiscation of neutral goods taken on Dutch ships before a declaration of war, and get his way by threatening to resign from the King's Council.[56]

In the eighteenth century there continued to be some variety in the choice of consultants, but reports by the King's Advocate alone became increasingly prominent. This was "the

[56] Below, pp. 113, 115.

principal law officer of His Majesty in the College of Advocates at Doctors' Commons and in the Admiralty and Ecclesiastical Courts,"[57] and an excellent illustration of his function and attitude is to be found in three reports made by holders of the office between 1740 and 1817.[58]

The first report is by George Paul, who was appointed King's Advocate in 1727. It is addressed to the question whether a British naval officer had trespassed on Portuguese jurisdiction when he took deserters from his man-of-war off an English merchantman in the River of Lisbon. Paul's advice was to the effect that "An English man of war's Commanding Officer in a Neuter Port, by the general Laws of Nations, has no authority, or coercive jurisdiction beyond the limits of his floating castle, . . ."

The second report is by John Nicholl, who came to the office in 1798. It has to do with the impressment of British seamen in a neutral port and, though less decisively stated, the opinion is again restrictive of British practice. Impressment being "an Act of Force and violence which may disturb the Peace of the Port, and its commerce, the Foreign State may have a just right to prohibit it."

The third is by Christopher Robinson, appointed in 1809, and it declares that the arrest of a deserter by a British officer at New Orleans could not be justified. ". . . the Act of detaining the man by British Authority within the American Port was a violation of Territory. . . ."

These three documents show the legal adviser in his role of disinterested counsellor impartially examining a situation in which British interests, important enough to figure among the causes of wars, were at stake. In each case the British Government was receiving instructions as to the limit within which executive action should be kept. Its view as to the appropriate norm of international conduct was being given a

[57] *Encyclopaedia of the Laws of England*, 2nd edn., London, 1906, vol. 1, pp. 225-226.

[58] Lord McNair, *International Law Opinions*, vol. 1, pp. 74-76.

shape that, in deference to rights said to be conferred by the law of nations upon another State, forbade a specific use of available power for British purposes.

The temper of the request for advice in such cases is especially significant, and a report of 1852 is worth notice on this account. The French Government had complained that the appointment by a British court of a commission to examine witnesses in France was a violation of international law. The Attorney General and the Solicitor General were associated with the King's Advocate in this instance, and the three joined in sustaining the action taken. They pointed out that such commissions, which had been in use for more than a century "throughout the civilized world," arrogated no authority abroad. They did not attempt to compel the attendance of witnesses and obtained information only in the measure that nationals of the country were willing to give it. This is so elementary that one shares the surprise of the Law Officers that the question should have been raised. The interesting point is the Law Officer's view of what they had been asked to do. They were "to report . . . whether the course which has been followed by the Court of Exchequer is contrary to international law, and if not, what arguments should be used by Her Majesty's Government to prove that the French Government have no just ground of complaint."[59] Here, as in many other matters so referred, the Government apparently stood ready to accept and act upon a finding that one of its agencies had overstepped the limits of national authority and encroached upon the exclusive jurisdiction of a foreign State.

Upon occasion, however, what is desired is a brief, and the advisers are not proof against the temptations of special pleading. A case in point is the famous reply of 1753 to the memorial from Frederick the Great justifying his seizure of funds hypothecated to the service of the Silesian loan. England and France being at war and Prussia neutral, British privateers had captured and brought in for adjudication Prussian

[59] McNair, *op.cit.*, vol. 1, p. 71.

ships carrying French cargo. It was another of the frequent clashes between the continental doctrine of "free ships, free goods" and the British practice of taking enemy goods, whether contraband or not, regardless of the flag under which they moved. Frederick claimed the right to use the hypothecated funds for compensation to his injured subjects.

No less than fifty-one vessels owned or chartered by Prussians had been detained; but an even greater interest at stake was the principle of a mode of belligerent pressure to which Britain was to cling *contra mundum* for another hundred years. The array of authority called in to answer Frederick's *pro-memoria* was suited to the occasion. Leading it was the Dean of the Arches, that is to say the judge of the ecclesiastical Arches Court of Canterbury who was also president of the College of Advocates.[60] His colleagues were the King's Advocate, the Attorney General and the Solicitor General. The last two were common lawyers, the Solicitor General being none other than William Murray, afterwards Lord Mansfield, who is still accounted one of the greatest of English judges.

None of these eminent counsel acknowledged anything in the law of nations to invalidate the British seizures or to justify the King of Prussia's counterstroke. They treated as quite beyond question the right to seize enemy goods, regardless of their nature, on neutral ships; and they would not admit that the circumstances justified Prussian reprisals, insisting that the right of reprisal arose solely from violent wrong or denial of justice. The partisan character of their argument is apparent in the light dismissal of a verbal statement by Lord Carteret that had been taken by Frederick's Government as an assurance of freedom for noncontraband French goods on Prussian ships.[61]

[60] Halsbury, *The Laws of England*, vol. XI, London, 1910, pp. 508-510.

[61] The Pro-Memoria and Reply are reproduced in full, with some comment and the observation that the case was one suitable for arbitration, in Sir Ernest Mason Satow, *The Silesian Loan and Frederick the Great*, Oxford, 1915, pp. 42-111.

In the early nineteenth century the signature most frequently found under legal advice addressed to the Secretary of State for Foreign Affairs is that of the King's Advocate. A description of the practice under Victoria prior to 1876 informs us that "cases which were not of the first importance were submitted to the Queen's Advocate, or, if they were more important, to the Law Officers and the Queen's Advocate in association."[62] But the office of Queen's or King's Advocate has been vacant since the resignation of Sir Travers Twiss in 1872,[63] and in 1876 much of the business that had formerly gone to him was taken into the Foreign Office itself with the appointment of a Legal Assistant Secretary.[64]

These functions are now performed by the Legal Adviser to the Foreign Office, whose rank is assimilated to that of Deputy Under-Secretary, and whose department in the Foreign Office has waxed in numbers and importance with the growing complexity of international affairs and the expansion of international organizations since the first world war. A corresponding growth has occurred not only in the United States and in Russia but in all countries actively concerned in world politics. Commenting upon this development, a recent writer on the Foreign Office, himself a British diplomat, observes: "In many foreign countries all candidates for the diplomatic and consular careers are required to possess legal degrees of one kind or another. With us it is not so. . . ."[65] Neither is it so, we may add, in the United States or the Soviet Union. The difference, however, is attributable to variation in the prominence of legal education as general preparation for public service—a prominence due at least in part to the attention given to economics and politics in the curricula of the law schools—rather than to greater or less use of the legal arts in the conduct of foreign policy.

[62] Tilley and Gaselee, *The Foreign Office*, London, 1933, p. 115.
[63] Halsbury, *loc.cit.*
[64] Tilley and Gaselee, *loc.cit.*
[65] Lord Strang, *The Foreign Office*, London, 1945, p. 159.

The records of consultation make it clear that it was an important function of the law officers, as it is now of the legal advisers attached to the Foreign Office, to make out the best possible case for action which the government has taken or decided to take. Like any lawyer, they must at times do this in conflicts where they personally consider that the weight of authority and the balance of justice is against the national position. Nor should this be held against the profession. In the international as in the national field, the balance of authority and justice is often a delicate one, and the establishment of a clear and viable rule then demands that all relevant considerations on both sides should be meticulously marshalled and weighed. The advocate who does his utmost for his employer though he prefers the opposing case may be lending vital aid in the clarification and consolidation of an operative international code.

Yet the features which stand out most impressively in the collections of letters addressed to the Foreign Office by its legal consultants is the frequency with which action is suspended pending dispassionate enquiry into international usage and doctrine, and the evidence here and there that action eventually taken has been determined by the advice tendered.

As evidence of the influence of law on foreign policy the public pronouncements of statesmen and governments have been habitually overestimated in the literature of international law. But intragovernmental communications of the sort with which we are here concerned are a different matter. When the Law Officers of the Crown advise the British Foreign Office that "nations cannot rightfully decide for themselves, or each for itself, what is the law of nations,"[66] some notion of a society and law transcending the nation is being actually brought to bear upon policy. The statement is not remarkable for its profundity; for, if there is a law of nations, nothing can be more obvious than that its content cannot be determined inde-

[66] November 18, 1859, quoted in H. A. Smith, *Great Britain and the Law of Nations*, London, 1932-1935, vol. 1, p. 12.

pendently by each of the entities subject to it. Unfortunately, moreover, even so simple a proposition cannot be taken as reflecting constant British policy. Cases will be cited in these pages where British governments, like all the others with which we shall be concerned, have persisted in a course of action which could only be called legal on their own subjective and unilateral interpretation of international law.

If these intragovernmental suggestions do not connote general and operative subordination of the State to a supranational society and law, what do they amount to? They constitute advice in a specific case to accept some widely accepted version of an international norm or to defer to impartial decision. If the executive department of government sees no interest at stake more precious than compliance with the norm, it will follow the advice. Most governments recognize to some extent in practice, as all do unreservedly in words, the virtues of a generally observed body of rules. The predictability of legally ordered conduct is a widely appreciated value. But the discretion to determine for themselves the point where the long-term advantages of conformity shall give way to considerations of immediate political expediency is an incident of sovereignty that governments show small sign of relinquishing.

In their function as counsellors helping to determine foreign policy, or advocates trying to establish the legality of policy already determined, the legal advisers draw upon a body of norms which they treat as binding upon States. They know or soon learn from experience the limits within which such norms actually operate; but their office affords what is perhaps the greatest opportunity to assist in expanding the system and increasing its efficacy. Theirs is the first chance to perceive those convergences of law and politics that can be made the steppingstones towards an effective law of nations.[67] Meeting frequently, as they do in these days of permanent

[67] Cf. Charles De Visscher, *op.cit.*, pp. 10-13, 132-139, 176-178; Corbett translation, pp. xii-xiii, 101-107, 138-140.

conference, the legal staffs of the various foreign offices constitute an active agency in the evolution of common working principles. Whether it is a case of disposing of a specific claim of one State against another, of setting up by bilateral treaty regulations to govern activities of mutual concern, or of drafting a multilateral code, these officials have a hand in all stages of the business. Not a few of them bring to their work a conviction of mission to speed the coming of a universal legal community. If with this conviction they combine courage and a shrewd sense of the possible, they can exert steady pressure in that direction upon their governments.

Prudent governments have always deliberated before taking decisive action, and an adventurous one will despise established routine; but the internal reference to legal advisers which is now normal constitutes one of the more constant factors making for order and peaceful settlement in the relations of States.

It has restored, modernized, and expanded the legendary Roman use of the fetial college, and the loss of supernatural reinforcement has probably not made its influence any less strong than that of its ancient prototype. Even if they had no further result, standing arrangements for consultation impose a *spatium deliberandi* between stimulus and response, a cooling-off period in which the impulse to violence often loses its force. But it would be quite unrealistic to rate their effect so low. Certainly the British record shows that the officers to whom the Foreign Office has turned for legal advice have not merely delayed action; they have at times determined policy.[68]

With the independence of the United States and the ensuing emergence of the Latin-American nations, the advisers of the Foreign Office entered upon a most active and creative period of legal construction. Relations with these newly sover-

[68] See, for example, Smith, *Great Britain and the Law of Nations*, vol. 1, pp. 221, 269, 278-281, 319, 330-331; vol. 2, pp. 29, 165-166; and for a particularly interesting case, in addition to those already cited from the same collection, McNair, *op.cit.*, vol. 3, pp. 322-327.

eign political communities called for re-examination, clearer definition, and fresh adjustment of the British position in a multitude of questions touching vital interests of all the parties. The conditions justifying recognition of a new State over the opposition of the former sovereign; the establishment of colonial boundaries against the claims of expansive young nations all the way from Canada to Argentina; rights of trade in war and peace between these nations and the British colonies; freedom of navigation and commerce on the St. Lawrence, Mississippi, Amazon, and Plate; the shifting rules of contraband, blockade, and neutrality in general; British impressment practice in ports and on ships under the new flags; the vast accumulation of private claims arising out of personal injury and loss of property during and after the wars of independence—all these and many other occasions of conflict challenged the sagacity and patience of the British Government and the knowledge and skill of its law officers.

In relations with the United States the range of peaceful adjustment after elaborate legal argument was especially notable. Here was the source of the great revival and development of arbitration in the nineteenth century, facilitated by a common legal heritage and a shared tradition of submission to law. The wasteful and halfhearted War of 1812 stands as a reminder that even such favoring circumstances cannot ensure that rational modes of settlement will prevail between sovereign States against political clamor for dramatic action.

British diplomacy in other parts of the world during the same period provided reminders that the international sphere is not quite such a realm of law as the letters of the Law Officers to the Foreign Office might lead one to suppose. British diplomatic historians have been at no pains to conceal cases in which governmental notions of national interest have led to "discreditable" and even "cynical" violations of treaty obligations or the general rules of international conduct. For the bombardment of Copenhagen and seizure of the Danish fleet in 1808, and even for the retention of Malta in contravention of the Treaty of Amiens, they find some hesitant justification in the anxiety and insecurity of the whole period of the Napoleonic wars. Even so, they reveal the special frailty of established rules in the international domain. The lawbreaker invariably considers himself in a state of emergency, and a prime function of law is to control conduct under unusual pressure. And there was a dearth of extenuating circumstances when in 1842 the Cabinet, though it "disapproved" Ellenborough's annexation of Sind in flagrant breach of treaties with the Indian rulers, made no move to restore this ill-gotten gain.[69]

We shall find in the diplomacy of the United States no scarcity of such reminders that governments reared on the strongest legal traditions can be led by notions of national interest to turn a blind eye upon international obligations. Usually the relevant interest is more or less obscurely linked with self-preservation, which American statesmen have been no less ready than those of Europe to recognize as "the first duty of a nation." It is one of the paradoxes of diplomatic discourse that this proposition, with its corollary that the nation is sole judge as to whether its existence is threatened, normally occurs in close juxtaposition with devout acknowledgments of a society of nations governed by law.

The screen of official euphemism is thus common to the diplomacy of the United States and Great Britain. Under it, the persevering student may discover processes of interaction that in the last century and a half have fashioned some of the firmer patterns of international practice. It is to these interactions, which provide a truer measure of legal influences than can be found in official declarations, that we now turn.

[69] See *The Cambridge History of British Foreign Policy*, Cambridge University Press, 1922-1923, vol. 1, pp. 325, 363; vol. 2, p. 211; and *passim*. In his article, "Machiavelli in Modern Dress," *History*, vol. xx, no. 78, September 1935, pp. 97-115, Professor W. K. (now Sir Keith) Hancock takes his anti-Machiavellian colleagues to task for their confused and ambivalent judgment of these and similar episodes and somewhat rhetorically asks the question, "Dare we assert, even to-day, that States do in all their major transactions behave as members of a community under the rule of law?"

CHAPTER II

ENTER THE UNITED STATES

Acceptance of the European law of nations

FROM the beginnings of the national history, the Government of the United States showed more than the average tendency to discuss relations with other countries in terms of law. An extraordinary number of the early leaders were lawyers, some of them steeped in the thought of Grotius, Pufendorf, Bynkershoek and Vattel. It was therefore to be expected that, as the young nation struggled for survival in the violent crosscurrents of great-Power politics, natural law and the law of nations should become a commonplace of its diplomatic intercourse. Shrewd and practical as these fathers of the Republic were, and skillful as they became in playing off against one another the colonial ambitions of Britain, France, and Spain, they clearly counted heavily upon a well-knit legal argument larded with the philosophy of the Enlightenment. Their hardheadedness has been contrasted favorably with the optimistic legalism and moralism of a later generation of American statesmen; but their writings, public and private, reek with those very qualities.

The function of legal adviser on foreign affairs, performed in England by the King's Advocate acting alone or in company with the Attorney General and the Solicitor General, was appropriated in the United States by the Attorney General,[1] and the style and substance of his communications to the

[1] In 1887, to replace the previous Examiner of Claims, the Department of State got its own Solicitor, who became general adviser on legal matters to the Secretary of State. By 1909 he was issuing as many as 165 communications a week on "every phase of international law and diplomacy." The Solicitor's Office became in 1931 the Office of the Legal Adviser, with 21 assistants and 3 clerks. (Graham H. Stuart, *The Department of State*, New York, 1948, pp. 215, 295-296). One distinguished service rendered

Secretary of State closely resemble those of the Law Officers of the Crown to the Foreign Office.

Opinions of the Attorneys General

As early as June 26, 1792, we find the Honorable Edmund Randolph, First Attorney General of the United States, laying the foundation for regular consultation on the law of nations. He had been asked his views on the arrest of the domestic servant of Mr. Van Berckel, Minister of the Netherlands, and sent the diffident reply that "the mere going into the house and executing a precept will probably sustain a prosecution; but, at best, it would be esteemed *summum jus.*" His doubts were justified; the international rule on the point has not been quite clearly established yet. There is, on the other hand, no hesitation in the general proposition by which this passage is preceded. "The law of nations," says the first Attorney General, "although not specially adopted by the constitution or any municipal act, is essentially a part of the law of the land. Its obligation commences and runs with the existence of a nation, subject to modifications on some points of indifference. Indeed a people may regulate it so as to be binding upon the departments of their own government, in any form whatever; but with regard to foreigners, every change is at the peril of the nation which makes it."[2] The last clause, it may be noted, is substantially identical in effect with the observation that the British Law Officers thought it neces-

by the legal advisers under their successive titles has been the series of *International Law Digests*, begun by Frances Wharton and carried on by John Bassett Moore and Green Hackworth. The two advisers last mentioned became judges of the Permanent Court of International Justice and the International Court of Justice respectively. Other cases in which this kind of "promotion" has occurred are those of Sir Cecil Hurst for Great Britain, Henri Fromageot for France, and John Read for Canada. That the legal advisers of the foreign offices should move on to the principal international tribunal is a further demonstration of the importance of these officials in the development of legal patterns in the relations of States.

[2] *Opinions of the A. G.*, vol. 1, pp. 27-28.

sary to convey to the Foreign Office almost seventy years later: ". . . . Nations cannot rightfully decide for themselves, or each for itself, what is the law of nations. . . ."[3]

Alexander Hamilton was no visionary, but he thought it worth while to write elaborate tracts on the law of nations to justify action taken or contemplated by the Government. Arguing against the confiscation of private enemy property, in most learned defense of the property clauses of Jay's Treaty, he asserted in much the same terms as Randolph the congenital membership of the United States in the legal community of Europe: "Ever since we have been an independent nation we have appealed to and acted upon the modern law of nations as understood in Europe. . . . It is indubitable, that the customary law of European nations is a part of the common law, and by adoption, that of the United States."[4]

The doctrine of incorporation

The "adoption" or "incorporation" of the law of nations in the law of the land has long been a favorite theme in the Anglo-American literature of international law. Its prominence was assured from the moment that Blackstone enunciated it. That great pundit, whose authority has been hardly less overwhelming in the United States than in England, enshrined in his *Commentaries on the Laws of England*[5] the dictum that ". . . the law of nations (whenever any question arises which is properly the object of its jurisdiction) is here adopted in its full extent by the common law, and is held to be a part of the law of the land."

The doctrine has a liberal and internationalist sound, and it is fortunate indeed for diplomatic relations that the English and American courts pay some attention to prevailing international usage, as they also do to rules of morals or comity. But

[3] Above, p. 33.

[4] *The Works of Alexander Hamilton*, Lodge edn., New York, 1904, vol. 5, 436-443.

[5] Book IV, chap. 5.

the practical significance of this "incorporation" can easily be exaggerated. It is as plain from the way that Randolph expressed it in the letter quoted above as it is from Lord Atkin's statement a century and a half later[6] that international law is part of the law of the land only in so far as the law of the land does not vary from it. This, as I have suggested, can equally well be said of any rule, regardless of its nature or source.

The bulk of the Law Officers' opinions was of course buried in the archives of the Foreign Office and inaccessible to the Attorneys General of the United States. There was no need, however, of an available collection of such opinions to bring about a continuity of approach among lawyers brought up on the same treatises, law reports and procedural traditions. And some at least of the more famous of the Law Officers' submissions were in the hands of their American counterpart. Thus Randolph in a letter of April 12, 1793 to the Secretary of State[7] disposes of a question of reprisals by quoting verbatim from the reply to Frederick's *pro-memoria* on the Silesian loan.[8] Two years later the same report was used by Hamilton in number 20 of the *Letters of Camillus* to support his argument that by the law of nations private enemy property was not confiscable.[9]

What was not quite so much to be expected was the familiarity, shown in the Attorneys General's letters as well as in the writings of Hamilton and other contemporaries, with the long line of continental European writers from Grotius to Georg Friedrich von Martens. Among these Grotius and

[6] *Chung Chi Cheung v. The King*, 1939, A. C., 160: "The Courts acknowledge the existence of a body of rules which nations accept among themselves. On any judicial issue they seek to ascertain what the relevant rule is, and, having found it, they will treat it as incorporated into the domestic law so far as it is not inconsistent with rules enacted by statutes or finally declared by their tribunals."

[7] *Opinions of the A. G.*, vol. 1, p. 32.

[8] Above, pp. 30-31.

[9] *Op.cit.*, vol. 5, pp. 439-440.

Vattel[10] meet the eye most frequently, but Pufendorf and Bynkershoek are also prominent. This is another feature common to these English and American documents, and it demonstrates that these interdepartmental communications were for writers on the law of nations a channel of influence at least as important as arbitral tribunals and national courts of justice confronted with international questions.

Divergence of advice and practice

Not that the advice submitted was uniformly followed. There is indeed evidence that in some cases it even escaped notice. No doubt breakdowns of communication, to say nothing of conflicts of view, occurred even in the early Republic's simple governmental structure.

Immunity of foreign warships

One of the clearest cases of divergence had to do with the immunities of ships-of-war in United States ports. William Bradford, who succeeded Randolph as Attorney General, wrote on June 24, 1794, to Randolph, now Secretary of State, to the effect that the writ of *habeas corpus* runs against the commander of a foreign warship in an American port unlawfully detaining an American citizen. The advice was based upon the general proposition, stated in no uncertain terms, that "the laws of nations invest the commander of a foreign ship-of-war with no exemption from the jurisdiction of the country into which he comes."[11] Yet within a month we find Randolph writing to Hammond, British Minister in Philadelphia, "A ship-of-war, when in a foreign friendly port, is ordinarily exempt from the jurisdiction of such port."[12]

[10] Ernest Nys, *Les Etats-Unis et le droit des gens*, Brussels, 1909, pp. 145-146, observes that Jefferson was responsible for the inauguration of instruction in the law of nature and of nations at the College of William and Mary in 1779, and that Vattel was the textbook from then until 1841.

[11] *Opinions of the A. G.*, vol. 1, pp. 47-48.

[12] Wharton, *Dig.*, vol. 1, p. 136.

Charles Lee, Attorney General in 1799, took the same position as Bradford. In a letter to the President on March 11 of that year[13] he supported it by passages from Vattel and Martens which, without mentioning men-of-war, merely assert the general subjection of every person and thing within the territory to the territorial law, with the exception of those enjoying extraterritorial rights, such as foreign princes and their ministers. Less question-begging was the argument that he based upon Article 23 of Jay's Treaty.[14] There it had been agreed that "the ships-of-war of each of the contracting parties shall be hospitably received in the ports of the other, their officers and crews paying due respect to the laws and government of the country." To disobey or resist duly authorized process would be inconsistent, Lee not unreasonably held, with such due respect. Finally—and this might have been thought conclusive in an American context—he was able to cite an Act of Congress passed on June 5, 1794. Tucked away amid miscellaneous provisions in Section 7 of this statute was authority to the President to use military power in any case where process issuing out of a court of the United States was disobeyed or resisted by any person having custody of a foreign man-of-war in an American port.[15] An Act of 1805,[16] that carried the same principle into great detail and applied it even to cases of mere misdemeanor, was allowed to expire in 1808; but the Act of 1794 was in 1800 continued without limitation of time and is still on the statute books. Clearly the Congress has not been unduly sensitive to any obstacle in the law of nations to the exercise of jurisdiction over foreign warships.

Yet, in addition to Secretaries of State, American courts have taken the opposite line, showing a marked inclination to avoid decisions at variance with what they have described as prevailing usage, comity or law among nations. It was indeed an American court that established the now prevailing doc-

[13] *Opinions of the A. G.*, vol. 1, pp. 87-92.
[14] Signed in London, November 19, 1794.
[15] 1 *Statutes at Large*, p. 384.
[16] 2 *Statutes at Large*, pp. 339-342.

trine on the subject, and American practice that consolidated the trend towards immunity.

This is all the more remarkable in that Chief Justice Marshall's reasoning in the much-quoted case of *The Schooner Exchange v. McFaddon*, March 3, 1812, was by no means unambiguous or clear-cut. He did indeed say: "It seems then, to the court, to be a principle of public law, that national ships of war, entering the port of a friendly power open for their reception, are to be considered as exempted by the consent of that power from its jurisdiction." But he hastily added: "Without doubt, the sovereign of the place is capable of destroying this implication. He may claim and exercise jurisdiction either by employing force, or by subjecting such vessels to the ordinary tribunals. But until such power be exerted in a manner not to be misunderstood, the sovereign cannot be considered as having imparted to the ordinary tribunals a jurisdiction, which it would be a breach of faith to exercise."[17] The most that Marshall's "public law" appears to do is to set up a presumption of immunity that is at once rebutted by a clear assertion of jurisdiction.

Nor did Mr. Justice Story, ten years later, add anything to the precision of the judicial position. His interpretation is to be found in *The Santissima Trinidad*, March 12, 1822.[18] It had been shown in *The Schooner Exchange*, he thought, that the exemption of warships "was not founded upon any notion that a foreign sovereign had an absolute right, in virtue of his sovereignty, to an exemption of his property from the local jurisdiction of another sovereign; for that would be to give him sovereign power beyond the limits of his own empire. But it stands upon principles of public comity and convenience, and arises from the presumed consent or license of nations, that foreign public ships coming into their ports, and demeaning themselves according to law, and in a friendly manner, shall be exempt from the local jurisdiction. But as

[17] 7 Cranch, 145-146.

[18] Wheaton, *United States Reports*, 7, 352-353.

such consent is implied only from the general usage of nations, it may be withdrawn upon notice at any time without just offense, and if afterwards such public ships come into our ports they are amenable to our laws in the same manner as other vessels."

The Geneva Tribunal followed the same devious path in 1872 when it declared that "the privilege of extraterritoriality accorded to vessels of war has been admitted into the law of nations, not as an absolute right, but solely as a proceeding founded on the principle of courtesy and mutual deference."[19] Like Story, it raised but did not answer the intriguing questions: "What is the difference between a right and an absolute right?" and "Can a matter be at once one of law and of mere courtesy?"

Law, morals, etiquette

Such vacillations between law, morals, and good manners have always been common in the search for international norms. They reflect, more faithfully than undiluted legal propositions, the nature and operation of those norms; for they correspond to the basic fact that governments determine for themselves the extent of their obligation. Neither for Marshall nor for Story, as far at least as may be judged from the language of these famous decisions, did the "general usage of nations," which is now known as "customary international law," create anything more than an implication that could be destroyed at will by unmistakably contrary act or, at most, by the courtesy of notice. The positivist who derives from consent, express or implied, the binding character of the international rule, has never been able to explain why the sovereign State should not cease to be bound on unilateral withdrawal of consent, or why the invocation of a rule in one situation should not be canceled by its denial in another.

[19] *Papers relating to the Treaty of Washington*, vol. 4, *Geneva Arbitration*, U. S. Government Printing Office, 1872, p. 50.

The weakness of the theoretical basis of the rule did not, however, prevent the growth of a firm pattern of practice. Immunity of their public vessels from foreign jurisdiction, like the privileged status of diplomatic agents, was something that governments wanted and could get only by reciprocity. Attorneys General and Secretaries of State became consistent in their support of immunity,[20] and a reinforcing interaction set in between American and English views. The *Parlement Belge*[21] was decided with an eye on *The Schooner Exchange*, and extended the privilege of warships to government-owned vessels employed in trade. This British decision had its influence when the Supreme Court of the United States in 1926 confirmed the dismissal for want of jurisdiction of a libel *in rem* against a ship owned and commercially operated by the Government of Italy.[22] It was these authorities that enabled Lord Atkin to make the confident statement in *Chung Chi Cheung v. The King*[23] that "the sovereign himself, his envoy, and his property, including his public armed ships, are not to be subjected to legal process." Lord Atkin had summarily rejected the fiction of extraterritoriality that Oppenheim, among others, had tried to fasten on the public vessel as a floating portion of its owner's dominions.[24] He was not prepared to accept the global exemption that might be inferred from such a fiction. Some alleged immunities were controversial.

[20] Cf. Hyde, *International Law Chiefly as Interpreted and Applied by the United States*, 2nd edn., 1947, vol. 2, pp. 826-828. It was in connection with *habeas corpus* proceedings that Attorney General Bradford had in 1794 denied the immunity of public vessels. The full cycle was marked by the incident reported here by Professor Hyde. In 1924 *habeas corpus* proceedings were begun in the U. S. District Court to secure the release of crew members detained on the Mexican gunboat *Bravo* in the port of New Orleans, and process was actually served on the Commander. The Department of State took steps to have the Court advised that the ship was not subject to the jurisdiction of United States Courts.

[21] 5 P. D., 1880, p. 197.

[22] *Berizzi Brothers Co. v. S. S. Pesaro*, 271 U. S. 562.

[23] A. C., 1939, p. 160.

[24] His Lordship was referring to Lassa Oppenheim, *International Law*, 5th edn., Hersh Lauterpacht (ed.), vol. 1, para. 450.

The Court was bound to respect only those clearly established.

The most recent development in this matter is reflected in Draft Article 22 of the United Nations International Law Commission's Report on its 8th Session.[25] This subjects government ships operated for commercial purposes to the same rules as privately owned merchant vessels when in foreign territorial waters. The Governments of the United States and Britain now seem disposed to abandon the position that the immunity of public vessels is not lost by trading. As was to be expected, the Soviet Government continues to demand immunity for all government vessels irrespective of employment.[26]

Treaties in the executive, legislative, and judicial branches of United States Government

One manifestation of the American leaning to legal formulation was the eagerness of the Continental Congress to have relations with the rest of the world speedily regulated by treaties. In this there was something of the conviction that written texts have in themselves a compulsive force that would protect the interests of a nation whose financial and military strength bore no comparison with that of the other contracting party. Though Hamilton would be glad to adopt that part of Pufendorf's doctrine which held that a nation was not bound to comply with a treaty of assistance if doing so would involve the risk of its own destruction,[27] he and his contemporaries were not deterred by the same philosopher's warning that only fools continue to rely upon observance of a treaty by a signatory whose interests it would no longer serve.[28] One of the earliest enterprises of the Continental Congress had been the

[25] GAOR, 11th Session, supp. no. 9 (A/3159).

[26] GAOR, 11th Session, 6th Com., 488th meeting, p. 37.

[27] Below, pp. 49-51.

[28] Samuel Pufendorf, *De jure naturae et gentium*, book VII, chap. vi, sec. 14.

"Plan of 1776," drawn up as a model for negotiation with foreign governments. Within nine years this was to provide much of the content of treaties of amity and commerce with France (1778); The Netherlands (1782); Sweden (1782); and Prussia (1785).

The French Treaties of 1778

The Treaty of Alliance with France, 1778, which counted so heavily in the struggle for independence, prohibited any separate peace; but within four years representatives of the United States were themselves giving a demonstration of Pufendorf's proposition. In 1782, three great men of the Revolution, Benjamin Franklin, John Jay, and John Adams, came to a settlement with Britain in secret negotiations, saving the appearances, as Professor Van Alstyne makes plain, by a device that shows the inheritance of something more than law from old-world diplomacy. "By signing a definitive treaty replacing the agreement of November 30, 1782 . . . the American commissioners were able to avoid charges of dishonor and to preserve the appearances, if not the realities, of cooperation with France."[29] But the obligation of cooperation was to suffer sharper repudiation yet at the hands of Washington and Hamilton.

Treaties in the Constitution

The Constitution that came into effect in 1789 seemed to express and to promise a special respect for treaties in the United States. The relevant clause was designed, among other purposes, to carry abroad the assurance that the division of power in the federation would not jeopardize the fulfillment of treaty obligations. Care was to be taken to avoid secret entanglements and to prevent treaties from being used as instruments for the usurpation of power by the executive branch. The advice and consent of the Senate, expressed by the af-

[29] *American Diplomacy in Action*, Stanford, 1944, p. 23.

firmative vote of two-thirds of the Senators present, was made a condition of validity. But once a treaty had been ratified with this consent, it was to be part of the supreme law of the land. Nothing in any state constitution or state law could alter its obligation.[30]

That these impressive provisions did not place treaties above administrative discretion was soon to be demonstrated.

Article 11 of the French Treaty had laid it down that "the two parties guarantee mutually from the present time and forever against all other powers, to wit: the United States to His Most Christian Majesty, the present possessions of the Crown of France in America, as well as those which it may acquire by the future treaty of peace: and His Most Christian Majesty guarantees on his part to the United States their liberty, sovereignty and independence. . . ." Previous wars had left no doubt that French possessions in America were imperiled by war with England. But on April 22, 1793, Washington, taking note of the state of war between Austria, Prussia, Sardinia, Great Britain, and the United Netherlands on the one part, and France on the other, declared "the disposition of the United States" to "pursue a conduct friendly and impartial towards the belligerent powers," and warned his countrymen that any who committed or abetted hostilities against either belligerent would be "liable to punishment or forfeiture under the law of nations."[31] This, though it did not use the word, was of course a proclamation of neutrality, and a negation of any duty to assist France in preserving her American dependencies. Many Americans thought it a shameful desertion of the Ally without whose aid independence could not have been won.

It was Alexander Hamilton who led the defense of the President's decision, the same Hamilton who had written so zealously in number 20 of his *Letters of Camillus* about the obligations of the law of nations.[32] Frequently as it was vio-

[30] Article 2, sec. 2; Article VI.

[31] Wharton, *Dig.*, vol. 3, p. 586.

[32] Above, p. 40.

lated, the sanctity of treaties always figured as an essential rule in statements of the customary law of nations, and Hamilton had assumed the task of showing why this rule did not mean that the United States must now enter the war on the side of France. He had one typical lawyer's argument, which was also not without moral cogency. It was that as France had been the first to declare and begin hostilities this was an offensive war, whereas the treaty had in its second article described the Franco-American alliance as defensive. But, being intent on tearing to shreds all the arguments of those who held that the proclamation was a violation of the treaty, he went on to give his real reasons for regarding the guarantee as of no effect in the circumstances. His arguments at this point are precisely those that Cecil had observed in use among sovereigns of the sixteenth century[83] and—such is the continuity of political response when basic national interests are at stake—they are identical with the excuse euphemistically known today as "impossibility of performance." He pointed out that France, having aligned most of Europe against herself, could not possibly spare the naval forces necessary to assist the United States and protect American trade. "This state of things alone," he writes, "discharges the United States from an obligation to embark in her quarrel." The President had not only the right but the plain duty to declare the country's neutrality. Machiavelli could not have improved upon this. "All contracts," Hamilton adds, "are to receive a reasonable construction. Self-preservation is the first duty of a nation; and though in the performance of stipulations relating to war, good faith requires that its ordinary hazards should be fairly met, because they are directly contemplated by such stipulations, yet it does not require that extraordinary and extreme hazards should be run, especially where the object to be gained or secured is only a partial or particular interest of the ally. . . . Good faith does not require that the United States should put in jeopardy their essential interests, perhaps

[83] Above, p. 11.

their very existence, in one of the most unequal contests in which a nation could be engaged, to secure to France what—? Her West Indian Islands and other less important possessions in America."[34]

Here was the advocate putting a prepossessing legal face upon ugly facts. The imaginary distinction between the ordinary and the extraordinary hazards of war, and the arrogant assumption that American plenipotentiaries in 1778 could not have contemplated that a guarantee of French possessions might involve their defense against extremely dangerous odds, betoken the jurist's craft. An unvarnished statement of the case might have run as follows: In 1778 the thirteen colonies were in desperate need of French aid. They were willing to assume any future risk to avoid immediate shipwreck in the great enterprise of independence. Now, in 1793, the whole outlook had radically changed. A France whose revolutionary extremes had forfeited something of America's affectionate gratitude had thrown down what looked like an insane challenge to Europe. What the young nation desperately needed now, especially to Hamilton's mind, was a period of peace in which to meet the perils of internal disintegration, develop commerce, establish financial solvency, and build up a merchant marine and navy. Reconquest by England seemed a probable consequence of joining France. Law or no law, promise or no promise, the United States must be neutral.

With such a statement the face of the United States might have been set against the twin casuistries of impossibility of performance and *rebus sic stantibus*. The frank admission of limits beyond which no pre-established rules govern State conduct, coupled with a refusal to dress up in a thin veil of legal interpretation the State's determination of the limit in any specific context, would have hastened the development of effective rules. Any growth favored by the penumbra in which an act of political expediency can parade as an exercise of legal right is apt to be of the mushroom variety.

[34] "Pacificus," nos. 2 and 3, *op.cit.*, vol. IV, pp. 447-451, 456-457.

In 1798 Congress went as far as it could to complete the destruction of the Treaty of Alliance and, with it, of the Treaty of Amity and Commerce also concluded in 1778. Declaring that France was continuing her repeated violations of these agreements and repelling all attempts at amicable adjustment, the Senate and House of Representatives enacted "that the United States are of right freed and exonerated from the stipulations of the treaties and of the consular convention, heretofore concluded between the United States and France, and that the same shall not henceforth be regarded as legally obligatory on the Government or citizens of the United States." With the approval of the President this became law.[85]

Congress was here exercising what it regarded as the unquestionable right of the injured party unilaterally to abrogate an international treaty that has been violated. The French Government of the time disputed the abrogation, and in subsequent negotiations the Government of the United States found it expedient to bargain for release from the treaties rather than insist that they had ceased to exist with the Act of Congress.[86] But that a right to abrogate for violation exists is an opinion supported by courts of the United States and Great Britain, by American and other Secretaries of State, and by a mass of literary authority.[87] The fact that each contracting State is allowed to decide for itself whether there has indeed been a breach of the treaty by another party is merely another manifestation that the aggregate of States is not in the usual sense of the term a society under a legal system. The proposal in the Harvard Research[88] to reduce the liberty of unilateral abrogation to a right to seek a declaratory judgment from a competent international tribunal, while

[85] 1 Stat., 578.

[86] Moore, *Dig.*, pp. 357-358.

[87] Recent statements of the American position will be found in the memorandum of the Legal Adviser, February 27, 1935, Hackworth, *Dig.*, vol. 5, pp. 345-346, and *Opinions of the A. G.*, vol. 40, p. 124. For a summary of opinions and decisions, see Harvard Research, *Law of Treaties*, comment on Article 27.

[88] *ibid.*

highly commendable in purpose, was based upon an exaggerated estimate of the effect of modern organization in creating a "community of nations."

President Franklin D. Roosevelt and *rebus sic stantibus*

On April 29, 1934, in the course of the long and ineffectual effort to persuade Japan to abandon its policy of aggression in China, the Department of State instructed the American Ambassador in Tokyo to make the following statement to the Japanese Minister for Foreign Affairs: "Treaties can lawfully be modified or terminated only by processes prescribed or recognized or agreed to by the parties to them."[39]

Presumably, the United States, consistently with its own practice, would acknowledge among "recognized processes" that of denunciation for violation unilaterally found by the denouncing party. It would also, if one may judge from the proclamation by President Roosevelt on August 9, 1941 announcing suspension of the Load Lines Convention of 1930, recognize the plea of *rebus sic stantibus*, again on the mere finding by a party that there had been a material change in conditions. What further latitude, it may be asked, could Japan have wished?

The Conference convened in London in 1871 to consider the consequences of Russia's denunciation of the clauses in the Treaty of Paris, 1856, neutralizing the Black Sea, being quite unready to take the action necessary to enforce compliance with the treaty, contented itself with a declaration recognizing "that it is an essential principle of the law of nations that no Power may release itself from the undertakings assumed in a treaty, nor modify its terms, without the consent of the Contracting Parties in the form of a friendly understanding." This would seem to rule out any automatic operation of the principle *rebus sic stantibus*, and the declaration forms part

[39] Department of State, *Press Releases*, 223-248A, 1934, pp. 244-245.

of the documentation upon which, after a comprehensive review of executive and judicial authority and of juristic opinion, the Harvard Research group based its finding that "the principle is well established that one party to a treaty does not have the right to terminate its treaty obligations unilaterally merely upon the ground that it believes that the doctrine of *rebus sic stantibus* is applicable to the treaty."[40] Yet, on the advice of the Acting Attorney General,[41] President Roosevelt thought it proper to frame the above-mentioned proclamation in these terms:

"Whereas the conditions envisaged by the Convention have been, for the time being, almost wholly destroyed, and the partial and imperfect enforcement of the Convention can operate only to prejudice the victims of aggression, whom it is the purpose of the United States of America to aid; and

"Whereas it is an implicit condition to the binding effect of the Convention that those conditions envisaged by it should continue without such material change as has in fact occurred; and

"Whereas under approved principles of international law it has become, by reason of such changed conditions, the right of the United States of America to declare the Convention suspended and inoperative;

"Now, therefore, I, Franklin D. Roosevelt, President of the United States of America, exercising in behalf of the United States of America an unquestioned right and privilege under approved principles of international law, do proclaim and declare the aforesaid International Load Lines Convention suspended and inoperative in the ports and waters of the United States of America, and in so far as the United States of America is concerned, for the duration of the present emergency."[42]

How very far from unquestioned is the "right and privilege" invoked by the President, and how dubious the adequacy

[40] *op.cit.*, comment upon Article 28.
[41] *Opinions of the A. G.*, vol. 40, pp. 119-124.
[42] DSB, vol. 5, August 9, 1941, pp. 114-115.

of the change in conditions from which it was said to arise, has been well shown by one of the United States' leading exponents of international law.[43] But if "international law" is formed, apart from treaties, by the actual practice of governments, there would seem to be little ground for condemning the action taken as illegal, however regrettable it might be judged. Even the *locus classicus* of 1871 was a mere declaration, to which the United States was of course not a party, and which contrasted with the actual acceptance of the change unilaterally brought about by Russia.

Panama, 1903

In one celebrated case where the Government of the United States took action at variance with a treaty, neither violation by another party nor *rebus sic stantibus* was pleaded in justification. It was under what he described as "a mandate from civilization" that President Theodore Roosevelt took steps to prevent the Panamanian revolt of 1903 from being crushed by Colombia (whose sovereignty in the area the United States had guaranteed in a treaty of 1846), and within three days of the outbreak recognized the newborn Republic of Panama. The object was liberty to build an Atlantic-Pacific canal. The Colombian Congress, holding out for better terms, had refused to approve ratification of the draft treaty negotiated in Washington, and Panama was confidently expected to be less exacting.

President Roosevelt's vigorous conduct of this affair had been encouraged by a memorandum prepared, prior to the revolt, by a jurist whose contribution to the study of international relations in their legal aspect has rarely been surpassed. This was Professor John Bassett Moore, a former solicitor of the Department of State, and he gave it as his opinion that "the United States, in undertaking to build the canal, does a work not only for itself but for the world." He apparently

[43] Herbert Briggs, "The Attorney General Invokes *Rebus Sic Stantibus*," AJIL, vol. 36, 1942, pp. 89-96.

felt, however, that the notion of world-mission needed some bolstering of a more orthodox legal type, and proceeded to find it in the treaty itself. The guarantee of 1846 had been given in return for an undertaking that "the right of way or transit across the Isthmus of Panama upon any modes of communication that now exist, or that may be hereafter constructed, shall be free and open to the Government and citizens of the United States." The United States had loyally performed its part of this bargain, intervening on several occasions to protect Colombia from foreign attack or to safeguard the proposed canal route against internal disorder. But, since no canal had been completed, the Government and people of the United States had never received their *quid pro quo*, namely the benefit of passage by ship across the Isthmus. The United States therefore had a right to build the canal, and Colombia had no right to obstruct the building. Thin as the legal argument was, it was no weaker than those that have served on similar occasions when great-Power convenience has overridden the protests of a small nation. As for the world-mandate, neither Moore nor the President mentioned the world service of treaty observance as any counterweight to that of an interoceanic canal. Subsequent administrations had twinges of conscience; but proposals to make some compensation to Colombia for the loss of Panama were defeated until 1921 when, oil discoveries having made it expedient to placate that country, a treaty providing for a payment of twenty-five million dollars was approved by the Senate.[44]

Treaties in the courts

Though, as we have observed, the special attention to treaties in the Constitution has not made their obligation invulnerable to political expediency, the kind of evasion practiced

[44] Samuel Flagg Bemis, *The Latin American Policy of the United States*, New York, 1943, pp. 150-151; Thomas A. Bailey, *A Diplomatic History of the American People*, New York, 1940, pp. 537-546. Dwight C. Miner, *The Fight for the Panama Route*, New York, 1940, reproduces the Moore memorandum on pages 426-432.

in this case has been rare in the diplomacy of the United States. In the main, both executive and judicial authorities have shown themselves scrupulously sensitive to the national duty of observance. The constitutional provisions, it is to be observed, did not place treaties on a plane with the Constitution itself in the matter of supremacy. They stand in the rank of laws made in pursuance of the Constitution and, like all such laws, are subject to repeal by later congressional enactment. This means that the internal laws of the United States may prevent fulfillment of a treaty and bring about a situation where the nation is exposed to penalties for the breach of its agreement. But neither executive nor judicial authority takes the position that the Act which repeals a treaty as law of the land destroys the international obligation. On the contrary, as Secretary Hughes put it in his memorandum for President Harding dated October 8, 1921,[45] the statute "does not of itself destroy a treaty as a contract binding upon the nation from an international standpoint. . . . Congress has the power to violate treaties, but if they are violated, the Nation will be none the less exposed to all the international consequences of such a violation. . . ." One implication of general importance is that whatever the nature of the obligations imposed by international norms they belong to a separate and distinct system. The theory of incorporation that holds international law to be part of the law of the land does nothing to exclude conflict between the international and national systems of obligations. This is as true of England as it is of the United States, for there also an Act of Parliament must be followed by the courts regardless of its discrepancy with their ideas of international law.

Here again is a context in which United States courts have shown a marked desire to preserve the international norm with its internal effect. They will not accept a mere suggestion of congressional intent to repeal; the intent must be clearly

[45] Hackworth, *Dig.*, vol. 5, p. 325.

expressed. This was the rule declared and followed by the Supreme Court in *Cook v. U.S.A.*[46]

The question before the court was the legality of the seizure on November 1, 1930, of a Canadian vessel, eleven and a half miles from shore, on suspicion of rumrunning. The Tariff Act of 1922, section 581, authorized the Coast Guard to make such seizures up to twelve miles. In 1924 a treaty had been concluded defining the limit for the seizure of Canadian vessels as the distance that the particular craft could steam in one hour. This, in the case before the Court, was ten miles. But section 581 had been re-enacted verbatim in the Tariff Act of 1930. Did this mean that the twelve-mile limit was in effect at the time of seizure?

The court held that "the Treaty, being later in date than the Act of 1922, superseded, so far as inconsistent with the terms of the Act, the authority which had been conferred by Sect. 581 upon Officers of the Coast Guard to board, search and seize beyond our territorial waters. . . . The treaty was not abrogated by re-enacting Sect. 581 in the Tariff Act of 1930 in the identical terms of the Act of 1922. A treaty will not be deemed to have been abrogated or modified by a later statute unless such purpose on the part of Congress has been clearly expressed."

Effect of war on treaties

Another expression of this judicial solicitude is to be found in decisions as to the effect of war upon treaties. The question presented itself concretely in the form of claims founded after the War of 1812 upon Jay's Treaty, 1794. One of these claims reached the Supreme Court in 1823, another as late as 1929, and the intervening century gave time for some interaction between American and British legal opinion and executive practice.

Article 3 of Jay's Treaty promised that "it shall at all times be free" to American citizens and British subjects dwelling

[46] *Supreme Court Reports*, October term, 1932, pp. 641 seq.

on either side of the Canadian boundary "freely to pass and repass by land or inland navigation into the respective territories and countries of the two parties . . . and to navigate all the lakes, rivers and waters thereof, and freely to carry on trade and commerce with each other." Article 9 was a guarantee of the real-property rights of British subjects in American territory and of American citizens in British territory. Article 28 declared the first ten articles of the Treaty permanent, whereas others were limited to twelve years.

After the War of 1812 it seems to have been the general view of British governments that prewar treaties with the United States had automatically come to an end with the outbreak of hostilities. One of the most irritating consequences, from the American standpoint, was the refusal to allow the free navigation and trading in the all-Canadian part of the St. Lawrence which the treaty had stipulated. The river was of course vitally important to the citizens of upper New York State as the main channel for their commerce in lumber and other commodities, and the British restrictions led to a lively diplomatic interchange in which the argument of "natural right," vigorously pressed on the American side, proved as unavailing as the treaty.

This British obduracy might have been expected to have some influence upon the Supreme Court when in 1823 it had to deal with the real-property claim brought by a British corporation, the Society for the Propagation of the Gospel, against New Haven. Quite apart from the human inclination to retaliate in kind, from which even judges cannot be supposed wholly free, the British position might have been taken as evidence of one party's intention when the treaty was concluded. Or, again, it might have been treated as an instance of rule-making practice. In fact, the Court refused to accept the proposition, for which there was both official and literary authority, that war brought a general abrogation. Mr. Justice Washington, who delivered the judgment, held instead that "treaties stipulating for permanent rights, and general arrangements, and professing to aim at perpetuity, and to deal with the case of war as well as of peace, do not cease on the occurrence of war, but are, at most, only suspended while it lasts; and unless they are waived by the parties, or new and repugnant stipulations are made, they revive in their operation at the return of peace."[47] It will be observed that there is no explicit reference here to the intention of the treaty-makers. The Court seemed to rely directly upon the objective nature of the transaction in question. If this was taken simply as a cue to intention, the judge failed to say so.

In England the Master of the Rolls rendered a similar decision in 1830 on a conveyance of real property by an American citizen. Unlike the Supreme Court, however, the English judge placed his decision squarely on the ground of intent, declaring it "a reasonable construction that it was the intention of the Treaty that the operation of the Treaty should be permanent, and not depend upon the continuance of a state of peace."[48] This was a far cry from the famous pronouncement of Lord Bathurst in a note dated October 30, 1815, to John Quincy Adams, Minister of the United States in London. Mr. Adams had expressed the opinion that the Treaty of 1783, with its grant of fishing privileges to Americans, had not been abrogated by the War of 1812. "To a position of this novel nature," wrote Bathurst, "Great Britain cannot accede. She knows of no exception to the rule that all treaties are put an end to by a subsequent war between the same parties."[49] Nor was the British governmental position altered by the judgment in *Sutton v. Sutton*. Bathurst's dogma was reiterated by Sir J. D. Harding, Queen's Advocate, in a Report of January 12, 1854: ". . . by the Law of Nations war abrogates all treaties between the belligerents." Not until 1864 did the Law Officers of the Crown admit by implication that some treaties might survive.[50]

[47] 8 Wheaton, 494-495.
[48] *Sutton v. Sutton*, 1 Russell and Mylne, 675.
[49] Moore, *Dig.*, vol. 5, p. 383.
[50] Lord McNair, *The Law of Treaties*, New York, 1938, pp. 533-535.

Presumed intent, "the policy of the statutes," partly of course to be gathered from the nature of the arrangement, is again suggested as the essential criterion in *Techt v. Hughes.*[51] Judge Cardozo's analysis of the problem in that case is hardly to be matched in the judicial literature of the common-law countries. The question before him was whether on December 27, 1917, an Austrian subject could, in virtue of the treaty of May 8, 1848, acquire title by descent to land in New York, or whether the treaty had been terminated by the state of war declared between Austria and the United States on December 7, 1917. In an elaborate survey of decisions and treatises the judge had found neither "uniformity of doctrine" nor "scientific accuracy of expression." The necessity of justifying a decision induced a major attempt to remedy these defects. The following excerpts give the gist of his reasoning:

> A treaty has a twofold aspect. In its primary operation, it is a compact between independent states. In its secondary operation, it is a source of private rights for individuals within states. . . . Granting that the termination of the compact involves the termination of the rights, it does not follow because there is a privilege to rescind that the privilege has been exercised. The question is not what states may do after war has supervened, and this without breach of their duty as members of the society of nations. The question is what courts are to presume that they have done. . . . It is not for them to denounce treaties generally, *en bloc.* Their part is, as one provision or another is involved in some actual controversy before them, to determine whether, alone, or by force of connection with an inseparable scheme, the provision is inconsistent with the policy or safety of the nation in the emergency of war, and hence presumably intended to be limited to times of peace. The mere fact that other portions of the treaty are suspended or even abrogated is not conclusive. The treaty does not fall in its entirety unless it has the character of an indivisible act. . . . We must consult in each case the nature and purpose of the specific articles involved. . . . Until the political departments have acted, the courts . . . are free to make choice of the conclusion which shall

[51] 1920, 229 *New York Reports*, pp. 242-247.

seem the most in keeping with the traditions of the law, the policy of the statutes, the dictates of fair dealing, and the honor of the nation.

The final passage in this admirable exposition can be taken as a statement either of certain general preconceptions that may guide the judicial search for intent or of considerations appropriate to the legislative function of filling a gap in the law. In either interpretation it emphasizes the scope for moral preference in the decisions of courts.

Cardozo's statement brings the whole question of the effect of war upon treaties into new and clearer focus. Though, as Mr. Justice Sutherland would point out (see *Karnuth v. the United States*),[52] "The law is still in the making"; the current now runs strongly against abrogation. Mere suspension, and then only of clauses so incompatible with a state of war as to justify the presumption that they were intended to operate solely in peace, is more and more widely regarded as the appropriate rule. Few now object to seeing a treaty partly operative and partly inoperative between belligerents, with the inoperative parts automatically reinstated, failing contrary provision, when peace supervenes. The only treaties in which total abrogation rather than partial or total suspension is still commonly considered appropriate are those setting up associations dependent upon a degree of mutual confidence that is rarely regained on the mere cessation of hostilities.[53]

[52] Below, pp. 64-67.

[53] But see Harvard Research, *Law of Treaties*, Article 35 and comment. The group of American jurists engaged in this enterprise took the bold stand that "there is no reason of public policy or national defense why any treaties should be regarded as *ipso facto* annulled or terminated by the outbreak of war between the parties." (*ibid.*) This would seem considerably in advance of the point reached either in practice or in prevailing doctrine. Cf. Hyde, *International Law*, vol. 2, p. 1551 and note 3; McNair, *Les Effets de la Guerre sur Les Traités*, ADI *Rec.* 1937, vol. 59, p. 576, and *The Law of Treaties*, New York, 1938, pp. 530-552. For a comprehensive study of American theory and practice, see Stuart H. McIntyre, *Legal Effect of World War II on Treaties of the United States*, a Columbia University Ph.D. dissertation, 1956, published in 1958 by Nijhoff, The Hague.

Judge Cardozo's approach would seem uniquely appropriate to courts operating under a constitution that makes treaties law of the land, yet accepting the principle of separate national and international systems of obligation. Since the international contract survives legislation repealing the treaty as law of the land, it might be argued conversely that abrogation or suspension of the international contract whether wholly or in part has in itself no effect upon the law of the land.[54] Is it quite clear that the occurrence of war can automatically annul or suspend a law of the land that contains no express provision to this effect?[55] Judge Cardozo saw the function of the courts in this context clearly as one of determining, from the nature of the arrangement in question or other evidence, whether or not the parties intended or should be presumed to have intended a specific treaty provision to go on producing its effects in wartime or, if not, to resume producing them on the advent of peace. The controversy, in other words, is just another occasion for the ordinary judicial task of interpreting a written enactment when its application in given circumstances is in dispute. That this is the true nature of the matter is still sometimes obscured by the lingering influence of the old notion of abrogation as a mechanical incident of war to which the intention of the parties at the moment of contracting had no relevance. The initial way of escape from undesirable consequences of that trenchant conception was the recognition of exceptions in favor of types of transaction thought to be not objectively incompatible with the state of war. If this classification was attempted simply as a clue to the intention of the parties, the failure to say so has been singularly frequent. And whether as itself the deciding factor or as index of intent, com-

[54] Cf. the judgment of the Swiss Federal Tribunal in *Lepeschkin v. Gossweiler & Co.*, 1923, translated in Herbert W. Briggs, *The Law of Nations*, New York, 1942, pp. 483-485.

[55] Professor Corwin offers no authority in support of his assumption (*The President: Office and Powers*; New York, 3rd edn., 1948, p. 238.) that "when a treaty or treaty provision has been discarded. . . , it ceases to be 'law of the land' for any purpose whatsoever. . . ."

patibility or incompatibility with war is no criterion at all by which to decide whether or not a treaty provision should automatically resume its operation with the cessation of hostilities, which is often the question in dispute. As Sir Cecil Hurst argued[56] intention has everything to recommend it for the role of decisive factor in the whole range of questions from total termination to partial suspension, and its clear recognition in the early decisions upholding the continuance of treaty obligations among belligerents might have rallied an international consensus that is hardly yet established.[57]

If and when such a consensus is established around the criterion of intent, there will of course still be national and international differences between courts and other authorities in their conclusions. In *Karnuth v. the United States*[58] Mr. Justice Sutherland, having quoted from both, seems to follow Mr. Justice Washington in *Society for the Propagation of the Gospel v. New Haven* rather than the Master of the Rolls in *Sutton v. Sutton.* The Supreme Court seemed, in other words, to rely upon the nature of the given arrangement as itself the criterion rather than as mere guide to the criterion of intent. But the decision need not have differed if it had been placed clearly on the latter ground. If the Court did not follow the liberal and well reasoned lead of the New York Court of Appeals in *Techt v. Hughes*, this may have been, as suggested in Harvard Research,[59] because it was aware of executive opinion in favor of abrogation of the relevant treaty right or because to have upheld that right would have been to defeat a part of the nation's immigration policy. But if these considerations explain, they hardly justify the decision. There were

[56] BYBIL., vol. 2, 1921-1922, p. 40.

[57] Treaty-makers sometimes adopt an ambiguous formula because a difference cannot for the moment be resolved. This is a mode of postponing resolution until a time when the difference may have diminished or disappeared. Where a court is called upon to interpret a treaty in which this has occurred, it will probably refuse to find any obligation not explicitly assumed by the parties. See below, pp. 176-177.

[58] 279 U.S., 236-242.

[59] *loc.cit.*

more creditable, though not necessarily conclusive grounds.

The question in *Karnuth v. the United States* was whether Article 3 of Jay's Treaty had survived the War of 1812 and was still in effect in 1927. As we have seen, British governments in the early nineteenth century had been adamant in their view that the right of free passage and commerce mutually granted in that article had come to an end with the outbreak of hostilities in 1812. But throughout the long intervening period, Canadians and Americans had been crossing and recrossing without hindrance. It was only after the supposed threat to American labor had brought about a shift of policy from free to restricted immigration that the idea of checking the movement of day labor from Canada to the United States took shape. In 1927 United States immigration officials took into custody two Canadian residents, one of Scottish and the other of Italian birth, who came daily to work in the United States. The charge was violation of the quota provisions of the immigration act, which were not applicable to Canadians born in Canada. *Habeas corpus* proceedings for release of the prisoners were dismissed in the District Court. The Circuit Court reversed this decision, holding that the immigration act should not be interpreted in a way inconsistent with Article 3 of Jay's Treaty. The case was then appealed to the Supreme Court.

A letter from Mr. Hackworth, Solicitor of the Department of State, to the Solicitor General on December 15, 1928, shows that the position taken by the British a hundred years earlier was regarded as relevant to the question of abrogation or survival. Mr. Hackworth wrote, "I have been unable to find that the British Government has ever taken any official action upon the assumption that Article 3 of the Jay Treaty survived the War of 1812. This, coupled with the attitude assumed by Great Britain in the correspondence between that Government and Mr. Adams, the American Minister to London, namely, that all pre-war treaties were terminated by the war, would seem conclusively to show that the British Government does not regard the Article as in force. The actions and expressions of opinion by authorities of the Government of the United States in this matter do not seem to have been altogether consistent."[60]

The Supreme Court reversed the Circuit Court judgment, holding that Article 3 had been abrogated by the War of 1812. Mr. Justice Sutherland, giving the Court's judgment, admitted that "the authorities as well as the practice of nations, present a great contrariety of views. The law of the subject is still in the making." He then proceeded to complete the process of lawmaking as far as the United States is concerned. There was, he thought, "fairly common agreement that, at least, the following treaty obligations remain in force: stipulations in respect of what shall be done in a state of war; treaties of cession, boundary and the like; provisions giving the right to citizens or subjects of one of the high contracting parties to continue to hold and transmit land in the territory of the other; and, generally, provisions which represent completed acts. On the other hand, treaties of amity, of alliance, and the like, having a political character, the object of which is to promote relations of harmony between nation and nation, are generally regarded as belonging to the class of treaty stipulations that are absolutely annulled by war."[61] There was no difficulty in classifying free passage as a liberty incompatible with war, but the elaborate attempt to establish that it is not of a sort to be automatically revived at peace is not convincing. The argument that, unlike the property rights protected by Article 9, the right of passage is not "vested" or "permanent in its nature" is unimpressive. In view of the words "at all times" in Article 3, and of the terms of Article 28 making this one of the permanent articles, the opposite reasoning would have been at least equally persuasive. A disposition to favor free intercourse between two traditionally friendly peoples could have been most respectably indulged.

[60] Hackworth, *Dig.*, vol. 5, pp. 382-383.
[61] 279 U. S., 236-242.

Given an inclination, on the other hand, to deny the survival of this provision, a stronger case could have been made out by frankly following Mr. Hackworth's cue. The British position in the years following the War of 1812 could have been taken as proving one party's view either of the nature of the arrangement or, in so far as this is a distinct question, of the intention of the treaty-makers.

Recognition of States and Governments

Since the aggregate of States lacks central authority, each State has to be left free to determine for itself the relevance to any set of facts even of such rules as are generally accepted. This is a recurrent difficulty in all the systems built upon the assumption of a community of States under law. To present this as merely a manifestation of the greater decentralization of the international as compared with the national legal order[62] is only to state the difficulty in different words, leaving unanswered the question whether so high a degree of decentralization does not negative both community and system.

One of many points at which this difficulty is encountered is at the very threshold of the alleged community and legal system, when we ask, "Who are the members of the community, the persons of its legal system, and how do they achieve membership and personality?"

For a long time the answer was thought to lie in recognition. But if a political society had to await recognition by existing State-members to become a member of the community and a subject of its law, this "constitutive" doctrine implied that until that moment it must remain rightless. This was morally disturbing, and did not seem to square with practice. Nor, if one asked how many recognitions were necessary to confer membership, was it entirely satisfactory to be told either that a "consensus" of recognition was the decisive thing, or that

[62] Hans Kelsen, *Principles of International Law*, New York, 1952, pp. 22, 36, 402-403.

the recognized State was a member and person only vis-à-vis those that had recognized it.

Considerations such as these brought adherents to the "declaratory" doctrine. At a certain point of development fixed by international law, a political society, regardless of recognition, is said to become a member of the community and a subject of its rights and duties.

As we shall see, some conscious or unconscious adherents of the declaratory doctrine have held that once a State has achieved the qualifications defined by international law it has a right to recognition. For others, recognition is always a "free act."[63] At least one eminent authority has contrived a constitutive theory that accommodates a right to recognition, though this means attributing a legal right to a still unconstituted body.[64] None of the theories can of course eliminate the role of unilateral decision, which can be replaced only by supranational authority. For even the doctrines that assert a right to recognition have to rely upon each existing State-member to answer the question whether any given society in fact presents the qualifications to which the alleged right attaches.

As the following rapid survey of American thought and practice since the eighteenth century will show, the doctrine which comes nearest to conformity with the present policy of the United States would not at all have suited the official positions taken in the early years of the Republic. What happened to prevent the building of a firm legal structure on the foundations first laid down makes an instructive study in the interplay of legal notions and political expediency.

Three quotations will indicate the swing of the pendulum from duty to convenience:

Thomas Jefferson, 1793:—We surely cannot deny to any nation that right whereon our own government is founded—that

[63] Cf. the "Resolutions of the Institute of International Law concerning the Recognition of New States and New Governments," Brussels, 1936, Articles 1 and 10.

[64] Hersh Lauterpacht, *Recognition in International Law*, Cambridge, 1947, especially pp. 72-78.

everyone may govern itself according to whatever form it pleases, and change these forms at its own will; and that it may transact its business with foreign nations through whatever organs it thinks proper, whether king, convention, assembly, committee, president, or anything else it may choose. The will of the nation is the one thing essential to be regarded.[65]

John Quincy Adams, 1818:— . . . there is a stage in such contests when the parties struggling for independence have, as I conceive, a right to demand its acknowledgment by neutral parties. . . .[66]

John Foster Dulles, 1957:—There are some who say that we should accord diplomatic recognition to the Communist regime because it has now been in power so long that it has won the *right* to that.

That is not sound international law. Diplomatic recognition is always a privilege, never a right.[67]

The mode in which the United States had made itself an independent nation predisposed its governments and citizens to regard self-determination as a "natural right" of every people, and to enter into diplomatic relations with any new regime that expressed the national will. There would inevitably be difficulty and dispute in determining when a group of human beings presented the characteristics of a people or nation to which the so-called right attached; but this has not deterred American statesmen from asserting the principle. It was the establishment of a republic by the National Convention in France that prompted Jefferson as Secretary of State to instruct Morris as he did. The subject was thus a change in the form of government of an existing State, not the formation of a new State; but the pronouncement, as indicated by the reference to the establishment of the United States, was broad enough to cover both occasions for recognition. It was to be reiterated by generations of American political leaders,

[65] Letter to Gouverneur Morris, United States Minister in Paris, March 12, 1793, Paul L. Ford, *The Works of Thomas Jefferson*, New York, 1904, vol. 7, p. 259.

[66] Letter to the President, August 24, 1818, Moore, *Dig.*, vol. 1, pp. 78-79.

[67] DSB, July 15, 1957, p. 93.

whose decisions on the recognition both of new States and of new governments afford an excellent measure of the practical significance in foreign policy of the principles laid down by Jefferson.

John Quincy Adams spent much of his time as Secretary of State in delicate negotiations with Spain for the acquisition of East Florida. While these were in progress he vigorously opposed the immediate recognition of the Latin-American States that was being urged not only by the governments of those countries but by commercially and sentimentally interested American citizens in and out of Congress. As we have seen, however, even he conceded the right. It was sufficient for his purpose to demand delay until the fact of independence was sufficiently established. This appears to have been the only condition in his mind. In the letter to the President quoted above he insisted that a revolutionary people attained the right to be acknowledged as an independent nation only when "the chances of the opposite party to recover their dominion" were "utterly desperate."[68] By 1822, having secured Florida by his 1819 treaty with Spain, he had seen no further reason for delay. Writing to the protesting Spanish Minister in Washington after the House of Representatives had approved the President's message recommending recognition, he felt free to assert that the United States had "yielded to an obligation of duty of the highest order."[69] In instructions a year later to the United States Minister in Buenos Aires, he emphasized the unconditional nature of recognition once independence was established. It was, he said, not something to be bargained for, "not a subject of equivalent; it is claimable of right or not at all." Another passage in the same document, contrasting the European and American approach to the question, claims the doctrine of national self-determination as something essentially American. "The European alliance of Emperors and Kings

[68] Moore, *loc.cit.*

[69] Manning, *Diplomatic Correspondence of the United States concerning the Independence of the Latin-American Nations*, New York, 1925, p. 157.

have assumed, as the foundations of human society, the doctrine of unalienable *right*. The European allies, therefore, have viewed the *cause* of the South Americans as rebellion against their lawful sovereign. We have considered it as the assertion of a natural right."[70]

If Adams was thinking of Great Britain in this context as one of "the European allies," he was doing that country some injustice. True, London, like Paris, had rebuffed suggestions from the United States for a joint policy in regard to the Latin-American nations. But Canning, for practical reasons touching commerce and the general interests of Britain in the Western Hemisphere, was by 1823 no less desirous than Adams had been to proceed to recognition. If the British Government advanced towards this goal with even greater deliberation than had been shown in Washington, this was due to considerations closely akin to those that induced Adams so long to delay the official act. Canning had to overcome some opposition inspired by a conservative distaste for revolutionary republicanism, reinforced perhaps by memories of obligations assumed in treaties with Ferdinand VII not to recognize any sovereignty other than his in the Spanish colonies or to assist them in their rebellion; but what really delayed recognition was the astute diplomat's expectation of developments that would reduce Spain's claims to absurdity, cut the ground from under the continental champions of legitimacy, and ensure the new States' friendship for Britain.[71]

The British correspondence on the subject uniformly assumes the right to recognize at least *de facto* without waiting for any Spanish acknowledgement of independence. In Lord Londonderry's letter to de Onis of June 28, 1822, there had even been a strong suggestion of the "obligation of duty" in-

[70] *ibid.*, pp. 191, 198.

[71] See H. A. Smith, *Great Britain and the Law of Nations*, vol. 1, pp. 115-170; Julius Goebel, "The Recognition Policy of the United States," Columbia University *Studies in History, Economics and Public Law*, vol. 66, New York, 1915, pp. 116-143; W. W. Kaufmann, *British Policy and the Independence of Latin America*, 1804-1828, New Haven, 1951, pp. 136-181.

voked by Adams. To leave such immense territories indefinitely without properly established relations, his Lordship had argued, would mean "fundamentally disturbing the intercourse of Civilized Society." A State that could not maintain control over dependencies must "be prepared to see those relations established themselves, from the over-ruling necessities of the Case under some other Form. . . ."[72]

The criteria that the British Government thought appropriate to a decision on recognition were essentially the same as those propounded by Jefferson and Adams. Like the Government of the United States, it was sending commissions to Latin America to report upon the progress of the struggle for independence. These were to ascertain, among other things, whether the revolutionary governments had (*a*) made public their will to independence; (*b*) achieved military control of their territories and "a respectable condition of military defense"; and (*c*) gained "a reasonable degree of consistency" and "the confidence and good will of several orders of the people."[73]

By 1836 another condition had made its appearance in statements of United States policy on the recognition of new States—a condition that is no less relevant to the recognition of new governments. This was the capacity "to perform the duties and fulfill the obligations towards foreign powers incident to their new condition."[74] How closely related British and American ideas on the subject now were is indicated by a letter from the British Ambassador in Paris to Lord Palmerston in reference to the French Republic proclaimed in 1848. The Ambassador reported telling Lamartine that "our rule was to recognize any form of Government which seemed to promise permanency, which maintained security within and gave no wanton cause of offence to its neighbors. . . ."[75]

[72] Smith, *op.cit.*, pp. 122-124.

[73] *ibid.*, pp. 129-130.

[74] Senator Clay, reporting a Resolution of the Senate Committee on Foreign Relations in favor of recognizing Texas as an independent Republic, Moore, *Dig.*, vol. 1, pp. 96-97.

[75] Smith, *op.cit.*, p. 107.

The dire possibilities of a principle of self-determination unless hedged about with definite and agreed conditions became painfully apparent to the government at Washington following the secession of the Southern States. Charles Francis Adams was about to proceed to London as Minister of the United States to the Court of St. James's and received elaborate instructions from Secretary of State Seward on his mission. He was in particular to do everything possible to dissuade the British Government from recognizing the Confederate States. Mr. Seward admitted the right, even the duty, to recognize "a new State which has absolutely and beyond question effected its independence," but he went on to say: "On the other hand, we insist that a nation that recognizes a revolutionary State, with a view to aid its effecting its sovereignty and independence, commits a great wrong against the nation whose integrity is thus invaded, and makes itself responsible for a just and ample redress . . . the several nations of the earth constitute one great federal republic. When one of them casts its suffrages for the admission of a new member into that republic, it ought to act under a profound sense of moral obligation, and be governed by considerations as pure, disinterested, and elevated as the general interest of society and the advancement of human nature."[76]

The student of policy as distinct from statements about policy must compare these declarations of the principle of self-determination, and of the conditions under which recognition becomes both a right and a duty, with, let us say, the recognition of Texas in 1837 and of Panama in 1903. The first followed a revolution which owed its success in large part to assistance from the United States which the government had not used due diligence to prevent, and its timing was determined less by considerations of general international interest than by the fear that delay would mean commercial discrimination in favor of other nations, especially Great

[76] *Diplomatic Correspondence*, Department of State, 1861, pp. 60-61, 63.

Britain.[77] The second was immediately preceded by official assistance to prevent successful intervention by the Colombian Government, was designed to ensure the success of the revolt, and awaited no proof either of ability to maintain independence or of intention and capacity to meet international obligations.[78] It is quite unnecessary at the present day to argue that, despite the reliance of the President and his *ad hoc* legal adviser on a mandate from civilization, the predominant motive was the national interest of the United States.

The contrast has been drawn here in the interests of a dispassionate estimate of the unquestioned influence of asserted principles and rules in foreign policy. It also serves to indicate the vast difference that must exist between systems of international law based upon what governments ask other governments to do and any system that can be built out of what they do themselves. If practice is to be the material for generalization, as most modern constructers of systems profess, then the latter kind of practice surely merits at least as much attention as the former. But the records of declaration, demand, and protest are voluminous and accessible, and the utopianism of many of the systems with which the literature of the subject abounds can in part be traced to an excessive juristic preoccupation with such material.

With a brief lapse in the Civil War, explained by a certain reluctance to recognize immediately the results of insurrectionary violence such as it was resisting at home,[79] the government at Washington remained faithful to the principle of recognizing any form of administration, regardless of its mode of establishment, supported by the popular will. If it was behind others in its recognition of the Diaz regime that came to power in Mexico in 1876, it could explain this as an applica-

[77] Cf. Bailey, *op.cit.*, pp. 247-253; Bemis, *op.cit.*, pp. 74-80.

[78] Above, pp. 55-56.

[79] See Moore, *The Principles of American Diplomacy*, New York, 1918, p. 212, for Secretary of State Seward's instructions to the United States Minister in Bolivia not to recognize any government which "was not adopted through the free will and the constitutionally expressed voice of the people."

tion of the conditions mentioned in the Clay Report of 1836[80] in reference to the recognition of Texas, namely that the new administration should have given evidence of firm establishment and of the capacity and intention to fulfill the international obligations of the State.[81] The same conditions were again asserted to be the only ones regarded by the United States in deciding whether or not to recognize when, in 1900, a *coup d'état* brought a change of regime in Colombia.[82] The idea of insisting upon constitutionality in the change, briefly entertained by Secretary Seward, reappeared only with the advent of Woodrow Wilson.

President Wilson's innovation was justified in his "Declaration of Policy with Regard to Latin America" of March 11, 1913, as being in the interest of "order based upon law and upon the public conscience and approval." The plan to discourage violent and unconstitutional changes of government by withholding recognition of administrations so established was especially designed as a sedative for the chaotic turbulence of Mexico since 1911; but it was stated in terms applicable to any Latin-American country. After Mexico, it was applied to the Dominican Republic, Ecuador, Nicaragua, and Cuba; but not outside the Western Hemisphere.[83] The criteria stated in connection with the recognition of the Chinese Republic in March 1913, are the classical three—actual control, popular acquiescence, will and ability to meet international obligations. No test of constitutionality is suggested. Even in regard to Latin America the test was soon abandoned except in Central America where it had been stipulated by treaty. In 1936 we find Secretary of State Hull declaring that the general policy

[80] Above, p. 72.

[81] Moore, *Dig.*, vol. 1, p. 148.

[82] *ibid.*, pp. 138-139. In this case government with the assent of the people is specifically stipulated, as it would be later in regard to the Chinese Republic. But this is nothing more than Jefferson's "will of the nation." The assent required is acquiescence, which may be proved by the absence of substantial resistance. Cf. Secretary Hughes to Mr. Gompers, Hackworth, *Dig.*, vol. 1, pp. 177-178.

[83] Hackworth, *Dig.*, vol. 1, pp. 174, 182-188.

of the United States was still that laid down in regard to the *coup d'état* of 1900 in Colombia and that this would be the policy in regard to Paraguay.[84]

In complete negation of the Jeffersonian principle, the constitutional criterion would on the face of it exclude self-determination realized by revolution. That this was far from being President Wilson's general intention is shown by the speedy recognition of the government formed in Peru, less than twelve months after his "Declaration," following the violent overthrow of the President in power. In this case the *coup d'état* was considered justified by the President's unconstitutional behavior. It could be described as a defense rather than a betrayal of government by law.[85] However that may have been, the episode reveals the true nature of what was verbally a sharp change in traditional policy. This was an assertion of the liberty to withhold recognition until *desiderata* determined by the recognizing government have been met. This liberty, as already demonstrated in relation to Diaz in 1876, is implicit in the ungovernably subjective application of the conditions of will and capacity to fulfill international obligations, firmness of establishment, and even national acquiesence. It has more recently been made quite explicit.

Mr. Hackworth, then Legal Adviser of the Department of State, introducing the subject in his *Digest of International Law*,[86] wrote: "Whether and when recognition will be accorded is a matter within the discretion of the recognizing State."

The sixteen-year postponement of the United States' recognition of the Soviet regime in Russia was defended as an application of two of the classical conditions, namely those demanding the consent of the people and the will to fulfill international obligations.[87] For some time these were cited again

[84] Hackworth, *Dig.*, vol. 1, pp. 174-175.

[85] Hackworth, *Dig.*, vol. 1, p. 274; Bemis, *Latin American Policy of the United States*, p. 173, note 10.

[86] 1940, vol. 1, p. 161.

[87] See the letter from Secretary Hughes to Mr. Gompers, Hackworth, *Dig.*, vol. 1, pp. 177-179.

as the chief reasons for ignoring the 1949 shift of power in China, and there is no reason to doubt the sincerity of the United States Government's statements on this subject. In relations with Latin America the withholding of recognition had been one means of encouraging regimes that would fulfill their international obligations and thus reduce the occasions for European intervention. To insist upon this condition would thus in some cases serve an interest of the United States. The government has also believed that general insistence upon it would make for a more law-abiding international community. There are grounds for Mr. Dulles' statement that "in this matter, as in others, the United States seeks to act in accordance with principles which contribute to a world society of order under law."[88] But the achievement of this condition, and of all the others ever mentioned, is no longer regarded as giving a right to recognition. "Always," says Mr. Dulles, "recognition is admitted to be an instrument of national policy, to serve enlightened self-interest."[89] The word "enlightened" does nothing to curtail the latitude offered by such a principle.

President Wilson's revival of legitimacy in the form of refusing recognition to governments that came into power by unconstitutional means was officially discarded in the presidency of Herbert Hoover.[90] In a closely related form, however, legitimacy was to reappear under the same Administration.

Secretary of State Stimson's note of January 7, 1932, to China and Japan was a warning that the United States would not recognize changes brought about in China by means contrary to the 1928 Pact of Paris and likely to "impair the treaty rights of the United States or its citizens." It was at once a protest and an attempt to check by moral suasion a specific alteration of the *status quo* by force. Repeated in a note of

[88] DSB, July 15, 1957, p. 94.

[89] *ibid.*

[90] The continued application of this condition in Central America was explained as a treaty obligation. Hackworth, *Dig.*, vol. 1, p. 185.

twelve members of the League of Nations Council to Japan, it was generalized by a Resolution of the Assembly dated March 11, 1932, into the statement that "it is incumbent upon the members of the League of Nations not to recognize any situation, treaty, or agreement which may be brought about by means contrary to the Covenant of the League of Nations or to the Pact of Paris."

What practical effect this generalization had upon the policy of leading members of the League may be gauged by their recognition of Italy's conquest of Ethiopia in 1936.[91] In the country of its origin, however, the "Stimson Doctrine" of nonrecognition of territorial and other changes achieved by "unlawful" violence has gone some way towards consolidation as a rule of international conduct. It was incorporated in the Anti-War Treaty, Rio de Janeiro, 1933, Article 2, the Convention on the Rights and Duties of States, Montevideo, 1933, Article 11,[92] and in the Treaty for the Fulfillment of Existing Treaties between the American States, Buenos Aires, 1936. The continued refusal to recognize the absorption of Latvia, Esthonia, and Lithuania in the Soviet Union is an application of the principle.

To sum up, the Government of the United States now handles recognition not as a right that accrues at a point of political consolidation defined by the law of nations, as Jefferson and John Quincy Adams regarded it, but as an advantage to be granted or withheld as official views of national interest dictate. The principle applied in the United States has thus come into harmony with that of most countries, remaining differences in practice depending on different assessments of the interests involved.

A memorandum prepared by the Secretariat of the United Nations in 1950 described the doctrine prevailing among governments in the following terms.[93]

[91] Below, p. 217.

[92] Repeated in Article 11 of the Declaration of the Rights and Duties of States drafted by the International Law Commission of the United Nations, GAOR, 4th Session, supp. no. 10, p. 8.

[93] SCOR, 5th year, special supp. no. 1, pp. 19-20.

The recognition of a new State, or of a new government of an existing State, is a unilateral act which the recognizing government can grant or withhold. It is true that some legal writers have argued forcibly that when a new government, which comes into power through revolutionary means, enjoys a reasonable prospect of permanency, the habitual obedience of the bulk of the population, other States are under a legal duty to recognize it. However, while States may regard it as desirable to follow certain legal principles in according or withholding recognition, the practice of States shows that the act of recognition is still regarded as essentially a political decision, which each State decides in accordance with its own free appreciation of the situation. . . .

The memorandum went on to quote a statement made by the representative of the United States in the Security Council, Mr. Austin, in defense of the recognition of the Provisional Government of Israel:

I should regard it as highly improper for me to admit that any country on earth can question the sovereignty of the United States of America in the exercise of that high political act of recognition of the *de facto* status of a State.

Moreover, I would not admit here, by implication or by direct answer, that there exists a tribunal of justice or of any other kind, anywhere, that can pass judgment upon the legality or the validity of that act of my country.

Mr. Austin, perhaps forgetting Secretary of State Seward's admonition to England in 1861,[94] even demolished the shadow of a rule that premature recognition may be an intervention in breach of international law. "I am certain," he said, "that no nation on earth has any right . . . to lay down a proposition that a certain length of time of the exercise of *de facto* authority must elapse before that authority can be recognized. . . ."[95]

On the other hand, the United States has gone furthest among the great Powers in practising and binding itself by treaty to practise nonrecognition as a means of discouraging

[94] Above, p. 73.
[95] SCOR, 3rd year, no. 68, 294th meeting, p. 16.

"illegal" violence. Thus while the movement in Washington has been away from any general rule of law limiting discretion in this matter, it has recently turned towards a form of treaty regulation that has this effect.

A recent British Government has reaffirmed the right to recognition. In his statement in the House of Commons on March 21, 1951, Mr. Herbert Morrison, Foreign Secretary, distinguished between the recognition of a State or government and entry into diplomatic relations. The latter he described as "entirely discretionary," whereas recognition "*should be accorded*" given "the conditions specified by international law," and "*should not be given* when these conditions are not fulfilled."[96] The conditions, as he saw them, were only two, effective control and firm establishment. But since, as the Foreign Secretary duly pointed out, "it is a matter of judgment in each particular case whether a regime fulfills the conditions," and since the relevant judgment is that of the recognizing government, plenty of room for discretion is in fact reserved.

Mr. Morrison's statement concluded with what amounted to a flat rejection of any principle of legitimacy: "The recognition of a government *de jure* or *de facto* should not depend on whether the character of a regime is such as to command His Majesty's Government's approval."[97] British recognition of the Chinese People's Government on January 6, 1950, leaves no doubt that the Minister was describing actual policy. British thought and practice are marked by the conviction that good relations demand the recognition of firmly established situations regardless of the mode of establishment. It has not followed the American use of nonrecognition. Justifying its adaptability to the facts of world politics, it can invoke early American principles no longer, it seems, in vogue in Washington.

[96] Italics mine.

[97] *Parliamentary Debates, House of Commons*, 1950-51, vol. 485, pp. 2410-2411.

On paper, Jefferson's principle has another champion among the great Powers. Like the revolutionary leaders in America, Lenin and Stalin proclaimed the right of national self-determination and the right of the self-determined to normal intercourse with established States and governments. A liberal nationalities policy has been the constant boast of the Soviet regime. In 1948 the Soviet delegation unsuccessfully pressed for self-determination as an item in the United Nations Declaration of Human Rights. Continued Soviet advocacy secured the anomalous insertion of this collective claim as Article 1 in a Draft Convention on Human Rights that has been oscillating for some years between the Human Rights Commission and the General Assembly.[98]

The most authoritative Soviet treatise on international law, published under the auspices of the Law Institute of the Academy of Sciences[99] derives from Marxist-Leninist doctrine the principle that every people establishing itself as a State must be regarded as a subject of international law with the right to be recognized and to enter into full relations with other States. It cites as examples Poland and Czechoslovakia in 1917-1918 and the Indonesian Republic and Vietnam in 1950.

This seems dogmatically clear. But a later section in the same chapter, written by a different hand, asserts with equal assurance that recognition is primarily a political act which States grant or withhold as their own interests prompt. Evidently the Soviet axe has not cut through the traditional ambiguity of the subject. Nor has the practice of the Soviet Government been demonstrably faithful to the self-determination so persistently propounded by its representatives. The Red Army's suppression of the Hungarian revolt in 1956 showed the same priority of policy over principle that has been the Soviet reproach against the capitalist treatment of

[98] GAOR, *6th* Session, 1951-52, Plenary Meetings, p. *516*.

[99] *Mezhdunarodnoe Pravo*, 2nd edn., Moscow, 1951, p. 158.

new States and governments. The Academy's treatise[100] had condemned Wilson's plan of withholding recognition from governments established by unconstitutional means as a device for encouraging Latin-American peoples to choose regimes "wholly subservient to Wall Street."

[100] Pp. 188-189.

CHAPTER III

THE SOVIET DILEMMA

THE Soviet Government took over the Russian Empire with the normal European inheritance of international legal lore. Russia, it is true, had come late into full intercourse with the Powers of the West. It was only in the early eighteenth century, little more than seventy years ahead of the entry of the United States, that she was received without question as a great Power in the "family of nations." This reception was in large part due to Peter the Great's innovations both in internal government and in international relations—innovations explicitly directed to winning for Russia a universally recognized place among the leading participants in world politics. Others, like Ivan III and Ivan IV, had glimpsed the same goal; but it took Peter's genius and his inexhaustible flow of consistently directed energy to achieve the long advance from Russia's seventeenth-century position to that which she occupied in the eighteenth.

International law under the Czars

But even before this swift accession of power and prestige, the principles and practices ascribed to a law of nations had by no means remained unknown in the realm of the Czars. First Kiev and then Muscovy had for many centuries maintained treaty relations with neighboring empires, kingdoms, and cities. They had sent and received ambassadors, drawn boundaries, negotiated rights of navigation and commerce, even insisted on occasion upon formal and substantive rules of war. In the sixteenth and seventeenth centuries business under these headings brought Moscow into relationships at one time or another with all the States of Europe.

Recent Soviet writers have been at great pains to emphasize prerevolutionary Russian contributions of doctrine and practice to the development of international law. F. F. Martens, best known of Czarist writers on the subject, was still at the end of the nineteenth century making light of the Russian literature in his field. His revolutionary successors have severely rebuked him for this manifestation of what they call the traditional prerevolutionary "kowtowing" to foreign culture.[1] Their histories of the development of international law closely resemble the Soviet chronicles that attribute so many advances in the physical sciences to subjects of the Czars.[2] And though, as they lead us didactically through this interesting material, they feel it necessary repeatedly to point out that the pioneering work of the Czarist jurists and diplomats was tainted with the fatal vice of capitalist inspiration, their nationalistic pride is evident. They have, moreover, formulated an apparently satisfactory Marxist explanation of the positive and lasting benefits accidentally resulting from this class-determined activity. The Czarist governments, they say, though always striving to make their foreign policy the servant of their class interests and to keep it in harmony with their reactionary domestic policy, could not with impunity ignore the national interests of the great Russian people. So, when their foreign policy coincided with those interests, it could not but have objective, progressive significance.[3]

All the way from the ninth to the eighteenth century bits and pieces of Russian practice could be found that bear some resemblance to patterns of international intercourse in our day. Soviet legal historians have devoutly made each of these fragments the starting point of a now generally accepted institution. Taken at its face value, their record would per-

[1] See F. I. Kozhevnikov, *Russkoe Gosudarstvo i Mezhdunarodnoe Pravo*, Moscow, 1947, p. 135, referring to F. F. Martens, *Sovremennoe Mezhdunarodnoe Pravo*, vol. 1, 1887, pp. iii-v; and for the general accusation, p. 158.

[2] See, in addition to the book by Kozhevnikov cited in the preceding note, the collective work published by the Akademiya Nauk SSSR, Institut Prava, under the title *Mezhdunarodnoe Pravo*, 2nd edn., Moscow, 1951, pp. 63-89.

[3] See the work last cited, p. 78.

suade the reader that but for Russian diplomacy there would have been little or nothing of the present accumulation of approved patterns. The exaggeration is obvious; but, at least towards the end of the period, there begins to be some substance in these characteristic claims.

Thus, to take a specific boast, we may accept the statement that Catherine II, when in 1780 she drew together the First Armed Neutrality, took the first practical step towards establishing the principles of maritime warfare eventually promulgated in the Declaration of Paris, 1856.[4] It seems clear that the Empress dreamed of developing her "darling child"[5] into a general code of war at sea. Her willingness in 1793 to abandon both child and dream in her overriding anxiety not to hamper England's war against the Revolution is only another instance of the way in which notions of law and leanings towards a coherent legal system yield to political exigencies. Her deranged successor, Paul I, under a different conjuncture of pressures, revived the armed neutrality. Alexander I reaffirmed its principles, and from his reign on, these were advocated by Russian governments.

The reasons for Catherine II's action in 1780 were complex, but some at least were concrete and substantial. Considered in conjunction with her more publicized solicitude for the general welfare of the family of nations, these are an object lesson in the motives that combine to produce the shifting norms of international conduct. Britain, at war with her American colonies and their allies, France and Spain, was seeking to gain full advantage of her strength in men-of-war and privateers. Enemy goods, contraband or not, were taken from neutral ships, and merchant vessels were captured and condemned for breach of thinly maintained blockades. The Anglo-Russian Treaty of Commerce, June 20, 1766, had laid

[4] *op.cit.*, p. 61. Cf. Charles De Visscher, *Théories et Réalités en Droit International Public*, 2nd edn., Paris, 1955, pp. 199-200; Corbett translation, p. 157.

[5] B. H. Sumner, *A Short History of Russia*, New York, 1943, p. 385.

it down that ships of one contracting party should be free to trade with an enemy of the other provided they did not carry "warlike stores." This liberty was not to extend to "places actually blocked up, or besieged, either by sea or land." A list of warlike stores was set out in Article 2. Together, these provisions meant that enemy goods should not be taken from Russian ships unless contraband, and that Russian ships should be captured only for breach of real blockade. British commanders were formally instructed to observe these rules, but complaints that they were being disregarded continued to come in.

The damage to Russian trade was perhaps more potential than actual; but Catherine was undoubtedly under pressure to take remedial measures. She was also concerned with the general growth of British power resulting from increasing command of the seas. A combination of suffering or threatened neutrals, prepared to assert with force principles such as "free ships, free goods" and "blockades, to be legal, must be effective" appealed to her more than the alliance that England was offering. Until it was too late, the British Government refused the one inducement that might have tipped the scale, namely aid in any forthcoming war between Russia and Turkey. Without this, all the advantages of Russia's entry into the war on the side of England promised to accrue to His Britannic Majesty, who with this assistance might contrive to keep his colonies and at the same time increase his naval predominance. The rules eventually codified in the Declaration of Paris were probably not the most substantial among the consequences of Catherine's decision in favor of the Armed Neutrality.[6]

[6] For a comprehensive collection of documents and opinions see James Brown Scott (ed.), *The Armed Neutralities of 1780 and 1800*, Carnegie Endowment for International Peace, 1918. For a British account of causes and effects, see Sir Francis Taylor Piggott, *The Freedom of the Seas, Historically Treated*, London, H. M. Stationery Office, 1920, pp. 42-60; and, for a study based upon an exhaustive search of Russian documents and sharply critical of Piggott's conclusions, Carousi and Kojouharoff, "The First Armed Neutrality," *National University Law Review*, vol. IX, no. 1, pp. 1-69.

Catherine's successors professed increasing zeal for international legislation. In his liberal period, Alexander I made a series of proposals on international codification, organization, disarmament, and the control of the slave trade. The reactionary interventionism of his Holy Alliance did not entirely annul the positive influence of his disparate efforts towards an operative and pacifying international order. England and the United States turned to him in 1820 for the arbitration of their dispute concerning the ownership of slaves in American territory that had been occupied by English troops. This was the first of a series of nineteenth-century arbitrations by Russian umpires, among whom both Alexander II and Alexander III figured. Proceedings under Professor F. F. Martens of the University of St. Petersburg led in 1896 to a unanimous award in the famous boundary dispute between Great Britain and Venezuela, and served as model for the Convention on the Peaceful Settlement of International Disputes adopted at The Hague in 1899.

The Brussels and Hague Conferences

The Brussels Conference of 1874, which tried unsuccessfully to establish a comprehensive set of rules for land warfare, was convoked on the initiative of Alexander II; and it was his grandson, Nicholas II, who brought together the Hague Peace Conference of 1899. This Conference succeeded in drawing up a Convention which, embodying much of the unratified Brussels draft, was eventually adopted by most of the world's States.

Nicholas II, in persuading the Queen of the Netherlands to issue invitations to a peace conference at The Hague, was interested chiefly in a measure of international disarmament. His announced objective was world peace, and his proposals, in addition to arms reduction, included an elaborate scheme for the peaceful settlement of disputes. Commenting upon this enterprise,[7] the Soviet historian E. V. Tarle seems clearly

[7] Vladimir P. Potemkin (ed.), *Istoriya Diplomatii*, Moscow, 1945, vol. 3, pp. 710-711.

to join in the ridicule with which, as he records, the Czar's essay in pacifist idealism was greeted by the diplomats and courts of Europe. These skeptics attributed the initiative to the weakness of Russia's army and finances, fear of Germany's rising military power, and the need of a quiet period in which to modernize armaments and consolidate the position in the Far East, where the occupation of Port Arthur was having dangerous repercussions. Tarle disagrees with the Soviet jurists who count the Hague Conferences a distinguished Russian contribution to a world order of law. He writes the results off as illusory.

Tarle's judgment errs on the negative side. No one disputes the frequent and shocking violations and evasions that have made the value of the whole movement to humanize war a debatable question. But the Declaration of Paris and the successive Hague Conventions and Regulations have had a mitigating effect upon belligerent practice. For what they have been worth, credit must go in considerable measure to Russia. Nor does the fact that the initiative was prompted or facilitated by the material needs of that country make the contribution any less real. Governments can rarely act upon motives of pure altruism.

The Revolution

In its general repudiation of bourgeois institutions, the revolutionary government of Russia might have been expected to reject the legacy of international norms which the deposed regime had helped to build up. In fact, it was compelled from the first to use the language and the forms that pass under the name of international law. It did not hesitate to complain of violations of international law by the capitalist States not only in the dire form of military intervention but also in such minor details as the unauthorized entry of warships into Russian territorial waters.[8] Merely to assert the illegality of

[8] Stalin, *Voprosy Leninizma*, 10th edn., p. 359. Quoted in Ivo Lapenna, *Conceptions Soviétiques de Droit International Public*, Paris, 1954, pp. 64-65; T. A. Taracouzio, *The Soviet Union and International Law*, New York, 1935, pp. 61, 63, 64.

intervention and the distinction between open sea and territorial waters of course logically implied acceptance to that extent of a system of international law. Another matter of immediate importance called for similar treatment. In the Commissariat of Foreign Affairs an elaborate argument in legal terms was devised to meet the claims for payment of Czarist debts. The key words were *fundamental change*, not just a shift from one government to another, but a social doctrine and structure so different that even the excessively frail rules of passive State succession became irrelevant. Nor, when it refused to admit that such a change would logically also bring into question the nation's succession to the rights of prerevolutionary Russia, was the Soviet Government more inconsistent than those creditors who asserted (*1*) that the Bolshevik society was a totally new phenomenon whose rights had still to be determined, and (*2*) that the pecuniary obligation survived. In a word, the scornfully new regime found itself in a world where it could not dispense with the language and forms of intercourse fixed under conditions which it proposed to abolish. Terms of peace had to be defined, boundaries drawn with old and new States, treaties of commerce and navigation negotiated, delegations sent and received. Marxist dialecticians who were not under the urgent necessity to get things done might worry about the orthodoxy of acts and communications that assumed the existence of a mutually binding law of nations. Government used the tools at hand.[9]

International law and Marxist doctrine

The ancient legal itch for system lured the Soviet jurists into a task of theoretical reconciliation the main product of which has been three decades of abusive polemic. In Marxist definition, law is a superstructure of norms and procedures based upon the economic organization of production in any given society. It is created and sustained by the dominant class

[9] Cf. Akademiya Nauk, *Mezhdunarodnoe Pravo*, Moscow, 1951, p. 9.

as an instrument for controlling the subordinate class or classes. This is not the place to enter upon an extended examination of this definition. It may be pointed out in passing, however, that, while the law of any society roughly corresponds to the will of the class ruling for the time being, it is designed at least as much to settle conflicts and maintain order within the same classes as to dispose of differences between them. It is also worth noting how little the legal system may change as political ascendancy shifts from one class to another. England under alternating Conservative and Labor governments provides a striking example.

Of limited validity in reference to national law, the definition stubbornly resists application to a law of nations. Is there such a thing as an international society divided, across national lines, into exploiting and exploited classes? To us who do not live in the Soviet Union, China, or their orbits, the answer seems clearly negative. We of course observe at times a measure of solidarity, transcending national boundaries, among ruling and employing classes, and, especially in the recent years of international unions, among employed classes. But we also observe not only how swiftly and completely this relatively frail sense of common interest has broken down when national groups have gone to war, but also how the executive, legislative, and judicial mechanisms of modern States are used to protect and enhance the interests of national groups of governors, employers, or workers against their counterparts abroad. The norms of international law so called, in so far as they operate at all, bear upon the conduct of persons acting for States regardless of their class provenance, and change only very gradually and indirectly with changes in the class affiliation of governing groups.

Since the nineteen-twenties, Soviet jurists have never ceased to worry the twin problems of a community of diametrically opposed social orders and a class origin for the law of such a community. We cannot here chart in detail the turns, twists, and reverses in this literature.[10] It will be sufficient for our purposes to trace the main shifts by which theory has tried to keep up with policy.

Korovin

Dean of the corps of tormented theorists is surely Professor E. A. Korovin, whose tireless capacity for solution and recantation has enabled him to navigate crosscurrents in which less adaptable pilots have foundered. In his short monograph on *The International Law of the Transitional Period*,[11] Korovin points out that from the Marxist point of view natural law is impossible as a source of international law, since no Marxist can recognize any universal, human, ideal law constituting a supraclass order.[12] For the mixed period of transition from world capitalism to world communism, what he calls the historical school provides a better cue. But this is only a cue, since community in the sense of solidarity of ideas cannot as a rule exist between countries of bourgeois and socialist culture and there is therefore no general content for a corresponding complex of rules.[13] A partial legal community is, however, possible, based upon common recognition of so-called common human values, that is to say, values not bound up with a limited epoch or with a sharply defined equipment of political and social forms. Thus, these countries may join in establishing and observing norms to guide the struggle against epidemics, or to ensure the protection of ancient monuments and treasures of art. The necessities of trade, and the obvious advantages of collaboration in the technical improvement of communication and transportation, may sustain some further legal community.

[10] Valiant attempts to do so have been made, for example, by Ivo Lapenna, *Conceptions Soviétiques de Droit International Public*, Paris, 1954; and, more briefly, by Hans Kelsen, *The Communist Theory of Law*, New York, 1955.

[11] *Mezhdunarodnoe Pravo Perexhodnogo Vremeni*, 2nd ed., Moscow, 1924.

[12] P. 25. References are to the Russian edition cited.

[13] P. 15.

Korovin was here carefully trying to fit the actual facts of Soviet relations with the outside world into some theory that would not be too patently heretical for Marxists. He was stretching a point in the recognition of values not intimately connected with a specific social and economic substructure.

But he was taking risks graver than this. Unable to admit the subjection of the new revolutionary State to an established capitalist law of nations, he made the fragmentary norms determining relations between it and the bourgeois States a new international law now being added to the several circles or systems already in existence. There was, he argued, no universal system. He specified four particular circles, European, American, imperial-colonial (the last named embracing relations between imperial States and their colonies), and, finally, the transitional Soviet-capitalist circle. In each of the prerevolutionary circles or systems, a general solidarity of ideas and interests existed between dominant classes that were essentially identical in nature, the State being in each case nothing more than a provisional form of class domination. As a person of international law, the State was simply the personification of the class for the time being dominant in the nation. Therefore, when a new class took over control, the State itself became another person. The class identity being thus broken, a new set of norms would be called for to govern relations with the new entity.

Here, Korovin insisted, lay the entire and only legal justification of Soviet refusal to pay the debts of the previous regime of Czar, landowners, and bankers.[14] Here too was a demonstration of the class origin of each of the older systems of international law. But what of the new system? The sparse components of this system were the product of a partial community of ideas and values between different classes. As E. B. Pashukanis was to point out, this must mean interclass

[14] P. 30.

law, a doctrine which, after an earlier provisional acceptance, he soon recognized as anti-Marxist.[15]

In addition to the dominant class, formally personified as the State, Korovin recognized many other persons of international law. He was particularly anxious to establish the personality of the workers' associations and other proletarian organizations that looked to revolutionary Russia for leadership. But he added the Vatican, the League of Nations, international unions and commissions, the Red Cross, and primitive peoples.[16] This generosity got him into trouble. Stalin was now laying down the doctrine that in order to liquidate the survivals of capitalism at home and break down the capitalist encirclement abroad the Soviet State must rise to a peak of power before withering away. Korovin's treatment of the State as nothing more than a personification of the dominant class and as only one of the persons of international law tended to reduce its importance, and this, though it seemed calculated to please orthodox Marxists, encountered growing disapproval. The author found it necessary to confess his errors, as he has had to do many times since, and to give his support to opposing theses. Among the concepts that had to be abandoned were those of the multiple circles or systems of international law, the diversity of persons subject to it, and the special law of a transitional period. Pashukanis found some passing favor with his condemnation of this last theory as a version of the reformist heresy that posits an evolution into socialism, and with his insistence that States alone are subjects and persons of international law. Prevailing Soviet doctrine

15 "The Soviet State and the Revolution in Law," translated in *Soviet Legal Philosophy*, Twentieth Century Legal Philosophy Series, Harvard University Press, 1951, vol. v, pp. 244 seq. In his introduction to this volume, pp. xxvi-xxxiii, Professor John Hazard tells the story of the rise and fall of Pashukanis, who at the height of his career was Vice-Commissar of Justice in charge of drafting the codes of law called for by the Constitution of 1936. In AJIL, vol. 51, 1957, pp. 385-388, he has the satisfaction of noting the posthumous rehabilitation of this jurist.

16 Pp. 33-34, and *Sovremennoe Mezhdunarodnoe Pravo*, Moscow, 1926, pp. 19-23.

now asserts a universal system of international law and makes States if not its sole, certainly its principal, subjects.[17]

Pashukanis

Having finally rejected Korovin's theses of 1924, Pashukanis had the courage to declare that a law of nations presented theoretical problems that had so far defied solution in Marxist terms.[18] But if he himself had desired to give up the struggle, he would not have been allowed to do so. One of the official reproaches leveled at the legal profession was its failure to produce a satisfactory Soviet doctrine of international law. To have followed the Marxist definition of law to its logical conclusion would have deprived Soviet society of any legal argument against the early Western inclination to regard it as something beyond the pale, unentitled even to the measure of community represented by the approved forms of international intercourse. How intolerable Moscow and its jurists found this situation is indicated by the eagerness with which they sought *de jure* recognition from Western governments. In this effort they were driven to the extreme of asserting that every nation in the stage of establishing its independence, regardless of its degree of civilization, has a right to such recognition. This position was not consistently adhered to. A comparison of Akademiya Nauk *op.cit.*, pp. 158 and 175, shows first the assertion of the right to recognition and then the statement that recognition is a political act determined by the recognizing State's own interests. The obvious desire to have the benefits of a system of law without being limited by its disadvantages is not peculiar to the USSR.

Pashukanis returned to the fray in 1935 with his *Ocherki po Mezhdunarodnomu Pravu*, and in that work he came so

[17] Pashukanis, *Ocherki po Mezhdunarodnomu Pravu*, Moscow, 1935, p. 15; Akademiya Nauk, *op.cit.*, pp. 5, 157; T. I. Tunkin, "Mirnoe Sosushchestvovanie i Mezhdunarodnoe Pravo," SGIP, 1956, no. 7, pp. 5-6, 11.

[18] "The Soviet State and the Revolution in Law," *loc.cit.*

close to an accurate assessment of the part played by legal institutions in the foreign policy not only of the Soviet regime but of governments in general that his treatment deserves special attention.

The book begins with a statement of the importance of studying international law and of the tasks that confront the student. The first task is the theoretical one of tracing the historical origin of the forms and institutions in use and discovering their real significance. Here Pashukanis strikes a note that is apparently compulsory for all Soviet writers on subjects with a political bearing. The main purpose at this stage is to "unmask the hypocrisy of bourgeois and social-fascist pacifism, which covers a policy of imperialist aggression and preparation for new wars."

The second task is the practical one of giving Soviet society a concise account of the forms and institutions of international law which the organs of the proletarian government can use. This will arm it for the defense of the interests of the Soviet State in its relations with the capitalist world. But the student must always remember that all legal forms, especially in the international sphere, have only a subordinate significance. Questions both of internal and of external policy are decided by the real correlation of class forces, by the hard class struggle. No legal formula, however solemnly proclaimed, has meaning in itself, apart from the relation of forces behind it. Thus, everyone should know that treaties of nonaggression or neutrality provide no guarantee that the Soviet Union will not be attacked.

Why, then, negotiate such treaties? At this point the author has recourse to a form of words to which the reader may attach any or no meaning. "In the definite concrete historical conditions of a specific stage in our relations with a given capitalist State, its acceptance of a legally formulated obligation of nonaggression, *a fortiori* of mutual assistance, has great political significance."

If the essential limitations mentioned are always borne in mind, an exact knowledge of appropriate forms, combined with the skill to choose, and when necessary to construe, the forms most suitable to the political purposes of the Soviet State, is extremely useful. It is for the Soviet science of international law to ensure that red diplomacy has full use of this auxiliary tool.

Pashukanis condemns the formal and scholastic doctrines still current in Russia on the nature of international law. These, he says,[19] are the result of the surviving influences of bourgeois-juristic methodology, in which law is treated as an independent essence. Law, he insists, is one of the weapons of class struggle, one of the forms of the politics practised by the ruling class. Instead of abstract scholastic attempts to construct systems of "international law of the transitional period," Soviet internationalists should make it their task to learn and publicize the practice of the Soviet State and, from the basic principles of its foreign policy, formulate its international-law positions. International intercourse does not presuppose any "community of values," or similarity of economic systems and social orders. In our epoch international law is a means of struggle not only between competing capitalist States, but between different and opposing economic and social systems.

After all this in the first chapter, it is not a little surprising to find the author in his second arguing the reality of international law as a system with custom and treaty as its sources. Despite Lenin's observation that law without machinery of enforcement is nothing, Pashukanis repudiates Austin's doctrine that the so-called law of nations is mere morality, and is led into the weak position of treating reprisals, self-help, war, boycott, and blockade as legal sanctions.[20] Yet he has to

[19] P. 16.

[20] In his "Polozhenie na Teoreticheskom Pravovom Fronte," *Sovetskoe Gosudarstvo i Revolutsiya Prava*, nos. 11-12, 1930, pp. 21-22, he had quoted this passage of Lenin and observed that international law could not exist for any who accepted it literally.

admit an almost complete lack of efficacy in this system. In the practice of the capitalist States, he says, questions are decided ninety-nine times out of a hundred by force, with no regard for any legal principle.[21] As if this were not enough, he proceeds to list peculiarities of international law which reduce to the vanishing point its character as a system. These are (*a*) lack of clarity and definition, due to the contradictory conduct of States; (*b*) the stagnation characteristic of customary law; (*c*) the large role of commentators, each speaking consciously or unconsciously for views which at the moment please his class and State; (*d*) rarity of realization in practice, due to the absence of any punishment for violation by great Powers against the weak; and (*e*) the frequent impossibility of final decision of any international-law dispute. He sums up with the observation[22] that "the mutual relations of capitalist States being based upon bitter competition, the most substantial questions, touching the material interests of the different groups of capitalists, belong to the inviolable sphere of State sovereignty. Problems of trade, customs, tariffs, markets, currency, export of capital, colonial policy, emigration and immigration are decided by each government in its own discretion on the basis of the factual relations of forces."

What all this taken together means is that the norms of international law are rarely more than particular and subjective formulations of the immediate interests of the governments invoking them. As Pashukanis describes their use, they are tentative legal propositions, advanced by one side and usually denied by the other, with no over-all authority giving a determining statement of their validity.

If he had been a free agent, Pashukanis would perhaps have avoided the tangle of contradiction into which he falls in his search for system. Developing the doctrine of the first chapter, which reduces what is euphemistically known as international law to the common practice of using legal argu-

[21] P. 22.
[22] P. 22.

ments and forms as instruments of national interest, he might have gone on to an objective analysis of the use made of these implements by the Soviet and other governments in the myriad types of business that draw them into conflict or collaboration. Carried on in a similar spirit by his colleagues, this would have been a challenging invitation to the lawyers of other nations to make the study a common scientific enterprise transcending national boundaries in object and method. One product might have been the clear delineation of matters in which long practice, embodying common notions of law, has set generally approved patterns that can be disregarded only at some cost. These are the points at which the legal propositions begin to take on the quality of rules. They are no longer merely instruments of policy: they influence policy. Out of such areas of agreement in the general discord might have grown a more certain knowledge of the roles of law and other modes in the formulation and execution of foreign policy in our competing systems, and of conditions favoring the expansion of the legal role.

But a consistent treatment along these lines would have done little to meet immediate official needs. A foreign office committed to the doctrine that the "norms" of international law are merely formulations of the interests of the governments invoking them could hardly maintain that they impose obligations. What the Soviet Government sought, as many others in their time have done, was a system of rules to which it could appeal in support of its demands but which would not compromise the doctrine that it was ostensibly following or embarrass it in the prosecution of its aims. Ordered to meet incompatible requirements, Soviet jurisprudence still squirms on the horns of this dilemma.

Vyshinski

By 1938, Pashukanis had been purged. An article in *Pravda* on January 20, 1937, had described him as an enemy of the people.[23] His conception of the international law of the time

[23] Hazard, *op.cit.*, p. XXIX and AJIL, vol. 51, 1957, p. 385.

as a compromise between two antagonistic class systems, an interclass law, had been condemned as counterrevolutionary.[24] Judging, however, by the big guns turned upon him by Vyshinski, who from this time to his death was to be the most authoritative mouthpiece of the official line in matters of law,[25] his more grievous sins lay in his theory of law and the State. There, says Vyshinski, he had "criminally deformed our law" with his argument that in the period of proletarian dictatorship, before the State has withered away, the law is bourgeois. Worst of all, he had cast doubt upon the very possibility of a Soviet system of law. In the simple Soviet logic of the great prosecutor, he was therefore a spy, saboteur, and traitor, and his repeated recantations and qualifications were evasive or, at best, merely partial.

Tunkin

Yet, with slight changes in wording, the doctrine of international law now approved in the Soviet Union reproduces with dogmatic certainty the tentative findings of Pashukanis as set forth in his *Ocherki po Mezhdunarodnomu Pravu* of 1935. T. I. Tunkin[26] assures us that while Soviet theory shows many disagreements on other points it is unanimous in the view that there now is a general law of nations, the rules of which regulate the relations between all States regardless of their social systems. In Akademiya Nauk, *Mezhdunarodnoe Pravo* (1951, p. 5), this law is defined as the "will of the ruling classes, expressed in a body of norms, treaty or customary, regulating the legal relations between States, developed in the process of their struggle and cooperation and guaranteed

[24] Rapoport, "Protiv Vrazhdebnikh Teorii Mezhdunarodnogo Prava," *Sovetskoe Gosudarstvo*, nos. 1-2, 1937, pp. 92 seq., quoted in Lapenna, *op.cit.*, pp. 100-101.

[25] "Polozhenie na Pravovom Fronte," *Sovetskoe Gosudarstvo*, nos. 3-4, 1937, pp. 38-39; "Voprosy Prava i Gosudarstva u Marksa" and "Osnovnie Zadachi Sovetskogo Sotsialisticheskogo Prava," in *Voprosy Teorii Gosudarstva i Prava*, Moscow, 1949, pp. 23, 24, 27, 78; all quoted in Lapenna, *op.cit.*, pp. 39, 54-55.

[26] "Mirnoe Sosushchestvovanie i Mezhdunarodnoe Pravo," SGIP, 1956, no. 7, pp. 5-6.

by individual or collective State compulsion." The sinful words "interclass" and "compromise" are avoided; but the sense is the same. To complete the irony, the authority cited for this pronouncement is Vyshinski, who in 1949 had achieved his ultimate eminence as Minister of Foreign Affairs.[27] In 1956, as one of the many rehabilitations of the destalinizing period, Vyshinski's charge of treason against Pashukanis was declared to be unfounded.[28] Unfortunately the victim was long since dead.

There is much vehement confusion in Vyshinski's oracular utterances on the nature of law and its relation to politics.[29] But the 1948 article just cited leaves no doubt that at that moment law was for him an instrument of politics, and legal theory a tool of diplomacy.[30] This doctrine was unquestioningly accepted by the joint authors of Akademiya Nauk, *Mezhdunarodnoe Pravo* (1951, p. 105). They quote from a speech delivered by Vyshinski at the United Nations on November 22, 1948, and printed in *Pravda* three days later: "Law in general is nothing but an instrument of politics. Politics operates in many cases with the help of law, legal institutions and norms; it uses law as a tool, an instrument of its achievement." The conclusion is that for the Soviet State international law is a means by which it carries its foreign policy into effect.

Neither Vyshinski, nor the jurists who took his word as gospel until he died, thought it necessary to reconcile law as an instrument of Soviet politics with law as "a body of norms, treaty or customary, regulating the legal relations between States." The definition is blatantly circular;[31] but it must be taken to mean that international law in some measure con-

[27] The definition reproduces almost verbatim that published by Vyshinski in 1948 "Mezhdunarodnoe Pravo i Mezhdunarodnaya Organizatsiya," SGIP, 1948, no. 1, p. 22.

[28] Hazard, AJIL, vol. 51, 1957, pp. 385-388.

[29] Cf. Lapenna, *op.cit.*, pp. 53-54.

[30] See especially pp. 2-3.

[31] Vyshinski was not responsible for this defect. The word "legal" was inserted before "relations" by his followers.

trols the conduct of governments. How else can it regulate? Only in the most general sense could such an objective system of law be described as an instrument of State politics. If in fact governments accepted general submission to such a system, they could be said to do so as a matter of policy, in the conviction that submission to law best serves their political purposes. But from that point on, international law, if it is to regulate, must operate as a limitation upon, rather than a tool of, national aims and practice. If it is an objective regulating device, it cannot at the same time be subservient to the passing purposes of governments.

International law as a weapon

In most of the Soviet literature on the subject, the emphasis is sharply upon international law as a tool rather than as an objective system of control. It is a weapon in the struggle between different States or different groups and kinds of States. The collective treatise of 1951, which brings together so many of the contemporary Russian specialists in the field and relies so heavily upon Vyshinski, merely repeats a familiar refrain when[32] it contrasts the use made of international law by the Soviet Union and its friends on the one hand, and the capitalist States on the other. In the hands of the former, described as the "really democratic States and governments," it is a "weapon for strengthening the democratic principles of law and peace in international relations." In the hands of the latter, described as the "antidemocratic and reactionary governments," it is a "means of deceiving the peoples, of concealing imperialist designs of expansion and aggression." Apart from its complete denial of the community without which an objective system of legal controls cannot exist, this commonplace of the treatises stretches the elasticity of legal systems beyond the breaking point. How can one body of norms implement such diametrically opposed purposes?

[32] P. 3.

Only in 1956 do we find an attempt at reconciliation. In the article already cited, Tunkin has this to say: "International law, besides being a fund of principles and norms binding upon States, is, like all law, an instrument of policy, and is so used *in some measure* by socialist and capitalist States in execution of their foreign policy. The generally recognized principles and norms, being democratic in essence, *can only be used as an instrument of policy within limits determined by the content of these norms.*"[33]

The title of Tunkin's article is "Peaceful Coexistence and International Law," and his writing is remarkable for its moderation. In harmony with the conciliatory tone of the Soviet Government in its international relations through most of the year 1956, the author largely omits the folklore of capitalist aggression and imperialist conspiracy, and moves a long way towards traditional Western views about the basis and nature of international law. In doing so he firmly rejects the more advanced thesis, ascribed to a list of recent Western writers on the subject, that the system can emerge from its inchoate and primitive condition and become real law only with the development of world government. This, he says, is contrary to the laws of social development in our epoch. He sees no possibility of creating general international organizations, embracing the States of the two opposed world social systems, with any substantial supranational powers. The conception of a world State is, he insists, not only utopian; it is reactionary, since it reduces the significance of sovereignty and nonintervention and facilitates in the strong imperialist Powers a policy of dictation and intervention in internal affairs.

The relative restraint of these last words does not conceal the fact that Soviet writers must still maintain the diabolistic explanation of Western policy. And, though Tunkin concedes that international law, as an increasingly universal system, cannot consist of socialist norms, since on that basis agreement is impossible between the two orders of States, he admits no

[33] P. 11. Italics mine.

doubt as to the direction in which the content of the system is moving or the source of recent improvements.[34] The contemporary development, he says,[35] proceeds under the increasingly marked influence of the socialist camp. It moves towards the liquidation of reactionary institutions and the recognition of principles and norms guaranteeing peace, cooperation, and free national development. The two greatest advances in the last decade he attributes to Soviet initiative. These are the prohibition of aggressive war and the reinforcement and extension of the principle of national self-determination. The capitalist world, he says, limited self-determination to the "civilized States," but Soviet stimulation has made it universal.

Self-determination and Hungary

Sovereignty and self-determination—Soviet doctrine has made much of them, and continues to do so notwithstanding the savage suppression by Soviet arms of Hungary's tragic struggle for free government in the autumn of 1956. Apart from the continual harping on this theme in Soviet legal and political writing, the USSR has two treaties with Hungary that forbid intervention. Article 5 of the Treaty of Friendship, Cooperation and Mutual Assistance concluded at Moscow on February 18, 1948, binds the parties to "mutual respect of each other's sovereignty and independence as well as nonintervention in each other's internal affairs." Article 8 of the Warsaw Pact of May 14, 1955, lays down the same rule for its eight parties, which include the USSR and Hungary. Yet Professor Korovin found no difficulty in justifying the slaughter and destruction with which the Red Army finally succeeded in beating down the national revolt as assistance requested by the Government of Hungary in self-defense against external aggression. He characterized the hopeless effort of

[34] Cf. E. A. Korovin, "Nekotorye Osnovnye Voprosy Teorii Mezhdunarodnogo Prava," SGIP, 1954, no. 6, pp. 38-41.
[35] Pp. 7-8.

the United Nations to check the Soviet Government by condemnatory Resolutions as an intervention in domestic affairs forbidden by Article 2, paragraph 7, of the Charter. He was of course dancing to an official tune, as so many of his colleagues have felt compelled to do; but some consciousness of the weakness of his case appears in his arrogant expansion of the domestic category to include relations between the Hungarian and Russian governments. To describe these as domestic rather than international is to abandon all pretence of Hungarian sovereignty.[36]

Soviet jurisprudence has for some thirty years been the ready servant of Moscow's propaganda. This has meant that books and articles whose titles promise the Western reader scholarly technical treatment of the role of law in the relations of States speedily reveal themselves as political tracts. Even in that role most of them are marred by a childish violence of expression and indifference to contradiction. As we noted in reference to the article written by Tunkin in 1956, both tone and content change with major shifts in national policy, demonstrating Vyshinski's conception of legal theory as a tool of diplomacy. It is too early yet to say whether Hungary's tragedy will reverse the move towards rational discussion that was beginning to appear in 1956. But amid all the uneasy shifts of doctrine, there has been one constant. For the Soviet jurist, his government is always right. No more than any other art or discipline does jurisprudence enjoy in the Soviet

[36] See his radio broadcast of November 26, 1956, and his article in *New Times*, Moscow, 1957, no. 1, pp. 16-17, both reproduced in English in International Commission of Jurists, *The Hungarian Situation and the Rule of Law*, The Hague, 1957, pp. 25-27. The same volume, pp. 23-25, contains excerpts from a broadcast by G. P. Zadorozhny, another Soviet writer on international law. He, like Korovin, makes the Warsaw Pact a textual justification for the Soviet armed intervention. Article 5 of that instrument provides that the parties shall "adopt other agreed measures necessary to strengthen their defensive power, in order to protect the peaceful labors of their peoples, guarantee the inviolability of their frontiers and territories, and provide defense against possible aggression." Neither advocate of course admitted any impediment in Article 8, which forbids the parties to intervene in each other's internal affairs.

Union the liberty of detached evaluation. There is not yet any neutral meeting-ground for the international lawyers of Russia and the West.

If the personality cult, and the worship of Stalin in particular, has really been abandoned in Russia, and if the softer tone in international relations is to endure, the writers of the 1951 edition of the treatise published by the Law Institute of the Academy of Sciences are probably engaged in a major enterprise of rewriting. Compared with the edition of 1947, that volume well illustrates the swift footwork that has been required of Soviet jurists. In 1947 it was admitted that the founders and major prophets of Marxism had not been specialists in international law and had left no systematic revelation upon it. In 1951 Stalin was a god and the official tone towards the West was one of total antagonism. So the 1951 edition condemns the 1947 version for belittling the contribution of Marx, Engels, Lenin, and Stalin to the law of nations, and seeks by some sparse and heterogeneous quotations, now loaded with Delphic significance, to credit this line of succession, and especially Stalin, with all that is new and hopeful in the system. Lenin and Stalin are particularly lauded for revealing "the imperialist character of the newest forms of enslaving peoples and taking away their sovereignty, such as unequal treaties, the mandate system, the doctrine of the open door and equal commercial opportunity, etc." To Stalin is given the credit of proposing a united front of the peoples which led to the creation of the United Nations,[37] and of course, the writers insist, it is only the strong diplomacy of the USSR under his inspired leadership that has prevented that organization from becoming the instrument of American world government.[38] What will become of all this in any new edition of this leading Soviet work on international law?

[37] Pp. 96-104.

[38] Pp. 9, 96-104, and *passim.*

The "Five Principles"

A new and for the moment safe theme for juristic discussion was provided by the joint communiqué issued by Nehru and Chou En-lai on July 1, 1954. Here were promulgated, with the almost supreme authority of the Chinese Communist leadership, the "Five Principles" that should govern relations between all peoples. Seized upon at once by Professor Korovin as an epoch-making endorsement of the generally recognized principles of international law applicable alike to socialist and capitalist States, and especially relevant to an historical era that finds the world divided between two great socio-political systems, the five principles are as follows: (*1*) mutual respect of territorial integrity and sovereignty; (*2*) nonaggression; (*3*) nonintervention in internal affairs; (*4*) equality and mutual advantage; (*5*) peaceful coexistence.[39] These commonplaces of diplomatic conference are now discussed in the Soviet literature of international law with the piety traditionally reserved for divine revelation. A typical specimen of this exegesis is the article by G. P. Zadorozhny in SGIP (1955, no. 8, pp. 89-96). It ends with the obligatory recital of the Soviet Union's proofs of unbroken fidelity to the principles, and the bland assurance that, if other States will but observe with equal consistency the generally recognized principles of international law, then peaceful coexistence will be secure.

For all their subservience, we should have had little legitimate complaint against the Soviet theorists if they had been content to treat the law of nations as a polite term for the practice of using legal language, concepts, and forms in the advancement of national policy. This might have passed as a creditable exhibition of frankness, admitting the facts not only of Soviet diplomacy, but of diplomacy in general. True, the Western Powers show a broader willingness than does the USSR and its allies to submit to impartially interpreted

[39] SGIP, 1954, no. 6, p. 37.

general norms—a difference particularly noticeable in the current development of international adjudication. True, also, the USSR has demonstrated its total disregard for any general norms that would impede its methods of spreading communism and the expansion of Soviet power. The enthusiasm reserved by Soviet jurists for the Socialist importations into the body of international rules, and their constant denunciation of any legal propositions tending to limit Socialist sovereignty, reveal the essential rejection of world community under a legal system not wholly of their own making. But in the democracies also the notion of national interest still outweighs the claims of a world community subject to law. In matters that concern them deeply, though law is still invoked, the specific rule always supports the national case, and no authority is permitted to gainsay the national interpretation. In these circumstances, with political considerations dictating the content of the rule, it becomes clear that law is being made a tool of policy and the notion of an objectively binding system abandoned in practice. Western jurists trying to reconcile national discretion and universal norms are also impaled on the horns of a dilemma.

It might have been hoped that the International Law Commission would be a body in which the root difficulties of establishing law in an aggregate of determinedly individualistic units would have been dispassionately recognized and defined, and the essential conditions of progress made clear to governments and peoples. The members of the Commission were supposed to be appointed not as representatives of governments but in their private capacity as persons of recognized competence in international law drawn from the principal civilizations and legal systems. Official propaganda and competitive politics were thus to be exorcized from the Commission's expert deliberations.

From the first session in 1949 it became obvious that hopes like these were vain. In an article on this session, V. M. Koretski, the member from the USSR, made out an elaborate indictment of the members from the United States and Britain as tools of "ruling circles" that were planning a new war as the decisive step in subduing the rest of the world. Their object in the Commission was, according to Mr. Koretski, on the one hand to check any advance towards the prevention of war and, on the other, to push every proposal that would destroy the sovereignty of all States except those leading the "capitalist-imperialist conspiracy."[40]

It is plain enough to the Western mind that private experts are in their championship of national purposes sometimes indistinguishable from official representatives. The contemporary Communist mind, however, is incapable of imagining an expert whose views are not always those of his government. To it the distinction between government representative and national chosen for personal qualifications to perform an independent task is wholly illusory. This Mr. Koretski demonstrated at the second session of the Commission, in 1950. He withdrew from the session when his proposal to oust the member from Nationalist China was defeated by a vote of 10 to 1.[41] He remained absent during the third session, in 1951, and thereafter resigned.[42] In 1952, he was replaced by F. I. Kozhevnikov, and from that point on a jurist from the Soviet Union was in attendance.[43] The nature of Soviet participation, however, has remained much as before, though the virulence of tone has moderated. In the deliberations on arbitration, and on maritime jurisdiction, to take two examples discussed elsewhere in this book,[44] the familiar line of Soviet propaganda appears again. As in the promotion of human rights, so in the development of international law in general, the agencies of

[40] SGIP, 1949, no. 8, pp. 12-29.

[41] GAOR 5th Session, supp. no. 12, p. 1.

[42] That this "boycott" was part of the general Soviet plan to have the Nationalist Government replaced by that of the Chinese People's Republic in all parts of the United Nations makes it no less indicative of the use made of a program designed for legal development.

[43] GAOR, 6th Session, supp. no. 9, p. 1; 7th Session, supp. no. 9, p. 1.

[44] Below, pp. 127-128, 170-172.

the United Nations are made to appear battlegrounds where delegates from the Soviet bloc heroically defend the rights of oppressed nations and other groups against an imaginary conspiracy of enslavement led by the United States and Britain. The posture is apparently proof against its own palpable absurdity.

CHAPTER IV

MARE CLAUSUM AND *MARE LIBERUM*

"... all Princes generally govern themselves as they find the Conjuncture of the Times to favour their attempts."—Sir Leoline Jenkins to Mr. Secretary Coventry, William Wynne, *The Life of Sir Leoline Jenkins*, London, 1724, vol. 2, p. 698.

IF there is one branch of international usage where the contribution of the United States, in close interaction with Great Britain, has been more substantial than in any other, it is that which concerns the exercise of national authority, in peace and war, on the sea. This subject is again very much to the fore, with the Soviet Union now taking a prominent part in discussion and developments.

We have seen Elizabeth and her counsellors in their role as champions of *mare liberum*.[1] The England of the following century argued a different law. Under the Stuarts the island kingdom was the stronghold of *mare clausum*, and its lawyers turned their learned ingenuity to the vindication of royal claims to sovereignty in a great belt of waters reaching on the east to the very shores of the continent.

James I began modestly enough. Having abandoned the Dutch alliance and made peace with Spain, he proceeded to mark out the coastal zone in which no warlike operations between the continuing belligerents would be considered lawful. At his command, Trinity House set about delimiting the "King's Chambers," twenty-six bays on the east, south, and west coasts of England, varying in size from the entire Bristol Channel to such minor indentations as that between East Ness and Orfordness in Suffolk.[2] These became the limits observed

[1] Above, pp. 11-13.

[2] For maps see Thomas W. Fulton, *The Sovereignty of the Sea*, Edinburgh and London, 1911, pp. 121, 123.

by the High Court of Admiralty in measuring the English jurisdiction within which no prize might lawfully be taken while England was neutral. Then, and long afterwards, the King's Chambers were regarded as what we now call territorial waters. As late as 1859 Lord Cockburn held in *Reg. v. Cunningham*[3] that the Bristol Channel lay within the counties of Glamorgan and Somerset. The great change that has taken place in British maritime claims is indicated by the Attorney General's answer, sixty-eight years later, to a question put to him by the Court of Appeal. The Court was concerned with a collision that had occurred roughly ten miles from shore in the Bristol Channel at a point where the breadth was about twenty miles. The Attorney General, under instructions from the Secretary of State for Home Affairs, informed the Court that the place of collision was "not within the limits to which the territorial sovereignty of His Majesty extends."[4]

It was not in connection with neutral rights and duties that James was to make his exorbitant demands. What he tried repeatedly to do, though with an infirmity of purpose that doomed him to ultimate failure in his struggle with the ever resilient Dutch, was to exact recognition of a general sovereignty in the "British seas," coupled with the particular right to dictate the terms of fishing there. For the general claim, he relied upon those royal assertions of dominion which stretched back in time to Edgar the Peaceful and which we have seen Elizabeth skating over so lightly in her negotiations with Denmark. Whether as a matter of pride or as a cover for other aims, James and his successors displayed a febrile resolution not to let the legendary title "Lord of the sea of England" go by default. Their naval commanders were required to exact the humiliating naval salute even in Dutch coastal waters. As for exclusive fishing rights, there James's plan was to extend to his new realm the policy that he had inherited as King of Scotland.

[3] Bell's Crown Cases, 72.

[4] "The Fagernes," 1927 Probate, Court of Appeals, 311.

The English kings had in so many treaties granted or acknowledged the liberty to fish off the coasts of England that this was thought to be universal. In Scotland, on the contrary, where the industry meant so much more to the diet and commerce of the nation, fishing within the sea lochs and in a marginal belt varying from fourteen to twenty-eight miles (one or two "land-kennings") was considered a Scottish preserve. There the intrusions of the Dutch were occasions of frequent and bloody violence, and it was from the United Provinces that all the efforts of the Stuarts to extend the same regime to England met with stubborn and ultimately successful resistance.

The United Provinces had become the world's greatest maritime trader. By their own account, the herring fishery around the British Isles was the largest single factor in their prosperity. One of the Stuart objects was to check this commercial expansion with its increasing usurpation of British markets and its threat to the naval power of England. But James and his successors were under another sort of pressure as well.

Even in Elizabeth's day there had been much concern about the decline of the English fishing industry and the consequent scarcity of experienced mariners readily convertible into naval personnel. An effort was made to increase the domestic market by prescribing additional fast days when no meat was to be sold or eaten. This proved ineffective. It was impossible to defeat the ruses by which the Englishman continued to satisfy his preference for flesh. A new kind of remedy was proposed. Fishing should be permitted only to those holding licenses from the Crown, and the foreign catch should be kept off the English market. The queen refused to adopt such measures. They would weaken the Dutch, her allies in the struggle with Spain, and they would undermine her own position in the controversy with Denmark.

James I yielded easily to increased pressure. A committee including the famous Sir Julius Caesar obligingly reported that a general requirement of license to fish would not violate any treaty then in force, or any general rule of law.[5] On the strength of this, a Royal Proclamation of May 6, 1609, forbade all persons other than natural-born subjects "to fish upon any of our coasts or seas" save on yearly license. This was the starting gun for a series of international legal conferences and a literary outpouring of contending legal views for which there can have been few precedents. Both sides fortified their official positions with elaborate briefs from their jurists. Grotius had written his *Mare liberum* to refute the ocean-wide claims of Portugal and Spain and establish the right of the Dutch to trade in the Spice Islands. If he did not actually coach his fellow countrymen for their negotiations with the British, his tract was so powerfully relevant to their case that Charles I in 1635 ordered publication of Selden's *Mare clausum* as the most imposingly learned of the several replies to it. Under Charles II, Sir Leoline Jenkins, an Admiralty judge hardly less illustrious in his day than Lord Stowell a century and a half later, was induced to make out a case for a customary obligation binding the whole Dutch fleet to strike to any British ship "Commissioned for war, tho' never so inconsiderable in its strength," and for including in the sea of England even the coastal waters of the United Provinces.[6]

The Dutch argued, temporized, made guarded concessions, showed themselves masters of every delaying tactic. Law was their favorite weapon. They were dealing with a government and people who, prizing respectable legal justification for what they did, were disposed to take the time to counter the legal arguments of their opponents. The envoys sent by the States-General of the United Provinces came heavily armed with the law of nations and the civil law. These laws made the sea common. Only that part of it that could be commanded

[5] Fulton, *op.cit.*, p. 147.

[6] William Wynne, *The Life of Sir Leoline Jenkins*, London, 1724, vol. 2, pp. 697-700.

by shore cannon was subject to the jurisdiction of the riparian sovereign. Here they were asserting, in 1610, a criterion adopted ninety years later by Bynkershoek and ever since associated with his name.[7] If this was not enough, why then the Dutch fishermen had, by the peaceful and immemorial pursuit of their calling in the waters now declared closed, acquired a prescriptive right.

The British were hard put to it to hold up their end in this legal debate. Against the *mare liberum* argument they had nothing better to offer than a reiteration of the legendary claim of the kings of England to sovereignty in the surrounding seas. Stripped of its array of learned special pleading, this is what Selden's *Mare clausum* amounted to. As for prescriptive right, the series of Burgundian treaties that the Dutch also relied upon were proof enough that any liberty to fish in the English seas had been acquired, not by prescription, but by explicit grant. But how then escape the treaty obligation? Here the multiplicity of the British arguments betrays a painful consciousness of their weakness. The Dutch had not succeeded to the right of the Burgundian treaties. If they had, then they had destroyed the treaties and their rights by violation of the stipulated terms. Besides, there had been a fundamental change in circumstances. The permissions given had been for a hundred fishing vessels: now the Dutch sent two thousand. And, anyhow, liberty to fish did not exempt a grantee from customary dues.[8]

The Dutch, it should be noted, had two almost totally incompatible objects in view. They were determined to defeat the British claims to exclusive fishing rights and general sovereignty in the ill-defined but far-reaching "sea of England"; but they also very much wanted to avoid formal hostilities. Once under the Commonwealth and twice under Charles II, their difficult policy broke down in naval war. The

[7] *Dissertatio de dominio maris*, Leiden, 1702, chaps. 2 and 5, *Quaestiones juris publici*, 1737, book 1, chap. 8.

[8] The classic account of these conferences is Fulton, *op.cit.*, especially pp. 155-159.

third of these conflicts was deliberately planned by Charles II to facilitate his desertion of the Triple Alliance of 1668 and enable him to earn the rewards promised by Louis XIV for joining him against the United Provinces. He calculated that the best way to offset British distrust of Louis and inflame the national temper against the Dutch was to provoke an open challenge to Britain's maritime claims. Jenkins' brief was designed for home consumption rather than to impress the Dutch. It was to give the British attack the appearance of retort to Dutch violations of an established and precious legal right.[9]

All the British efforts to get an article obliging the Dutch to pay for fishing licenses into the successive treaties of peace that followed these wars were defeated by the diplomacy of their opponents. As for the maritime salute, though the Dutchman William of Orange, as King of England, was hardly less insistent than his predecessors, the target shifted to France. And this claim, like that to exclusive fishing rights, was becoming too patently inconsistent with the general British position on the freedom of the seas, and too expensive and disturbing in implementation, long to survive the Stuarts, who had made such indecisive and costly attempts to enforce it. By the middle of the eighteenth century, the salute was being described as "but an indifferent honorary ceremony." After Trafalgar (1805), instructions to demand it were dropped from Admiralty regulations.[10]

How was it that these great claims, which even so independent a jurist as Sir Leoline Jenkins was willing to champion, came to be replaced by the modest assertion of sovereignty in a three-mile marginal belt and in bays marked off by treaty or historically acknowledged as possessions of the riparian State?

[9] David Hume, *History of England*, chap. XLV.

[10] Fulton, *op.cit.*, pp. 147-159, 500-522; C. John Colombos, *International Law of the Sea*, 3rd edn., London, 1954, p. 45.

As Gidel observes,[11] the present admitted sovereignty of riparian States over a minimum marginal belt of three miles is not the residue of earlier claims to entire seas. The notion of a coastal zone where special rights exist had its own independent origin.

The Roman-law texts were of no help in this domain. They declared the sea, like the air, common, free *jure gentium* for use by all men, reducible to ownership by none;[12] and they made no distinction between coastal and distant waters. The owner of land running down to the sea had no right to prevent strangers fishing on the shore in front of his home.[13] This was private law, but it meant that the Roman State claimed no exclusive rights for its citizens even in coastal waters. On the other hand, Rome assumed jurisdiction to the extent of preventing interference with the general liberty of fishing and navigation and protecting shipping from the pirates that then as later infested the Mediterranean. It was the need of such protection, particularly where the approach to busy ports brought many ships together, that eventually brought recognition of the State's special authority in its coastal sea.[14]

Raestad[15] finds the first mention of a maritime zone belonging to the riparian State in the gloss attributed to Johannes Andreae, an eminent canonist of the fourteenth century, on the sixth book of the Decretals of Boniface VIII. No limit was specified. This had to await the authority of Bartolus of Sassoferrato who, towards the end of the same century, held that the territorial sovereign had jurisdiction and protection for a hundred miles to sea. This, he reckoned, was less than two days out, and according to him any place within two days' journey was in canon law "neighboring."[16] The wording sug-

[11] *Le Droit International Public de la Mer*, vol. 3, Paris, 1934, pp. 24-25. Cf. M. W. Mouton, *The Continental Shelf*, The Hague, 1952, pp. 193-194.

[12] *Digest* 1, 8, 4; 43, 8, 3, 1; 47, 10, 13, 7; Inst., 2, 1, 1.

[13] *Digest* 43, 8, 2, 9; 47, 10, 13, 7.

[14] A. Raestad, *La Mer Territoriale*, Paris, 1913, pp. 8-9, 51-52.

[15] *op.cit.*, p. 13.

[16] *ibid.*, pp. 14-15.

gests that he was translating into miles an existing doctrine that gave the State special powers of control in the *neighboring* sea. His pupil, Baldus Ubaldus, would have reduced the distance to sixty miles and given the territorial prince sovereignty rather than a merely protective jurisdiction; but the hundred-mile measure seems to have found more favor among the jurists. Alberico Gentili, the Italian refugee who became Regius Professor of Civil Law at Oxford, argued in the High Court of Admiralty that the Crown's duty to restore Spanish prizes taken by the Dutch extended far beyond the King's Chambers to a distance at least one hundred miles from shore, that being the extent of Britain's jurisdiction and responsibility—in a word, of its territory.[17] The same limit appeared even in official communications, as when the Earl of Salisbury, briefing the English Ambassador in Madrid on the fisheries proclamation of 1609, wrote that sovereignty extended that far seaward,[18] and when, two centuries later, the Czar of Russia claimed exclusive control and sealing rights within one hundred Italian miles of his Alaskan lands. Russia abandoned this claim in negotiations of 1824 and 1825 with the United States and with Great Britain,[19] but the Department of State at Washington was not above using it seventy years later in justification of the seizure of Canadian sealers.[20]

This measure, however, failed to establish itself in the general practice of Europe. It had rivals, especially in the northwest. The middle-distance doctrine has already been mentioned, and we have seen how decisively Elizabeth rejected it. There was also the range of vision, that is to say the distance at which land came into view from an approaching ship or, alternatively, the horizon as seen from shore.[21] Here again

[17] *Hispanicae advocationis libri duo*, book 1, chap. 8.

[18] Fulton *op.cit.*, p. 514.

[19] *Fur Seal Arbitration*, U. S. Government Printing Office, 1895, vol. 1, pp. 76-78.

[20] See Percy E. Corbett, *Law and Society in the Relations of States*, New York, 1951, pp. 124-126.

[21] Cf. Colombos, *op.cit.*, p. 70, note 5.

was a criterion hardly less imprecise than "neighboring." The range of vision varied with the elevation of the viewer and the viewed, with weather conditions, and of course with the keenness of sight. Nevertheless it served to distinguish coastal waters from the open or high sea for various domestic legal purposes, such as the distribution of salvage monies, the rights of the sovereign or his grantees in the matter of wrecks and jetsam, and the fixing of the time at which a charterer became liable to pay the shipowner for an entire voyage.[22] We have seen, also, how the Scots claimed exclusive fishing rights within one or two "land-kennings," each reckoned at fourteen miles. More important for our purposes is the fact that the range of vision was adopted in a number of treaties as the distance from neutral shores within which belligerents undertook not to capture enemy ships. One of these was the treaty of December 8/18, 1691, between Denmark, Norway, Great Britain, and the United Provinces.[23] The same measure appears also in treaties of Great Britain with Tripoli, March 5, 1676, and July 19, 1716; with Algiers, April 10, 1682, April 5, 1686, and August 17, 1700; and with Tunis, August 30, 1716.[24] In these treaties Great Britain obtained from the other parties an undertaking that their ships would not "remain cruising near or in sight" of His Majesty's roads, ports, or towns.

The defects of the range of vision as a measure of territorial waters have been noted. A more successful aspirant to general acceptance was the range of cannon. This was invoked as early as 1610 by the Dutch negotiators in London.[25] Only a century later, however, after it had been formulated by Bynkershoek,[26] did it become frequent in international transactions. It had the advantage of being based upon an ac-

[22] Raestad, *op.cit.*, pp. 46-47.

[23] Henry G. Crocker, *The Extent of the Marginal Sea*, U. S. Government Printing Office, 1918, p. 518.

[24] *ibid.*, pp. 534-535. [25] See above, pp. 113-114.

[26] *Dissertatio de dominio maris*, chaps. 2 and 5; *Quaestiones juris publici*, book 1, chap. 8.

tual mode of physical control. In this aspect it had, in addition to Bynkershoek's persuasive advocacy, the vast intellectual authority of Grotius. For Grotius had not thought of the coastal sea as something that could not be reduced to dominion. His *mare liberum* was the vast ocean, and the purpose of his essay under that title was to combat the sweeping claims of Portugal and Spain. What could be seen from the land was not necessarily *liberum*, for it was subject to appropriation by effective control.[27] What the two passages from Grotius suggest is not that the sea within sight belongs *ipso jure* to the territorial sovereign, but that so much of that area as is in fact controlled no less effectively than land should be regarded as under the jurisdiction of the riparian State. *De jure belli ac pacis* (book 2, chap. 3, 11) is explicit on the point that title to adjacent sea does not follow directly from title to the land: there must be actual control.

Bynkershoek, however, was not merely repeating and adding concrete detail to a suggestion left by his great predecessor when, in 1702, he wrote the famous sentence, *imperium terrae finiri ubi finitur armorum potestas*. He was making a generalization from practices which probably owed very little to any legal theorizing.[28] Cannon range was in the seventeenth century displacing the range of vision as the distance within which foreign men-of-war would not be permitted to hover or engage in belligerent operations. The point of reference was at first a fortress or a fortified port. Within range of his existing batteries a sovereign was regarded as having not merely the right but even the duty of preventing acts of war against the shipping of nations with which he was at peace.[29]

Bynkershoek's generalization did not find immediate or uni-

[27] *Mare liberum*, Magoffin edn., Carnegie Endowment, 1916, pp. 37-38; *De jure belli ac pacis*, book 2, chap. 3, 11-13; and see P. T. Fenn, *The Origin of the Right of Fishery in Territorial Waters*, Harvard, 1926, pp. 153-154, 165.

[28] For a detailed study, see Wyndham L. Walker, "Territorial Waters: The Cannon Shot Rule," BYBIL, vol. XXII, 1945, pp. 210-231.

[29] Raestad, *op.cit.*, pp. 108-110.

versal acceptance. Distances defined in terms of miles, or the range of sight, were still used in laws and treaties having to do with the administration of customs, fishing rights, and even neutral rights and duties.[30] Under pressure from France, Britain, and Holland, Denmark gradually reduced much broader claims and accepted four miles, while Sweden was content with three. The Danish reduction, it seems, was quite independent of any calculations about the range of guns.[31] But from 1762 on, treaties more and more made cannon shot the distance within which belligerent action was prohibited.[32] In a report to the Earl of Shelbourne, Secretary of State from 1766 to 1768, Sir James Marriott, King's Advocate, wrote that "jurisdiction is always understood to reach as far as the power of protection reaches—that is to say, within the command of gunshot from the shore. . . ."[33] When the Czar of Russia, on protests from the United States and Great Britain, abandoned his claims to one hundred miles in Bering Sea, it was upon cannon range that he fell back.[34]

By 1793 the United States had entered the discussion with the provisional adoption of a three-mile limit. That was the year in which Mr. Jefferson, as Secretary of State, wrote to the British and French Ministers in the United States defining the marginal belt within which the American Government proposed to prohibit hostilities between foreign belligerents. His note recalled the great differences of opinions and claims still existing and went on as follows: "The greatest distance to which any respectable assent among nations has been at any time given, has been the extent of the human sight, estimated at upwards of twenty miles, and the smallest distance, I believe, claimed by any nation whatever is the utmost range of

[30] *ibid.*, pp. 114-120.

[31] H. S. Kent, "The Historical Origins of the Three-mile Limit," AJIL, vol. 48, 1954, pp. 537-553.

[32] Crocker, *op.cit.*, pp. 537-632.

[33] Lord McNair, *International Law Opinions*, Cambridge University Press, 1956, vol. 2, p. 142.

[34] See above, p. 117 and the arbitration document cited there.

a cannon ball, usually stated at a sea league." The ministers were then informed that while the United States might after "respectful and friendly communication" fix a further distance it would for the moment rest content with this minimum "of one sea league, or three geographical miles, from the sea-shores."[35]

Within the next twelve years we find Sir William Scott (Lord Stowell) declaring Bynkershoek's dictum to be the legal rule and adding that "since the introduction of fire-arms, that distance has usually been recognized to be about three miles from shore."[36] In the "The Brig Ann," Story, J., on the other side of the Atlantic, takes the same line in 1812: "All the writers upon public law agree that every nation has exclusive jurisdiction to the distance of cannon shot, or marine league, over the waters adjacent to its shores." He adds Azuni to Bynkershoek for authority.[37]

Professor Jessup[38] has recounted how the three-mile limit became fixed in the practice of the United States. By 1864, when the French Foreign Minister argued that a battle between the Alabama and the Kearsarge more than three miles off the French coast would be a violation of French neutrality, we find Secretary of State Seward approving a reply to the effect that "no other rule than the three-mile rule was known or recognized as a principle of international law."[39] In the main, the United States has been no less staunch a champion than Great Britain of this principle as the seaward limit of the State's general sovereignty. As in regard to so many of the alleged rules of international law, however, the record has not been wholly consistent. From 1886 to 1890 the United

[35] Mr. Jefferson to Mr. Genet, Nov. 8, 1793, *American State Papers, Foreign Relations*, vol. 1, p. 183.

[36] C. Robinson, *Reports of Cases Argued and Determined in the High Court of Admiralty*, 3, 163, 5, 385c, the "Twee Gebroeders" and the "Anna," 1801 and 1805.

[37] John Gallison, *Circuit Court Reports*, vol. 1, p. 63.

[38] *Law of Territorial Waters and Maritime Jurisdiction*, New York, 1927, pp. 49-60.

[39] *Diplomatic Correspondence*, 1864, vol. 3, p. 104.

States claimed the right to control seal fishing in Bering Sea anywhere within one hundred Italian miles of the lands purchased from Russia in 1867. This could of course be presented as a claim, not to general sovereignty, but to protect a fishery threatened with extinction. The assertion of the three-mile general limit has never been deemed inconsistent with the exercise of special control in the enforcement of tariff and sanitary laws. But the United States was unable in 1890 to persuade Great Britain that fisheries protection should, in the peculiar circumstances obtaining in Bering Sea, be added to these permitted limited controls. Moreover, when, under the threat of forceful resistance, Washington agreed to arbitration, a tribunal of five members, including three neutrals, found that the United States had no right of property or protection in seals outside the three-mile limit. This decision was loyally accepted and compensation paid for the seizure of Canadian vessels.[40] But, as we shall presently see, a similar claim to control asserted in 1945 was to have a different fate.

The United States took its customs enforcement zone of twelve miles from the British Hovering Acts, in which this had long been the normal limit of operations, though until 1876 enforcement was authorized in exceptional circumstances as far out as three hundred miles.[41] But in 1935 United States legislation moved back towards the less restricted British practice prior to 1876. The Anti-Smuggling Act of 1935[42] empowered the President to establish enforcement areas as much as sixty-two miles from shore.

On September 28, 1945, President Truman issued a proclamation asserting the right to establish fisheries-conservation zones in "areas of the high seas contiguous to the coasts of the United States wherein fishing activities have been or in the future may be developed and maintained on a substantial

[40] Cf. Corbett, *op.cit.*, pp. 124-127.

[41] The Act of 1876 made twelve miles the outside limit. See 39-40 Victoria, C. 36, secs. 53 and 179; and *U. S. Statutes at Large* for Acts of March 2, 1799, sec. 25; and Tariff Acts of 1922 (sec. 581) and of 1930.

[42] 49 *U. S. Statutes at Large*, part 1, p. 517-Title 1, sec. 1(a).

scale," and to establish similar zones in agreement with other States at any place where fisheries have been developed and maintained jointly by Americans and the nationals of such States. In the latter case all fishing is to be subject to regulation and control as provided in the agreements. Arrangements made by the United States itself or jointly with one or more other States, that is to say, are to be enforced against fishermen of all nations.[43]

On the same day a second proclamation declared jurisdiction and control over "the natural resources of the subsoil and sea bed of the continental shelf beneath the high seas but contiguous to the United States."

These proclamations disowned any intent to change the high-sea character of the waters in conservation zones or over the continental shelf or to curtail the general right to navigation there. But many of the States that took the cue for similar declarations asserted their sovereignty not only in the contiguous continental shelf but in the waters above it. The most flamboyant of these sequels was the declaration signed on August 18, 1952, by Peru, Chile, and Ecuador asserting sovereignty in waters, sea bed, and subsoil to a minimum distance off their coasts of two hundred nautical miles.[44]

Against this and similar individual claims by Latin-American governments and by Saudi Arabia, the United States lodged protests still denying any obligation under international law to recognize sovereignty in waters beyond the three-mile limit.[45] Great Britain added her objections. Though the British Government had not protested the Truman proclamations, its note to Ecuador on September 14, 1951, was in the most general terms: "In the conception of His Majesty's

[43] Cf. M. W. Mouton, *The Continental Shelf*, The Hague, 1952, p. 66.

[44] For the spate of declarations, especially Latin American, that followed and for the most part far exceeded the Truman Proclamations, see Richard Young in AJIL, vol. 42, 1948, pp. 849-857, vol. 43, 1949, pp. 530-532, 790-792, vol. 45, 1951, pp. 225-239; Mouton, *op.cit.*, pp. 63-96, 250-260; Herman Phleger, DSB., June 6, 1955, pp. 935-939.

[45] Cf. Selak in AJIL, vol. 44, 1950, pp. 670-681; Phleger, *loc.cit.*

Government in the United Kingdom, there is no right under international law to control fishing outside the limit of territorial waters unless the right forms part of a historic claim to the regulation of sedentary fisheries, and even then such regulation does not affect the general status of the area as high seas."[46]

There were always States that refused to accept three miles as the outward limit of their maritime sovereignty, and for many years before 1945 the argument had been heard that a boundary originally determined by cannon range should move as that range increased. It took the Hague Codification Conference of 1930 to reveal how far the supposed rule was from the general consensus regarded as the lawmaking fact in the so-called community of States. Phleger[47] finds that the States "still adhering to the 3-mile rule represent about 80 percent of the merchant shipping tonnage of the world and most of its naval power." This would not constitute general consensus even if we ignored the fact that the Soviet Union, with its claim of twelve miles, is among the dissenters. There would now seem to be little chance that the three-mile limit can ever gain general acceptance as a rule of law. The current runs too strongly towards extension. Nor, if enlarging assertions of special rights of administration and exploitation of the type advanced by the United States itself are to continue, would there seem to be much point in positing a general rule to be riddled with exceptions.

There was adequate justification for admitting the right of a nation to exclusive exploitation of the resources of its continental shelf and for regulating high-seas fisheries in such a way as to conserve stocks. The purposes of the Truman proclamations were laudable. Their sequel, however, demonstrated the extreme difficulty, if not impossibility, of achieving such purposes by unilateral acts. The "continental shelf" is a term of uncertain definition, and current proposals for fixing the

[46] Mouton, *op.cit.*, pp. 88-96.
[47] *loc.cit.*

limit of exploitation would give immense and overlapping areas of sea bed to some countries and little or nothing to others.[48] Moreover, installations for the extraction of oil and other resources will in all probability give rise to disputes on the score of interference with navigation or fishing. As for fisheries conservation by single States or small groups of States, that can hardly fail to generate chronic conflict. An infinite succession of questions as to the justice of claims to the fisheries concerned, as to what measures of conservation are necessary and effective, and as to the impartiality of their application, can be foreseen. Many nations will be involved, and without a central and specialized organization for supervision and adjudication, the implementation of the claims now being put forward can only exacerbate what we have seen to be an age-old occasion of international strife.

The problem is eminently one for collective solution. What steps have been taken?

The outpouring of arbitrary declarations on fisheries, the continental shelf, and territorial waters after the Truman proclamations of 1945 stimulated a strenuous international effort to bring about general agreement on these subjects before the advance laboriously won since the middle of the eighteenth century should be completely wiped out.

The United Nations International Law Commission drew up and submitted to governments a series of drafts on the regime of the high seas and territorial waters, on the exploitation of the continental shelf, and on fisheries. The General Assembly arranged for an International Technical Conference on the Conservation of the Living Resources of the Sea, which met in Rome in 1955 under the auspices of the Food and Agriculture Organization. In the light of that Conference's report, the International Law Commission revised its earlier drafts, and in 1956 combined in one report and submitted to the General Assembly seventy-three draft *Articles Concerning*

[48] Cf. Mouton, *op.cit.*, pp. 6-45.

the Law of the Sea.[49] These deal successively with the territorial sea, the high seas, the contiguous zone, the continental shelf, and the conservation of living marine resources.

In submitting these final draft articles to the General Assembly, the Commission recommended that it "should summon an international conference of plenipotentiaries to examine the law of the sea, taking account not only of the legal but also of the technical, biological, economic and political aspects of the problem, and to embody the results of its work in one or more international conventions or such other instruments as it may deem appropriate." The Commission added the opinion that its work constituted adequate preparation for such a conference.

The General Assembly's Sixth Committee spent most of the eleventh session discussing the draft articles, and though these were referred without alteration to the International Conference that met at Geneva early in 1958, the discussion revealed the position likely to be taken by the governments on that occasion. A brief survey of the principal points upon which disagreement still existed will be enough to suggest that the Conference would demand miracles of reconciliation to mark any substantial progress towards a universal law of the sea. The International Law Commission's verdict that adequate preparation had now been made may prove to mean nothing more than that the limits of useful discussion had already been reached. For what the record most clearly demonstrates is that after ten years of laborious effort, the drive towards an over-all sea code has been halted by the major political antagonisms that have frustrated so many recent plans of international construction.

Breadth of the territorial sea

At the very outset of any enterprise seeking to establish a uniform law for the sea stands the vexed question as to the

[49] Report of the International Law Commission covering the work of its 8th Session, GAOR, 11th Session, supp. no. 9 (A/3159).

breadth of the marginal belt. Until 1958, the United States and British Governments were at one in the position, which now seems a minority one,[50] that three miles should be the outer limit. But at the Geneva Conference of that year the British, by way of concession to accumulating pressures, suggested the compromise of six miles. Russia since 1911 has been asserting increasing powers in a twelve-mile margin. Beginning with a Czarist prohibition of foreign fishing for twelve miles off the Pacific coasts of Russia, the claim has grown since the Revolution into one of general jurisdiction in a zone of that breadth measured from low-water mark on all mainland and island shores.[51]

In its final draft articles (no. 3) the International Law Commission notes the divergence of practice, records the opinion that "international law does not permit an extension of the territorial sea beyond twelve miles," and proposes that an international conference should fix the limit. The Soviet Union dissents. Its representative in the Sixth Committee (Mr. Morozov) declared that "the breadth of the territorial sea had always been decided by the coastal state itself, in the light of its security requirements, its economic interests and a number of historical, geographical and other factors, including the interest of international shipping," and made it clear that his government would demand that this liberty should continue.[52]

[50] A majority of the States answering the questionnaires preparatory to the Hague Codification Conference of 1930 favored the three-mile limit (League of Nations, C. 74, M. 39, 1929, V). By 1956 the majority appears to have been on the other side, demanding more than three miles. See Morozov in GAOR, 11th Session, 6th Com., 488th meeting, p. 36, and Fitzmaurice, *ibid.*, 499th meeting, p. 107.

[51] See Jessup, *op.cit.*, pp. 27-30, and the British Parliamentary Debates cited there, *House of Commons*, 1923, vol. 163, pp. 958-962, for disputes over seizures of British fishing vessels and crews in 1921-1923. For more recent Soviet legislation and treaties, see Akademiya Nauk, *Mezhdunarodnoe Pravo*, Moscow, 1951, pp. 306-307; A. N. Nikolaev, *Problema Territorailnykh Vod b Mezhdunarodnom Prave*, Moscow, 1954, pp. 167-238. Translations of some of the Soviet decrees will be found in U. N. Legislative Series, *Laws and Regulations on the Regime of the High Seas*, vol. 1, 1951, pp. 116-130.

[52] GAOR, 11th Session, 6th Com., 488th meeting, p. 36.

The representatives of Great Britain and the United States contradicted this statement of the present law and left no doubt that their governments would oppose any recognition of such latitude as a long step towards chaos.[53] As usual, the Russian attack characterized the Anglo-American advocacy of the three-mile limit as part of a general plan of imposing an imperialist will on the rest of the world.

Fisheries conservation

The International Law Commission (Arts. 49-60) would recognize the right of States to "adopt measures for regulating and controlling fisheries" on the high seas when necessary for the conservation of living resources. Any State aggrieved by such measures would be entitled to demand settlement by an arbitral commission of seven members, failing agreement on some other mode of peaceful settlement. The Secretary-General of the United Nations, in consultation with the President of the International Court of Justice and the Director General of the Food and Agriculture Organization, would be empowered to name arbiters if the parties failed to agree on the composition of the arbitral commission.

Continental shelf

As for the continental shelf, the International Law Commission (Arts. 67-73) would allow the coastal State "sovereign rights for the purpose of exploring and exploiting its natural resources." These rights would not, however (and here the phrasing of the Truman proclamations is adopted) "affect the legal status of the superjacent waters as high seas, or that of the air-space above those waters." Assuming that disputes in this context would not require the expert knowledge and technical adjustment that might be called for in regard to fisheries conservation, the Commission referred disputes not to an *ad*

[53] *ibid.*, 492nd meeting, p. 59 and 498th meeting, pp. 99-101.

hoc arbitral body but to the International Court of Justice.[54]

Both the United States and the British representatives in the Sixth Committee considered these provisions for compulsory arbitration or adjudication an essential part of the whole plan. Governments would not accept the proposed "restriction on their sovereign rights" unless they were given effective means of defending their interests.[55] The Soviet representative, on the contrary, true to the general position of his government in regard to arbitration,[56] rejected both the compulsory principle and the mode of constituting the arbitral body. As for submission to the International Court of Justice in disputes touching the continental shelf, here he gave explicit expression to the principle to which the Soviet Union adheres: "A State's expression of its willingness to submit to the jurisdiction of the International Court of Justice was part of its sovereign prerogative, and no State could be required to indicate such willingness in advance."[57] "Such a conception of sovereignty," said M. Francois, the Commission's Rapporteur, ". . . seemed irreconcilable with the needs of the international community."[58] Irreconcilable indeed; but, M. Francois might have added, a conception still controlling practice even among governments that have formally subscribed to the Optional Clause.[59]

The Article (no. 66) proposed by the Commission in regard to a zone of the high seas contiguous to territorial waters, in which coastal States may enforce customs, fiscal, and sanitary regulations, would drastically curtail such claims as that made in the United States Anti-Smuggling Act of 1935.[60] The zone would be limited to twelve miles from shore. This would conform to British practice since 1876. The United States representative in the Sixth Committee raised no objection; but

[54] See the Commentary on Art. 73 in the Commission's Report on its 8th Session.

[55] 498th meeting, p. 100; 499th, p. 107.

[56] See below, pp. 170-172. [57] 488th meeting, p. 38.

[58] 500th meeting, p. 115.

[59] See below, p. 173.

[60] Above, p. 122.

the Soviet delegate did. The Soviet Union will, it seems, oppose any international limitation of customs and sanitary enforcement zones, or of territorial bays.[61] For bays the Commission proposes a fifteen-mile criterion, and designates as "internal" waters within the fifteen-mile line (Art. 7).

The United Nations Conference on the Law of the Sea, meeting at Geneva from February 24 to April 27, 1958, was unable to realize the hope for an agreed limit to territorial waters. When the United States adopted and submitted to the Conference the British compromise suggestion of six miles, the Soviet Union continued its resistance, and though the vote was 45 to 33 in favor with 7 abstentions, this did not constitute the required two-thirds majority. The chairman of the United States delegation accordingly declared that in view of this failure his Government took the firm position that the three-mile limit would continue to be the established law, and that no State adhering to this rule would be under any obligation to recognize wider claims.

On a number of points the Conference was able to draft conventions embodying proposals very close to those submitted by the International Law Commission. Thus it recognized a contiguous zone, limited to twelve miles from the territorial-waters baseline, for the enforcement of customs, fiscal, immigration, and sanitary regulations; permitted coastal States unilaterally to adopt urgently needed fisheries-conservation measures in the high sea adjacent to their territorial waters when negotiations with the other States concerned failed to produce agreement within six months; and declared that the coastal States exercise "sovereign rights for the purpose of exploring" the continental shelf "and exploiting its natural resources." Its liberal definition of the continental shelf extends these rights "to a depth of 200 metres or, beyond that limit, to where the depth of the superjacent water admits of the exploitation of the natural resources of the said areas."

[61] 488th meeting, p. 36.

But it follows the Truman proclamations and the Commission's proposals in preserving "the legal status of the superjacent waters as high seas." In bays, the Conference stretched the Commission's fifteen-mile limit of "internal waters" to twenty-four miles.

How much of these regulations will come into effect, and how broadly they will apply, must depend upon the accumulation of ratifications. Those that do come into effect will leave ample room for dispute. In the matter of fisheries measures, the relevant draft convention provides for the compulsory reference of disputes to special commissions to be constituted in close accordance with the proposals of the International Law Commission. Apart from fisheries, however, all that the Conference could do by way of provision for the settlement of differences was to attach an optional protocol, the parties to which will accept the jurisdiction of the International Court of Justice.[62]

Freedom of the seas as freedom from national sovereignty

"Freedom of the seas" has been used in two principal senses. One is freedom from the sovereignty of any nation. The closest analogy is the *res communis* of Roman law, not the *res nullius*; though practice wavers between these two categories. In *res communis*, while use is open to all, none can acquire title. *Res nullius*, on the other hand, becomes the property of the first effective occupant.

In regard to that part of the sea washing national territory, theory and practice alike admit appropriation, the theoretical justification being (*a*) the moral consideration that sovereignty in the marginal belt is essential to national security and welfare, and (*b*) the legal consideration that effective control, equivalent to occupation, is possible there. Here, then, theory moved away from the *res communis* classification, without,

[62] DSB, June 30, 1958, pp. 1110-1125.

however, adopting that of *res nullius* with all its consequences. For nations are admitted to have sovereignty in the marginal belt of territorial sea for at least three miles from shore whether or not they have the means of effective control. And, as effective control is not made a condition, there is no question of territorial waters becoming subject to occupation by a non-coastal State by reason of dereliction on the part of the coastal State, as there would be if they were subject to the rules affecting *res nullius.*

In regard to the high seas, that is to say the sea beyond territorial waters (on the limits of which there is not, as we have seen, any general consensus), theory still clings to the classification *res communis.* Practice, however, is making this classification more and more inappropriate, since, as we have also seen, the assertion by States of more and more extensive claims to control are in fact making the use of the high seas less and less open to all. There is clearly an element of appropriation in establishing fisheries-conservation zones, in spite of clauses disowning sovereignty, and this is in some degree true even of the installation of equipment for working the continental shelf. Roman-law analogies have perhaps in this context served their turn, and might better be abandoned as now more misleading than constructive. But, if they are to continue in use, it may be suggested that *res publica* is becoming more appropriate than *res communis*, especially in view of the trend to multilateral conventions subjecting common use to collective regulation.[63] Effective implementation of a conception of the high seas as the public property of a universal community is of course still far ahead. With each step in that direction, the freedom of the seas must become increasingly a freedom of use subject to conditions and restraints defined and imposed by

[63] As regional arrangements moving in this direction, see the 1949 International Convention for the Northwest Atlantic Fisheries (Canada, Denmark, Iceland, United Kingdom, United States), and the 1952 Convention for the High Seas Fisheries of the North Pacific Ocean (Canada, Japan, the United States).

something analogous in the international sphere to the public law of States. This is the distant ideal towards which official and unofficial plans touching the use of the seas and providing for supervision and the compulsory adjudication of conflicts are moving.

Freedom of the seas as freedom of navigation and trade

The other principal sense of "freedom of the seas" has been freedom of navigation and trade in peace and war. Obviously a corollary of the absence of State sovereignty in the high seas, this principle has had a life of its own. All governments from time to time have not merely admitted but asserted the freedom of the high seas from national sovereignty, and in the interval between the abandonment of ancient claims and the recent assertion of new ones, peacetime practice largely conformed to the principle. In wartime, on the other hand, belligerent governments have asserted a right and exercised a power of control that have steadily expanded since the eighteenth century. The treatment of these assertions as exceptions to the general freedom of the seas made as concessions to the needs of belligerents cannot conceal the movement here towards *mare clausum.* Long checked by powerful States that might join the enemy if their complaints were ignored, the usurpation of neutral interests suffers little restraint in wars that range all considerable Powers on one side or the other. When the use of the high seas is so effectively controlled by belligerents that neutrals must apply for "navicerts" and "mailcerts" in order to carry on maritime trade in ordinary commodities, it no longer makes sense to talk of *mare liberum* in time of war.

In this matter, the practice of the United States has followed a course parallel to that of Great Britain. In the Napoleonic Wars, the United States resisted the contraband and blockade measures applied by Great Britain. In the Civil War it adopted and expanded those measures.[64]

In the first world war, it joined the Allies in practices which as a neutral it had condemned and protested.[65] In the second world war it abandoned its classic conceptions of neutral rights and duties long before it became a belligerent,[66] and then, as a belligerent, actively participated in the substantially successful effort to close the seas to all traffic not approved by itself and its allies.[67]

These developments in United States policy marked the triumph of what were regarded as requirements of self-preservation over established rules. Professor Hyde's comment is as instructive as it is restrained. Referring to the transfer of destroyers to Great Britain on September 2, 1940, he says: "The consummation of the arrangement signified that in the opinion of the American Government the normal international obligation resting upon the United States as a neutral had, under the existing circumstances, become inapplicable as a deterrent."[68] Two things combined to make the triumph especially conspicuous. One was the abandonment of interwar domestic legislation imposing upon American citizens neutral abstentions far more exacting than those called for by any international rules on the subject; the other was the final defeat of the century-old movement in the United States to secure freedom of private, noncontraband enemy property. The government had been sufficiently committed to this effort to make it the ground of refusing to adhere to the Declaration of Paris, 1856, which went only so far as to exempt innocent enemy property

[64] Cf. Philip C. Jessup in *Neutrality*, vol. 3, Edgar Turlington, New York, 1936, p. VII.

[65] Cf. Harvard Research, *Neutrality in Naval and Aerial War*, sec. 5, Neutral Trade, with Commentary; Hackworth, *Dig.*, vol. 7, pp. 23-24.

[66] Charles Cheney Hyde, *International Law Chiefly as Interpreted and Applied by the United States*, 2nd edn., Boston, vol. 3, 1947, pp. 2155-2158, 2202, 2230, 2234-2237.

[67] Cf. Julius Stone, *Legal Controls of International Conflict*, New York, 1954, pp. 485, 504-507, 603-607.

[68] *op.cit.*, p. 2235.

under neutral flags.[69] At the Hague Peace Conference in 1907 the United States delegation pushed the proposal with great vigor against the opposition of Britain, France, Russia, and Japan.[70] Finally, the principle emerged in vastly expanded form as the second of the "Fourteen Points" enunciated by President Wilson in his address to Congress on January 8, 1918, as his peace program:

> Absolute freedom of navigation upon the seas outside territorial waters, alike in peace and war, except as the seas may be closed in whole or in part by international action for the enforcement of international covenants.

This item got as far as the Paris Peace Conference of 1919, where, confronted with the combined opposition of Lloyd George and Clemenceau, it was indefinitely postponed.[71] The principle is still as remote as the vigorous world government which could alone give it reality.

[69] Hackworth, *Dig.*, vol. 6, p. 598.

[70] *ibid.*, p. 599.

[71] Samuel Flagg Bemis, *Diplomatic History of the United States*, 1936, p. 623.

CHAPTER V

THE DIPLOMACY OF ARBITRATION

ONE mode of handling international conflicts that has shown interesting development in recent years is reference to *ad hoc* or standing arbitral tribunals. Since 1922, when the Permanent Court of International Justice was set up, to be succeeded in 1945 by the International Court of Justice, it has been usual to distinguish between judicial and arbitral settlement. But for some time before 1922 there had come to be sufficient of the judicial quality in arbitration, and there continues to be enough of the arbitral in contemporary adjudication, to make the distinction one of little substance. What we have before us is a very long process of development, in the last century of which arbitration has been taking on more of the characteristics of judicial proceedings under municipal law. The highest point reached thus far—and it is a notable advance—is represented by the International Court of Justice and its proceedings. Since, however, submission to the Court remains voluntary, since the litigants are represented on the bench, and since judgments are not, despite Article 94 of the United Nations Charter, supported by any operative machinery of enforcement, it is difficult to recognize any difference in kind from the arbitral bodies which since the early nineteenth century have been justifying their awards by reference to "international law." Even the distinction often made, to the effect that adjudication is by a fixed bench, whereas arbiters are appointed *ad hoc*, is dulled by the addition of *ad hoc* judges when litigants have no national in the International Court of Justice.

Justification of decisions by reference to international law is the commonly recognized mark distinguishing between settlement by good offices, mediation, or conciliation on the one hand and arbitration on the other. This distinction is again hardly more than skin-deep. The mediator or conciliator may recommend his solution by reference to law as well as the mutual advantage of the parties; while the judge or arbiter may decide in accordance with his idea of the general advantage and appeal to law essentially as a means of making that idea palatable by subsuming it under a universal principle. Even municipal law can accommodate a wide choice of decisions, and the body of material known as international law is so vague and debatable that justification can be found in it for any award a reasonable man would be likely to make.

Significant theoretical differences do now exist between the two kinds of settlement proceedings. The first attempts to bring the parties into agreement on terms, while the second authorizes a third person or body of persons to decide terms. In the first there is no obligation to accept any suggested solution; whereas, once arbitration has been agreed upon, there is wide recognition and usual observance of a duty to comply with the award. These differences explain the fact that treaties frequently make provision for submission of all disputes not otherwise disposed of to conciliation proceedings, whereas the obligation to arbitrate is limited to "legal" or "justiciable" disputes.

These sharp distinctions are modern, and even now they are not always observed in practice. In the thirteenth and fourteenth centuries, when the practice of arbitration reached a temporary peak in frequency and scope, the persons chosen to settle a dispute were described indifferently as arbiters or conciliators and, though empowered to dispose of the matter finally, were given the widest choice of method and principle.[1] Nor was any distinction made between justiciable or legal, and nonjusticiable or political disputes. Where treaties made provision for a general settlement by arbitration, they covered all the differences between the parties, even (sometimes specifically) those touching security and honor. Moreover, sanctions

[1] See Mileta Novacovitch, *Les Compromis et les Arbitrages Internationaux du XIIe au XVe Siècle*, Paris, 1905, *passim.*

were explicitly provided for noncompliance, castles, money, and other valuables supplementing the oaths of the parties. It is to be noted, however, that arbitration was rare among the greater Powers, and that one of the famous cases of noncompliance with an award was Philip the Fair's rejection of the decision rendered by Boniface VIII in favor of Edward I of England, on the ground that the Pope had shown flagrant partiality.[2]

The comparative rarity of arbitration between great States in the Middle Ages suggests some of the reasons for choosing this way of settlement. The parties may doubt their power to exact satisfaction. They may, especially if they are conscious of weakness, have a general and decided preference for peaceful modes of pursuing their interests. Similar considerations often, however, weigh importantly with great Powers. They are not always or everywhere in positions of strength.

In the early years of the nineteenth century, it was Great Britain and the United States that did most to revive the ancient practice of arbitration. The story has been repeatedly and authoritatively told. There is still room, however, for a succinct re-examination of some of this familiar material with the attention focused upon the nature of the arbitral procedures employed, their relationship to other processes of adjustment, and the measure in which they can be said to have imported canons of judicial decision into the settlement of international disputes.

On the American side was at first weakness that might have tempted the more powerful State to dictate terms. But the United States was a huge and distant country where it was difficult and costly to bring overwhelming force to bear. Canada presented an exposed British flank—a valued possession that might easily be lost. During the early years of the new republic, European politics continued to be too threatening to Britain to permit the detachment of large military and naval resources for trans-Atlantic action. Moreover, the rising Amer-

[2] Novacovitch, *op.cit.*, pp. 18, 33, 59-60, 82-83, 97, 111-112.

ican nation was a valuable market and an immensely important source of food and raw materials that war would cut off. Reinforcing these considerations was a common tradition of respect for law and legal procedures. Even so, as the United States grew in strength and confidence, the choice of arbitration or renewed negotiation rather than war hung delicately in balance on several occasions, and once, in 1812, resort was had to arms. There is no pair of strong nations between which arbitration has been so frequent or has embraced such substantial issues. The habit of peace now stretches back for nearly a hundred and fifty years. It is therefore particularly instructive to find that in the repeated British-American clashes of important interest arbitration or another form of peaceful adjustment was never to be taken for granted. The governments took their decisions only after earnest calculation of the values at stake, the minimum and maximum results to be anticipated from an arbitral or negotiated settlement, and the risk and probable cost of war. Instructive also is the intermingling in one process of negotiation and arbitration, with the threat of force at times in the not remote background.

Arbitration under Jay's treaty

The circumstances in which the development of British-American arbitration begins could hardly have been less propitious. The formal peace of 1783 had left rankling grievances, the bitterest of which were the retention of the western fur-trading posts by Great Britain and the murderous raids of her Indian allies. On the other side were complaints over unpaid debts and the confiscation of loyalist property. To the American grievances were added, after 1793, the Orders in Council that, in addition to calling for the detention of neutral ships carrying food to France and the forced purchase of their cargoes, applied the Rule of War of 1756 to ships engaging in the trade between France and her colonies. In the United States, Washington and the Federalists, while deploring British outrages, favored Britain as against revolutionary France, which was also capturing American shipping and cargoes and imprisoning crews, and held that to push their just grievances to the point of war would be not only to ruin the struggling young nation financially, but to expose it to re-conquest. Against them Jefferson and the Republicans carried on an unbridled campaign of anti-British agitation. Only with great difficulty was the anti-British faction prevented from forcing through Congress retaliatory legislation to stop trade with Britain, and it was to blunt its attack that the Administration agreed to send a special embassy to London.

The choice fell upon Chief Justice John Jay, whose Federalist ties and friendship for England set the Jeffersonians against his mission from the first. To him was assigned the impossible task of persuading the British not only to return the fur-trading posts and restrain rather than incite their Indian allies, but to pay compensation for seizures made "under color of" the Orders in Council, curtail drastically their interference with neutral commerce, and relax their prohibition of trade with the West Indies. Rather than make substantial concessions on all these issues, the British Government would clearly have preferred to see her late colonies join the enemy. While therefore, as Professor Bemis says,[3] an abler negotiator might have won better terms, the Chief Justice was far from meriting the execration that so many of his countrymen poured upon him.

He secured a fresh promise to surrender the posts; and this promise was fulfilled. Arrangements were made for settling the debt and spoliation issues by arbitration. But because the British would not forego the capture of enemy goods on neutral ships or suspend the "Rule of 1756," refused to undertake not to use Indian allies, and would open West Indian trade only to vessels of seventy tons' burthen or less, the treaty that Jay brought home was the signal for a battle of the parties which in its vituperative bitterness has few parallels

[3] *Jay's Treaty*, New York, 1923, pp. 267-271.

in American political history. In the storm of personal abuse for surrender to England, Washington preserved sufficient influence to win the necessary two-thirds vote in the Senate; but the opposition then moved to the House, where, after two months of stormy debate, with the British and French ministers competing for votes, the appropriation to implement the treaty was passed on April 30, 1796, ten months after the Senate's narrow approval.[4]

In view of the intense feeling in the United States, it is hardly surprising that the treaty's arbitral arrangements were not uniformly successful. The commission charged with settlement of the debt issue gave up in acrimonious failure, revealing how arbitral proceedings may be simply a continuation of negotiation by other means.

In its composition, this commission adopted a pattern which is still more or less standard in arbitration. Article 4 of the treaty provided that two commissioners each should be appointed by His Britannic Majesty and the President of the United States. A fifth was to be appointed by unanimous vote of these four or, if they could not agree, selected by lot from two persons named respectively by the American and the British commissioners. All decisions were to be by majority vote of the commissioners present, provided that those present included the fifth commissioner and, in addition, at least one British and one American commissioner. The four original commissioners met in Philadelphia in May, 1797, and the lot to which, failing agreement, they had to resort, fell upon John Guillemard, a British subject resident in that city. Thus constituted, the commission began examining claims in January, 1798.[5]

[4] See Samuel Flagg Bemis, *Diplomatic History of the United States*, 1936, *passim*; Thomas A. Bailey, *A Diplomatic History of the American People*, New York, 1940, pp. 53-69.

[5] For facts and references touching these early arbitrations, I am indebted to John Bassett Moore, *History and Digest of the International Arbitrations to which the United States has been a Party*, Washington, Government Printing Office, 1898, vol. 1.

Within three months the proceedings had taken on a tone of acerbity and distrust. In his written answer to one statement of claim the American agent took it upon himself to caution the commission (which, as we have seen, consisted of three British subjects and two Americans), against making any decision so palpably absurd or so obviously partial or corrupt as to justify either party, on the authority of Vattel, to disregard it. An order of the commission repudiated these suggestions with restrained indignation, whereupon the United States Attorney General wrote enquiring whether this meant that "it belonged not to the Board to consider what the United States might think of their awards." To this Thomas Macdonald, one of the British commissioners, replied in a private note to the American agent. In his turn citing Vattel, he emphatically rejected the notion that the validity of an award could depend upon what either party thought of it. The incident passed; but shortly the same commissioner, whom Secretary of State Pickering later described as "in the highest degree overbearing and arrogant, and not very delicate towards our country," initiated a succession of increasingly sharp disagreements by submitting some notes on the general principles which he thought should govern the commission's deliberations. At least as much as opposing views on specific cases, these arguments about abstract principles, such as what constituted impediments to ordinary proceedings for debt, whether claimants should be denied if ordinary remedies had become available since the Jay treaty, and whether persons alleged to have owed allegiance to any of the States were entitled to claim as British subjects, contributed to a state of tension within the commission that brought about its dissolution. Taking advantage of the rule that at least one American commissioner must be present to render proceedings valid, the two Americans, by withdrawing at first temporarily to prevent particular decisions and then finally, brought the commission's activities to an end. This action may have been suggested by the withdrawal of the two British commissioners from the mixed board sitting in London under the same treaty to deal with maritime spoliations. There the lot for a fifth member had fallen upon an American, and the British members walked out to prevent the decision of a case which they thought outside the jurisdiction of the commission. They returned when their reasons for withdrawal were overruled by the Lord Chancellor.

The questions of principle on which the American commissioners in Philadelphia had so sharply differed from the majority were all necessary to the decision of claims before the commission, and to halt proceedings by withdrawal was to deny the tribunal power to make any decision which did not please the representatives of one party. In connection with the temporary withdrawal of the British commissioners from the London commission, Lord Granville, Secretary of State for Foreign Affairs, who had been the British negotiator of the Jay treaty, had suggested that the clause requiring the presence of at least one commissioner for each side perhaps gave each government power to prevent the decision of any question which in its opinion lay outside the commission's jurisdiction. But, far from dogmatic on the subject, he proposed consultation with Loughborough, Lord Chancellor, who had advised in the treaty negotiations. Loughborough was emphatic in the legal view that "the doubt respecting the authority of the commissioners to settle their jurisdiction was absurd; and that they must necessarily decide upon cases being within, or without, their competency." The American Government, in accepting the withdrawal of their commissioners at Philadelphia, took advantage of a clause which, despite Granville's very tentative suggestion, can hardly have been intended as a means of putting the commissions under the complete control of either party. Subject to such control, their proceedings would not differ in any essential from direct negotiation. In the London commission the American members, taking a diametrically opposite view where they were in a majority, were upholding that body's power to determine its own jurisdiction

—a position supported, as we have seen, by the head of the British judicial system.

Lord Granville had immediately accepted Loughborough's views on the powers of the London commission; but in 1799, on hearing of the withdrawal of the American commissioners in Philadelphia, he withdrew the British members of the London body by way of protest and in order to stimulate an agreement that would permit a resumption of proceedings. This proved impossible. The two governments could not get together on criteria for the admission of claims. The matter was finally disposed of by direct negotiation, Great Britain accepting a lump sum of £600,000. Thereupon, in 1802, the British members rejoined the London commission, which proceeded to pass upon the spoliation claims. Its suspension pending settlement of the debts issue had re-emphasized how narrow may be the distinction between arbitration and diplomatic bargaining unmixed with legal forms.

The Northeastern boundary dispute

In sharp contrast with the debt proceedings was the smooth course of the commission charged with determining "what river was truly intended under the name of the river St. Croix, mentioned in the said treaty of peace, and forming a part of the boundary therein described; . . ." The arrangement for manning this body was precisely like that for the two other commissions, except that only one member was named by each government. These two were to agree upon or select by lot the third member. They had no difficulty in agreeing upon their man, and, after two and a half years of surveys, personal visits to the region, and study of the myths, legends, and rumors that had to do duty for evidence, the three issued a unanimous declaration on October 25, 1798, which was accepted as identifying the St. Croix. There remained much still to be done before the entire northeastern boundary could be marked out on the ground, and the business had not yet aroused the passions that later made it a *cause célèbre*. This particular phase was marked by a sweet reasonableness that has not been a common characteristic of arbitral proceedings. A readiness to give and take, rather than any application of legal norms, was the secret of success, and the method of reaching a decision was one of urbane bargaining rather than adjudication as adjudication is conventionally described. This is perhaps the more remarkable in that all three commissioners were lawyers. Egbert Benson, the New York lawyer who had been chosen as third commissioner, reported to President John Adams in part as follows:

> . . . the reference, as it respected the source of the River, being as it were an appeal to mere judgment or opinion, is in that view analogous to cases of assessment of damages not capable of being liquidated by *calculation*, or *definite* Rule, and therefore to be assessed according to discernment or discretion; a latitude of arbitrament is in such cases supposed to be permitted to the Jurors, but as they must at the same time agree in a precise sum, accommodation of sentiment among them to a degree is necessary, and consequently justifiable.[6]

It is to be observed that the United States Government in this case made no objection to so amiable a way of fixing a boundary when there was no means of ascertaining "the meaning" of terms used in a treaty. That was not because all the concessions had come from the other side. Of two possible rivers, the commission had fixed on the more westerly, which meant less territory for the United States. This was balanced by their decision that the boundary should run along the northerly rather than westerly branch of their St. Croix. A similar spirit would have brought the rest of the northeastern boundary problem to a conclusion eleven years earlier than actually happened and would have saved the United States approximately nine hundred square miles of territory.

The treaty of peace (1783) had left another problem of the same sort in its description of the point from which the

[6] Benson's report is reprinted in full in Moore, *loc.cit.*, pp. 33-43.

east-west boundary between Canada and the United States was to start. This was the angle "formed by a line drawn due north from the source of the St. Croix to the Highlands; along the said Highlands which divide those rivers that empty themselves into the river St. Lawrence, from those which fall into the Atlantic Ocean, to the northwesternmost head of Connecticut River. . . ." Unfortunately, there was no well-marked mountainous ridge clearly answering this description; and of the two rough approximations, the Americans not unnaturally chose one about one hundred miles north of that which the British thought most nearly in conformity with the intention of the treaty-makers. Article 5 of the Treaty of Ghent, 1814, made provision for determination by two commissioners, one British and the other American. If these could not agree, the question was to be referred to a friendly sovereign or State, whose decision the two governments agreed to consider "final and conclusive on all the matters so referred."

After six years of surveys, hearings, and study, the two commissioners reached final disagreement. On September 29, 1827, the parties concluded a convention to refer the dispute to a friendly sovereign and, on its ratification in 1828, agreed upon the King of the Netherlands as arbiter. The American Government had in the interval given some consideration to proposing a compromise division of the territory in dispute. Gallatin, Minister to the Court of St. James's, had thought this unwise. If the proposal were rejected, the matter would still be subject to arbitration under the Treaty of Ghent, and any concession offered meanwhile would count against the United States. He made this point in a letter to Henry Clay, Secretary of State, dated October 30, 1826.[7] Having first confessed it impossible to fulfill the letter of the Treaty of 1783, he went on to say: "An umpire, be he a King or a farmer, rarely decides on strict principles of law: he has always a bias to try if possible to split the difference, and, with

[7] *American State Papers, Foreign Relations*, vol. 6, pp. 647-650.

that bias, he is very apt to consider any previous proposal from either party as a concession that his title was defective, and as justifying a decision on his part that will not displease too much either party, instead of one founded on a strict investigation of the title." This was shrewd psychology, and it presents the arbiter as carrying on with himself the kind of negotiation by which the parties themselves at times succeed in composing their differences. Gallatin knew, as did his government, that compromise, whether by the parties or by an arbiter, was the only way short of violence out of this particular dispute.

The Convention invited the arbiter to investigate and make a decision upon the points of difference. There was nothing to indicate that his decision must be strictly a finding as to the meaning of the Treaty of 1783. True, the decision was to be "sound and just," and the arbiter was authorized to order additional surveys if he thought them necessary.[8] But the documents strongly suggest that the parties were essentially asking the King of the Netherlands to dictate a compromise which they had been unable to reach by themselves. Article 7 had repeated the agreement, first set down in the Treaty of Ghent (Arts. 4 and 5), that his decision "shall be taken as final and conclusive," adding for greater assurance that "it shall be carried, without reserve, into immediate effect by Commissioners appointed for that purpose by the contracting parties."

As Gallatin had anticipated, the arbiter could find no basis in a study of the language of the Treaty of 1783 and the nature of the ground for a categorical statement as to where the treaty-makers intended the dividing line to run. There was nothing in any of the documents, maps, or arguments to give preponderant weight to either of the cases presented. Nor could further surveys provide a *ratio decidendi*. To adopt either of the lines advocated would, as the arbiter put it,

[8] Convention of September 29, 1827, Articles 1, 6, and 7, *American State Papers, Foreign Relations*, vol. 6, pp. 643-644.

"violate principles of law and equity" to the detriment of one party. It was this honest confession that gave the United States Senate its pretext for rejecting the frankly compromise boundary which the arbiter proceeded to recommend.

Though the King's proposal gave 7908 square miles of the disputed territory to the United States and only 4119 square miles to Canada, the British Government was willing to accept it, intimating at the same time that acceptance by both parties need not preclude subsequent adjustments. President Jackson would have fallen in with this suggestion but for the loud protests of Massachusetts and Maine. The decision was left to the Senate, which in a vote of 35 to 8 repudiated the award as failing to decide the question put and constituting a mere recommendation which the arbiter had no authority to make.[9] Ten years later, when the continuing quarrel over this boundary had risen to a point of dangerous tension, the same body would give its approval to a compromise, negotiated as part of the Ashburton-Webster Treaty, which cost Maine 893 square miles of the territory that it would have had under the Dutch award, but consoled it with minor frontier adjustments elsewhere, rights to float timber down the St. John River, and a payment of $300,000 from the United States treasury.

Formally, Maine had a case. How insubstantial it was, how much it depended on one form of words rather than another, is made apparent in a letter of Edward Livingston, Secretary of State, to Charles Bankhead, the British Minister in Washington, dated July 21, 1832. "No question," wrote Mr. Livingston, "could have arisen as to the validity of the Decision, had the Sovereign Arbiter determined on and designated any Boundary as that which was intended by the Treaty of 1783. He has not done so, not being able, consistently with the evidence before him, to declare that the Line he has thought the most proper to be established was the Line intended by the Treaty of 1783; he seems to have abandoned the character

[9] *British and Foreign State Papers*, vol. 22, pp. 772-871.

of the Arbiter, and assumed that of Mediator, advising both Parties that a boundary which he describes, should be accepted as one most convenient to them. But this Line trenches, as is asserted by one of the States of the Union, upon its territory, and that State controverts the Constitutional power of the United States to circumscribe its limits without its assent. If the Decision had indicated this Line as the Boundary designated by the Treaty of 1783, this objection could not have been urged, because then, no part of the Territory to the North or East of it, could be within the State of Maine. And however the United States, or any individual State might think itself aggrieved by the Decision, as it would in that case have been made in conformity to the submission, it would have been carried into immediate effect. The case is now entirely different, and the necessity for farther Negotiation must be apparent, to adjust a difference which the Sovereign Arbiter has, in the opinion of a co-ordinate Branch of our Executive Power, failed to decide."[10]

The Treaty of Washington, 1871, has been described as "the greatest triumph for arbitral methods that the world had yet witnessed."[11] A triumph for peaceful settlement by one means or another, yes; but anyone looking for a historical turning point from age-old modes of diplomatic negotiation towards the more objective and impersonal judicial method will hardly find it here. In two of the arbitrations for which the treaty made arrangements, one or other of the parties assumed a continuing discretionary right to appraise the proceedings and determine its own conduct accordingly—in short a continuing control of the issues submitted—which was quite consistent with mediation or conciliation, but did nothing to establish arbitration as a distinct procedure. In one, the tribunal itself acted as a negotiating mechanism, this time at the suggestion of the United States which, in the northeastern boundary dispute, had condemned the arbitrator's assumption of the role of mediator.

[10] *ibid.*, p. 789.
[11] Bailey, *A Diplomatic History of the American People*, p. 422.

The Halifax Commission

Among its miscellany of arrangements, the Treaty of Washington granted American fishermen certain rights along the Canadian coasts, and some compensating rights to the British fishermen along the coasts of the United States down to the thirty-ninth parallel. There was strong feeling in Canada that the United States was getting much the better of this bargain, and it was provided in the treaty that a joint commission should decide whether and how much compensation should be paid for the alleged advantage. The commission was to consist of one member appointed by the United States, one by Great Britain, and a third by the two governments acting together. It was not set up until 1877, the governments having at last, after much negotiation, agreed upon a Belgian diplomat as third commissioner. After five months of deliberation, the commission by a majority awarded five and a half million dollars to Great Britain. The American member, holding that the British gained more than the Americans from the treaty, attacked the validity of the award on the ground that the commission had no power to decide by majority.

In appropriating the money to satisfy this award, Congress stipulated that it should be paid only if the President, after corresponding with the British Government regarding the conformity of the decision with the treaty, should "deem it his duty to make the payment without further communication with Congress."[12] The American protest was conveyed to the British Foreign Minister, Lord Salisbury, through the American Minister in London. The concurring commissioners had not revealed the manner in which their award had been computed, and Mr. Evarts, Secretary of State, expressed his conviction that to have done so would have exposed beyond all question the "infirmity" of their finding. He went on to support in detail, but with somewhat less assurance, the American

[12] Moore, *op.cit.*, p. 748, quoting *Foreign Relations*, 1878, 291.

commissioner's rejection of a majority decision.[13] Lord Salisbury's reply pointed out that Mr. Evarts' aspersions on the methods and findings of the commission amounted to re-opening a judgment which the treaty intended to be final, and went on to cite authority for the proposition that a majority arbitral award is always valid in the absence of previous stipulation to the contrary. That this was the intention of the treaty-makers was moreover apparent, he held, from the mode of constituting these commissions, an odd number being secured by adding one member by agreement or lot to those appointed separately by the parties. Salisbury might have added, if he had known, that in 1796 the American Government had overruled the opinion of its Attorney General that unanimity would be necessary in decisions of the commission set up under Article 5 of the Jay Treaty, where the text reads: "The said Commissioners shall, by a declaration, under their hands and seals, decide what river is the river St. Croix, intended by the treaty."[14]

The President proceeded to pay the award, but with a notice characterized by a notable moral and legal ambiguity. The payment "is made upon the ground that the Government of the United States desires to place the maintenance of good faith in treaties and the security and value of arbitration between nations above all questions in its relations with Her Britannic Majesty's Government as with all other governments.

"Under this motive the Government of the United States decides to separate the question of withholding payment from the considerations touching the obligation of this payment, which have been presented to Her Majesty's Government in correspondence, and which it reserves and insists upon.

". . . Her Britannic Majesty's Government should be distinctly advised that the Government of the United States cannot accept the result of the Halifax commission as furnishing

[13] *Foreign Relations*, 1878, pp. 292, 305-308.

[14] Moore, *op.cit.*, p. 751, note.

any just measure of the value of a participation by our citizens in the inshore fisheries of the British provinces; and it protests against the actual payment now made being considered by Her Majesty's Government as in any sense an acquiescence in such measure or as warranting any inference to that effect."[15]

What this involved language seems to mean is that, while the government recognized no obligation, legal or moral, flowing from the award, it was making payment in the interests of dependability in treaty relations and arbitral arrangements. Though doubtless less damaging than a refusal to pay, the repudiation of the decision as a just measure of obligation, on something decidedly less than overwhelming evidence that the commission had exceeded its terms of reference, casts doubt upon the transaction as a step towards the triumph of arbitral method.

The Alabama Claims

Equally unorthodox by the canons of arbitration, though useful in a long and difficult process of negotiation, were the proceedings in settlement of the Alabama claims.

Article I of the Treaty of Washington, 1871, reads in part as follows: "Now, in order to remove and adjust all complaints and claims on the part of the United States, and to provide for the speedy settlement of such claims which are not admitted by Her Britannic Majesty's Government, the high contracting parties agree that all the said claims, growing out of acts committed by the aforesaid vessels, and generically known as the 'Alabama Claims,' shall be referred to a tribunal of arbitration to be composed of five Arbitrators, to be appointed in the following manner, that is to say: One shall be named by the President of the United States; one shall be named by Her Britannic Majesty; His Majesty the King of Italy shall be requested to name one; the President of the Swiss Confederation shall be requested to name one;

[15] *Foreign Relations of the United States*, 1878, p. 316.

and His Majesty the Emperor of Brazil shall be requested to name one."

The justice of the claims was not, however, to be determined by the tribunal simply in accordance with its notions of existing international law. The United States Government was unwilling to take such a risk. It got the British Government's assent in Article 6 of the treaty that the tribunal should be governed by three rules there stated. These were to the effect that a neutral government is bound: (*a*) to use due diligence to prevent the fitting out within its jurisdiction of vessels which it has reason to believe are intended to carry on war against a Power with which it is at peace, and to prevent departure from its ports of vessels adapted within its jurisdiction to warlike use for the same purpose; (*b*) not to permit belligerents to use its ports and waters as bases of operations, sources of supply or arms, or for recruitment; and (*c*) "to exercise due diligence in its ports and waters and as to all persons within its jurisdiction, to prevent any violation of the foregoing obligations and duties."

In the same article, the British Government recorded its refusal to recognize these as principles of international law in force when the claims arose, but, for the sake of good relations and in order to establish a precedent likely to be useful in the future, instructed the arbitrators to assume that it had undertaken to act upon them. The decision, in a word, was to be based upon the propositions stated, regardless of whether they were law or not, and the British Government was willing that they should in future be regarded as law.

The tribunal, duly constituted, held its first meeting in Geneva on December 15 and 16, 1871, and, after receiving the written American and British cases, adjourned with the intention of meeting again on July 15, 1872. Then the storm broke. The American case included claims for indirect or consequential damages which, according to the British plenipotentiaries at the Washington conference, had been dropped in the negotiations leading up to the treaty. The claims were not computed, but were so described as to embrace "the prolongation of the war and the addition of a large sum to the cost of the war and the suppression of the rebellion." Seven per cent interest was asked on any principal amounts that the tribunal might allow.

There was in all probability an honest misunderstanding here; but the case for the British contention that consequential damages had been excluded was weak. As Lord Cairns pointed out in the House of Lords[16] there was nothing in the wording of the treaty to prevent pressing such claims. Normally a claimant can be expected to demand compensation for all the damage he has suffered, leaving it to the court to rule out any of his claims as too remote. The British plenipotentiaries argued that they had not pressed for explicit exclusion because they had judged that this would be so politically embarrassing to the American negotiators and Government that no treaty would have been possible. But there had not been so much as a clear-cut verbal renunciation, and to depend upon a vague understanding in so substantial a matter argues an almost incredible slackness.

In the House of Commons, Gladstone and Disraeli described the indirect-damage claims as exceeding anything that even conquest could exact. To submit would be an abdication of the nation's honor. With the injustice characteristic of public agitation, the unexpected magnitude of the American demand was popularly ascribed to a rapacious Yankee trick. The common view was that it would be better to take all the risks of war than to pay so exorbitant a bill, or, apparently, even to let an arbitral tribunal pass upon it. The tension rose to the point of touching off a panicky liquidation of American securities, and in the United States the press began to take the line that the Government should trim its demands. But direct negotiations produced no compromise.[17]

When the tribunal met again in June, Lord Tenterden, the

[16] Hansard, *Parliamentary Debates*, 3rd series, vol. CCVI, p. 1889.
[17] Bailey, *op.cit.*, pp. 420-421.

British agent in the case, asked for an eight months' adjournment to permit the parties to revise their submission. This, the Americans feared, would end the attempt at peaceful settlement. It was a ruse within the tribunal itself that saved the situation. Developing an earlier hint from Tenterden,[18] Charles Francis Adams, the American member, suggested that the tribunal, while carefully refraining from deciding whether it was competent to pass upon indirect damages, should declare that, if it were competent, it would rule them out. This happy deviation from the judicial norm made it possible to proceed with the arbitration without subjecting either government to the odium of backing down.

How truly judicial the parties considered the proceedings at Geneva may be gathered from contemporary accounts of the steps taken to sway general opinion and, directly or indirectly, the views of the neutral arbitrators. On this subject the letters of Bancroft Davis, the American agent, to Secretary of State Hamilton Fish are especially revealing. In one, Mr. Davis tells how he cultivated the Brazilian member of the tribunal. In others, he reports on British efforts to win friends for their case in Berlin and Paris and the countermeasures adopted by himself. An excerpt from the letter on Paris will be sufficient illustration: ". . . I have decided to close an arrangement by which we shut up at least some of the organs which England is trying to control. I enclose articles from the *Constitutionnel* and the *Soir*. I have already sent you the *Memorial Diplomatique*. I shall have the *Courier Diplomatique* in the same train, and shall have the support of the *Moniteur*, the *Patrie*, the *Presse* and *Bien Public*. This list includes all the important political papers except the *Debats* and the *France*, and the *Journal de Paris*. The first two are bought by England; the latter I don't know about. All this costs money, but I shall take the responsibility, under Washburne's advice, of spending it. . . . The attacks from England were so steady and so persistent in misrepresentation that pub-

[18] Moore, *op.cit.*, p. 641.

lic opinion was beginning to set in strongly against us. It is now decidedly turning."[19]

Whether this competitive propaganda had anything to do with the final award of $15,500,000 in favor of the United States would be difficult to determine. Sir Roundell Palmer, afterwards first Earl of Selborne, was leading counsel for Great Britain and has left an intimate (and partly versified) account of the proceedings. His tone is mild; but his narrative conveys a clear conviction of prejudice in the neutral arbitrators. But then he was the losing advocate. There may indeed have been some initial *parti pris* due to general sympathy with the United States or to accumulated grievances against Britain. But if anything was needed to sharpen tendencies of this sort, it was supplied in abundance by the hot-tempered arrogance of Chief Justice Sir Alexander Cockburn, who had been chosen as British arbitrator. As Selborne says, the Chief Justice took no pains to conceal his impatient sense of intellectual superiority over his fellow arbitrators; and the contrast that he presented with the impressively able, calm, and consistently courteous Adams did no good to the British case.[20]

The Alaskan boundary arbitration

One of the best known instances of arbitration so called is the settlement of the Alaska boundary between the United States and Canada. The facts of the dispute and the general tenor of the majority decision of the body that disposed of it in 1903 are too well known to require anything but the briefest mention here. Our interest in it lies in its classic demonstration of the use of arbitral forms not for the purpose of obtaining an impartial decision on points of difference, but as a means of enabling one side to surrender without a politically costly loss of face.

The forms here were of the most judicial. The Washington

[19] Quoted by Allan Nevins, *Hamilton Fish*, New York, 1936, p. 555.

[20] *Memorials, Personal and Political*, London, 1898, chap. xii, especially at page 247.

Convention of 1903 stipulated a tribunal made up of "six impartial jurists of repute, who shall consider judicially the questions submitted to them." Three were to be appointed by each side, yet they were to "answer and decide" the submitted questions by majority vote. Their decision was to be "final and binding upon all parties."[21] On the face of it, another triumph for arbitral method. But, as so often happens, it was not the constituent instrument that determined the nature of the proceedings. Some nonjudicial elements entered the transaction even before the convention was ratified.

The Senate was doubtful. Unless "the right men" were appointed, the decision might go against the United States. Before approving the convention the Senators learned from President Roosevelt the names of those whom he proposed to nominate, and were satisfied. The Americans appointed were Elihu Root, Secretary of War, George Turner, who had just finished a term as Senator from Washington, the state most interested in the matter, and Senator Lodge, whose general hostility to England was well known and who had publicly derided the Canadian case. Of the three, only Root was a jurist of repute, and, in spite of his official position, his was the appointment least complained of on the other side. The choice of Turner and Lodge was regarded as an outrage in Canada, and even in the United States it was recognized with public satisfaction that there would be no question of impartiality in their case.

The President made no secret of his conception of "judicial consideration." He made it clear to Americans in London, and through them to the British Government, that rather than permit any substantial concession, he would run the boundary as he saw it and occupy the territory so delimited. To him the principal Canadian contention, namely that the boundary cut across the inlets, leaving their heads in Canadian territory, was ridiculous. If he could be sure of Lord Chief Justice Alverstone's vote, he would yield something on

[21] Articles I, IV, V, VI.

the Portland Canal Islands; but that was as far as he would go for the sake of a peaceful settlement.[22]

Apparently the Senate had not been so divinely convinced that the American case was legally irrefutable. If they had been, they need hardly have been so anxious that the "right" Americans should be appointed to the tribunal. But Roosevelt, in consenting to the forms of arbitration, was doing so with the reservation that the award must be in his own terms. He assigned no weight at all to the judicial wording of the convention, regarding the London proceedings as a mere continuation of negotiations in a form which would make defeat a little easier for the British to take.

In the face of bitter Canadian attacks on his conduct in this affair, Alverstone, who provided the one vote necessary to an American victory, stoutly maintained that he had acted in a purely judicial spirit. This may well have been so on the main issue, for there was nothing unreasonable in the view that the words in the Anglo-Russian Treaty of 1825, which laid it down that the boundary should be "a line parallel to the windings of the coast," were intended to mean not merely the windings of the general coast, as the Canadians argued, but all the inlets. But his negotiations on the minor points were perhaps more judicious than judicial, and these were quite enough to create the conviction on the inevitably sensitive losing side that he had been acting throughout as a diplomat rather than an excessively diplomatic judge.[23]

Marred as it has often been by the quarrelsome maneuvering so characteristic of the political dealings of States, the record of Anglo-American arbitration provides some recognized models of rational settlement. The Fur-Seals Arbitration of 1893 and the North Atlantic Fisheries Arbitration of 1911 exhibited an admirable combination of legal decision and

[22] Cf. J. B. Bishop, *Theodore Roosevelt and His Time, Shown in His Own Letters*, New York, 1920, vol. 1, pp. 260, 261; Philip C. Jessup, *Elihu Root*, New York, 1938, pp. 396-398.

[23] Cf. Lionel M. Gelber, *The Rise of Anglo-American Friendship*, Oxford, 1938, pp. 140-165.

equitable adjustment. Some of this distinction they owed to the quality of the tribunals, especially perhaps to the strong neutral element in their composition; but some of it was due to the fact that in both cases the arbiters were empowered to draft regulations for the future guidance of the parties. This provision made the arbitral arrangements by design what they had in other instances become in practice, namely a mechanism of negotiation. The award was in terms of existing law; but the attached recommendations recognized the loser's case for equitable interpretation or modification of the legal situation and paved the way for an adjustment acceptable to both sides.[24]

The Chamizal case

The retention of control after formal submission to arbitration, which we have noticed in a number of Anglo-American disputes, appears again in the Chamizal case. There the Government of the United States refused to accept "as valid or binding" an award rendered in 1911 by the Mexican and neutral members of the tribunal over the dissent and protest of the American member, leaving the dispute to lie unsettled though dormant.[25]

Treaties of 1848 and 1853 made the Rio Grande the boundary between the United States and Mexico from a point above El Paso to the Gulf of Mexico. Changes in the channel made necessary a further convention in 1884, Article 1 of which reads thus: "The dividing line shall forever be that described in the aforesaid treaty and follow the center of the normal channel of the rivers named, notwithstanding any alterations in the banks or in the course of those rivers, provided that such alterations be effected by natural causes through the slow and gradual erosion and deposit of alluvium and not by the abandonment of an existing river bed and the opening of a new one."

[24] Cf. Percy E. Corbett, *The Settlement of Canadian-American Disputes*, Yale University Press, 1937, pp. 34-49.

[25] *Foreign Relations of the United States*, 1911, p. 598.

In 1889 the two governments established an International Boundary Commission consisting of one Mexican and one American commissioner, and to this body was referred in 1894 the complaint of one Garcia. Garcia alleged that he had inherited a tract of land known as El Chamizal which, until 1873, had been on the south side of the Rio Grande, but "in consequence of the abrupt and sudden change of current of the Rio Grande, was now on the north side of the river and within the limits of El Paso." He said that he feared to occupy the property because certain Americans, believing it to be in the United States, had usurped possession. The question before the Commission was whether the change of current was of the sort that left the property in Mexico or transferred it to the United States, or, in other words, of the sort that the boundary followed or that left the boundary where it had been. Witnesses and an engineer's report indicated that erosion up to 1864 had been slow, but in subsequent floods had been visible and sudden. The Mexican commissioner took the view that it was the kind of avulsive shift that left the boundary *in situ*; the American, that it was a case of accretion where the boundary moved with the current. They were unable to reach agreement, and in 1897 recommended that the two governments should add a third commissioner, who should not be a national of either party, and that the Commission thus enlarged should arbitrate the difference. This recommendation was finally accepted in 1910, and an arbitral convention was concluded in that year.[26]

The 1910 convention provided for the enlargement of the Commission by the addition of a Canadian jurist "for the purposes of the consideration and decision of the aforesaid difference only." Article 3 ran in part as follows: "The Commission shall decide solely and exclusively as to whether the international title to the Chamizal tract is in the United States

[26] See Charles A. Timm, *The International Boundary Commission United States and Mexico*, University of Texas publication no. 4134, 1941, pp. 132-134.

of America or Mexico. The decision of the commission, whether rendered unanimously or by majority vote of the commissioners, shall be final and conclusive upon both Governments, and without appeal."[27]

The commission held sittings in El Paso between May 15 and June 2, 1911, and rendered a majority award to the effect that, since the accretions up to 1864 had been slow, the boundary changed with them, leaving the Chamizal tract in the United States up to the middle of the river-bed as it was before the flood of that year, but that, since the changes from that point on could not, in the opinion of the presiding and the Mexican commissioner, "by any stretch of the imagination, or elasticity of language, be characterized as slow and gradual erosion," the balance of the tract belonged to Mexico.[28] The American commissioner based his protest mainly upon two grounds, (*a*) that the convention of 1910 gave the arbitrators no power to divide the tract, authorizing them solely to find whether title to the whole lay in the United States or in Mexico; and (*b*) that the award was void as being "equivocal and uncertain in its terms and impossible of accomplishment," because it would be "as impossible to locate the channel of the Rio Grande in the Chamizal tract in 1864 as to relocate the Garden of Eden or the lost Continent of Atlantis."

The United States Government agreed with its commissioner that the award was invalid. It also pointed out that, since the commission had made no attempt to "locate the boundary line at the tract in dispute" the effect was "to remit once more this all-important matter to the two parties for settlement." It then went on to propose negotiation of a new boundary convention. Given that the actual fixing of the line on the ground was going to require a negotiated agreement, it would have seemed possible to accept the award and count upon negotiation for a reasonable settlement. Perhaps the Department of State was sincere in the belief, which it professed

[27] *Foreign Relations of the United States*, 1911, pp. 566-567.
[28] *ibid.*, pp. 584-587.

to share with its commissioner, that acceptance by the two governments of the commission's interpretation of the treaty of 1884 would "throw the international boundary line along the Rio Grande into inextricable confusion and cast doubt upon the private title of well nigh every foot of land on both sides of the river. . . ." But all this would have been true also, if at all, if the commission, remaining unquestionably within its powers, had decided that the whole of El Chamizal belonged to Mexico. It is the kind of consideration that is normally taken into account before a decision to submit to arbitration.

The American protest and rejection had all the appearance of expressing simply a strong distaste for the decision. The commissioner had made the points about excess of powers and uncertainty plus impossibility in the course of the hearings,[29] and the majority had held against him. It is surely less than obvious that one who has power to find title wholly in one party or the other has not the power, unless this is explicitly excluded, to find it partly in one and partly in the other. This was the commission's majority view of what the treaties compelled it to do. The United States Government was not only denying the commission's power to decide its own jurisdiction under the treaty (a power which it had asserted for the London Commission under Jay's Treaty[30] and again, in 1895, for the Mixed Commission dealing with claims between the United States and Chile),[31] it was denying its authority to determine the meaning of the instruments which it had to interpret to decide the case. Here again was no real submission to arbitral decision.

U.S.-Norway arbitration of 1923

In a letter dated February 26, 1923, to the Norwegian Minister to the United States, enclosing a draft in payment

[29] *ibid.*, p. 586.
[30] Above, p. 143.
[31] Moore, *Dig.*, vol. 7, pp. 34-35.

of the award of an arbitral tribunal on the claims of certain Norwegian nationals arising out of requisitions by the United States Shipping Board Emergency Fleet Corporation in 1917, Secretary of State Charles E. Hughes wrote as follows:

> By this action the Government of the United States gives tangible proof of its desire to respect arbitral awards and it again acknowledges devotion to the principle of arbitral settlements even in the face of a decision proclaiming certain theories of law which it cannot accept. Faithful to its traditional policy, my Government is most desirous to promote the judicial determination of international disputes of a justiciable character and in this interest to give its due support to judicial determinations.[32]

After this edifying exordium, the letter is given over to an attack on the award. Behind this lies a story similar in its essentials to those related in the preceding pages. The decision had gone against the United States. The American member of the tribunal had refused to be present while the award was announced on the ground that the terms of submission had been disregarded, and the American agent, who was present, had "reserved all the rights of the United States arising out of the plain and manifest departure of the award from the terms of submission and from the 'essential error' . . . by which it is invalidated."

It is in the letter from Secretary of State Hughes to President Harding, recommending payment, that we must look for the arguments supporting these objections. Because the compromise had made no provision for filing dissenting opinions, the tribunal had refused to permit the American member to make his opposing views part of the record. The Secretary's letter, dated January 11, 1923,[33] examines the arguments *seriatim*, presumably as communicated by the American arbitrator and agent, and finds in none of them clear grounds for holding the award invalid.

A treaty concluded by the United States in 1827 with Swe-

[32] *Foreign Relations of the United States*, 1923, vol. 2, pp. 626-628.
[33] *ibid.*, pp. 617-625.

den and Norway had guaranteed that no property of their respective nationals should be embargoed, detained, seized, or taken without the owner's consent "on account of any military expedition, or any public or private purpose whatever." The two governments had, however, agreed that no question of the violation of this treaty should be submitted to the tribunal, which was to decide upon the claims "in accordance with the principles of law and equity"—that is to say, without regard to any special treaty rights. The tribunal took note of this agreement and declared that it had acted in accordance with it. Nevertheless, the Americans participating in the case asserted that the majority decision, in recognizing in Norwegian nationals rights greater than those accorded by the law of the United States to its citizens suffering under the same requisitions, had in effect brought the treaty in as an element weighing upon judgment. Secretary Hughes advised the President against imputing such "fraudulent purpose" to the tribunal.

The agreement to arbitrate had been made under the Hague Convention of 1907 for the Pacific Settlement of International Disputes and therefore incorporated by reference the provision in Article 79 of that instrument to the effect that "the Award must give the reasons on which it is based." The American participants complained that this rule had been disregarded, especially in respect of the manner of calculating the amounts awarded. The Secretary of State advised the President that, although he too regarded the reasoning and explanation as "loose, ill-constructed, prolix and unsatisfactory," he could not conclude that the award "would be held by an impartial tribunal to be invalid upon the ground that it failed to meet the requirement in question."

The last serious criticism considered by the Secretary was that the tribunal, in increasing damages for detention after the signature of the peace treaty in June, 1919, had usurped the right of the United States to determine the existence and duration of emergency, thus applying, not a principle of international law, but "an erroneous rule of its own making."

The Secretary reported: "I have carefully considered this point, and I recognize that, in view of various statements in the Award, the argument may be urged with great force, but I am constrained to the conclusion that it is not so clearly established that this Government can assume that an impartial tribunal would decide the award to be invalid upon this ground."

Having thus concluded that if there were an appeal court, it would probably confirm the decision, the Secretary of State, instead of paying with good grace, repeated in his letter to the Norwegian Minister all the American objections, in an apparent effort to make payment appear as an act of grace performed by the United States Government out of devotion to "the judicial determination of disputes." The presiding arbitrator had been a Swiss jurist, appointed by the President of Switzerland at the request of the United States and Norway. The tone and content of the letter to the Norwegian Minister amounted to an attack upon the professional capacity and integrity of the appointee and an offense to the Head of State who had chosen him. This is no service to the cause of judicial settlement. The expressed anxiety to prevent the award being regarded as a precedent binding on the United States is not impressive. There is no rule of *stare decisis* in litigation between States.

Where a judicial system is so rudimentary as to offer no appeal, it is useless to expect that States will uniformly and unquestioningly accept the decision of a tribunal. There can be cases where the terms of reference have been so palpably disregarded, or the grounds of decision so vitiated by error or partiality that no disinterested and competent observer would hold an award valid. But the obvious course, for a government having the cause of judicial settlement truly at heart, is to discount heavily in itself the distortion due to the jaundiced eye of the loser.

The Secretary's letter to President Harding reveals grounds other than devotion to arbitration for complying with this award and, in doing so, shows the affinity that still exists in the actual practice of governments between arbitration and undisguised diplomatic negotiation. Supposing, said Mr. Hughes in effect, that we practically compelled Norway to submit the validity of this award to a second arbitration, the decision might well go against us, and this would be "highly injurious to the prestige and interests of our government." If, on the other hand, we won, we should then be back where we began. Last time, we were able "upon adequate consideration" to persuade Norway to leave the Treaty of 1827 out of account. But this time she might stand on the Treaty. Thus, in any subsequent proceedings for settlement, it might be "decided that the United States not only owed a certain amount of money but had been guilty of a breach of its Treaty obligation."

"I confess," concluded Mr. Hughes, "that, unsatisfactory as is the present Award, I see no satisfactory alternative to its payment."

Russia and arbitration

Russia participated in the nineteenth-century revival of arbitration. Between 1884 and 1887 the Russian and British Governments settled by joint commission a disputed section of the boundary between Afghanistan and the territories of the Czar. Six years later a dispute about the Russian and Afghan use of the river Kuskh, on the same boundary, was referred to another joint Anglo-Russian commission. In 1900, the United States and Russia submitted to Professor Asser of Amsterdam American claims arising out of the seizure of four American sealing-vessels in the Bering Sea. Asser's award, of about $115,000, was in favor of the United States.[34]

When in 1898 the Czar's government proposed to the Powers represented at St. Petersburg a conference to discuss

[34] W. E. Darby, *International Tribunals*, 4th edn., London, 1904, pp. 809, 821, 837.

the limitation of armaments, this initiative probably owed less to Nicholas II's devotion to world peace than to financial embarrassments that made it difficult for Russia to keep pace with the military establishments of enterprising neighbors. Whatever the dominant motive was, the projected agenda was soon enriched with an item calling for the elaboration of a detailed scheme of arbitration. The result was the Hague Convention of 1899 for the Pacific Settlement of International Disputes, followed by the revised Convention of 1907. Russia ratified the first on September 4, 1900, and the second on November 27, 1909. In 1912 she was party to a full-dress arbitration at The Hague with Turkey, the question in dispute being whether Turkey owed moratory interest on amounts overdue under the peace treaty of 1879. A tribunal composed of two Russians, two Turks, and a Swiss umpire rendered in 1912 an award dismissing the Russian claim.[35]

Under the Czarist regime, to sum up, Russia was playing an active part in developing the practice of arbitration. We may indeed add to the above brief record a peaceful settlement not in form an arbitration but essentially of the same nature. That was the submission of the question of responsibility and damages for the Dogger Bank incident of 1904 to a commission of enquiry suggested by France under Articles 9-14 of the 1899 Hague Convention. Admirals of five navies, including those of Great Britain and Russia, found that the opening of fire upon British trawlers on suspicion that they were Japanese torpedo boats was not justified, and the Russian government undertook to pay some $300,000 damages.[36] In this period also the ruling Czar was from time to time called upon by other governments to arbitrate disputes or to appoint arbiters, indicating that the Emperor of all the Russias was one of the band of eminent personages thought likely to fill such roles with disinterested justice.

[35] J. B. Scott, *The Hague Court Reports*, New York, 1916, pp. civ-cv, 297-328.

[36] Scott, *op.cit.*, pp. 403-412.

The Revolution changed all that. True, Soviet governments entered into a number of treaties providing for conciliation or other amicable modes of settlement.[37] As late as 1939, the nonaggression treaty with Germany (Art. 5) contains the obligation to settle all differences either by friendly negotiation or, if necessary, by arbitral commissions,[38] and their jurists now insist that the official attitude towards international judicial institutions and procedures is in principle a positive one. By way of evidence, they cite Soviet membership in the League of Nations and United Nations, acceptance of the Statute of the International Court of Justice, and the presence of a Soviet judge on the bench of that tribunal.[39] But in truth there has been no change in what Korovin, as early as 1924, described as the systematic opposition of Soviet Russia to arbitration. In the edition of his *Mezhdunarodnoe Pravo Perekhodnogo Vremeni* published that year in Moscow[40] he quotes a speech by Litvinov at The Hague in 1922 about the great abyss existing between the Soviet and non-Soviet worlds and the resulting impossibility of finding an unprejudiced judge for any dispute between them. Korovin explains:

> The indispensable minimum and fundamental postulate of any arbitration is a community of legal views and normative criteria. Failing such community, every attempt to find an arbitral authority between two halves of humanity speaking different languages is *a priori* hopeless.[41]

Korovin, a corresponding-member of the Academy of Sciences, has survived a long series of bewildering and dangerous shifts in Soviet views about the nature and sources of international law. But in the matter of arbitration he has been forced

[37] See, e.g., T. A. Taracouzio, *The Soviet Union and International Law*, New York, 1935, pp. 239-297 and Appendix XXIV.

[38] Leonard Shapiro, *Soviet Treaty Series*, Washington, vol. 2, 1955, p. 208.

[39] See, e.g., G. P. Zadorozhny, writing under the general editorship of E. A. Korovin in *Mezhdunarodnoe Pravo*, Moscow, 1951, pp. 487-488.

[40] pp. 47-48. [41] My translation.

to make nothing more than a formal and painless change of position. When the International Court of Justice on March 30, 1950, gave its advisory opinion affirming the obligation of Bulgaria, Hungary, and Romania to participate in the procedures set out in the peace treaties of 1946 for the settlement of disputes regarding observation of the human rights articles, he took the cue for a slashing attack on the Court as a tool of Anglo-American imperialism.[42] The book in which he collaborated as general and contributing editor in 1951 proclaims, as we have seen, the "in principle positive" attitude of the Soviet Union towards arbitration. But it goes on to warn its readers not to think that arbitral tribunals or the International Court of Justice can guarantee impartiality and justice in the settlement of international conflicts. For Soviet jurists, proof to the contrary is provided by the history of arbitration in the League of Nations and the so-called conspiracy to use the Court where capitalist judges are in a majority as a capitalist-imperialist instrument. The examples given are the reference of the Eastern Carelian question for an advisory opinion in 1923, and the advisory opinion of 1948 on the interpretation of Article 4 of the United Nations Charter.

The Soviet Government had refused to participate in an examination by the League or by the Permanent Court of International Justice of the question whether the 1920 Treaty of Dorpat and an annexed Declaration regarding the autonomy of Eastern Carelia constituted engagements of an international character placing Russia under an obligation to Finland. In view of the refusal, the Court declined to give the opinion requested by the League Council; but the author, G. P. Zadorozhny, gives it no credit for thus defeating what he has dutifully described as a step in the grand strategy of imperialism.

In the second example, the International Court of Justice complied with the request of the General Assembly, and its advisory opinion was to the effect that States-members of the United Nations are not legally entitled to make their vote

[42] SGIP, 1950, no. 5, pp. 57-60.

for admission of a new member dependent upon conditions other than those specified in Article 4 of the Charter.[43] In the Soviet Union it was orthodox to condemn this as a corrupt decision removing one obstacle to packing the United Nations with friends of the United States. Zadorozhny sums up by declaring that the USSR, while not rejecting the principle of international adjudication, does consistently fight putting it to such uses as these, which, he says without burdensome explanation, mask preparations for another war.

In another onslaught[44] Zadorozhny credits the Soviet delegates to the United Nations with a glorious victory over the imperialist plot, and again feels no inconsistency in calling the Court a tool of the Western Powers and at the same time admitting that it has given several opinions against them.

The same vituperative note runs through the attack by F. Ivanov in SGIP (no. 11, 1952),[45] upon the International Law Commission's draft procedure for arbitral tribunals. This article, under the title "The Fourth Session of the International Law Commission," is a general condemnation of the Commission and its work on the ground that it represents an American design to pervert international law to the aims of contemporary aggressors. It is a typical Soviet product of the period. Written perhaps six months before Stalin's death, it reeks with that adoration of the leader which was then the obligatory refrain of Russian writing in the social sciences. Professor Scelle's draft on arbitral procedure, like the other productions of the Commission, is linked by the author with the legendary conspiracy of the United States, aided and abetted by its satellites, to master the world politically and economically—a conspiracy consistently unmasked, denounced, and resisted by Stalin the omniscient. Professor Scelle is presented alternately as a "learned lackey" of the American imperialists and as a "passionate champion" of the world

[43] ICJ Reports, 1947-48, p. 65.
[44] SGIP, 1951, no. 2, pp. 60-69.
[45] pp. 72-79.

government under which the United States vainly hopes to conceal its all-embracing tyranny. The staid subject of international law is doubtless enlivened for Soviet readers by these touches of melodrama.

When we look for specific objections to Scelle's draft, we find that the principal complaint is that it establishes the principle of compulsory arbitration.[46] This is not so. The text is a draft of a convention which would make the procedure set out in its articles compulsory for any ratifying States which, by separate agreement either general or *ad hoc*, have undertaken to arbitrate existing or future disputes. In other words, any obligation to arbitrate will spring, not from this convention, but from a distinct and independent act of will. This must have been obvious to anyone understanding the French or English language.[47]

The real basis of Soviet opposition is that Moscow wishes not only to avoid any obligation to arbitrate, but, if it should participate in arbitration, to preserve its discretion at each stage of the proceedings. Clearly, for the Government of the USSR, arbitration is nothing more than negotiation in another form. Anything designed to make it more than this is to be resisted. A principal object of the draft is to prevent the original obligation from being evaded by refusal to join in a compromise, refusal to participate in the composition of a tribunal, withdrawal of an arbiter, or the unilateral and uncontrollable assertion that the award is invalid. Among the devices adopted in the draft to prevent such evasions, Ivanov singles out for special attack the power given to the President of the International Court of Justice to appoint arbiters if the parties fail to agree, and the power given to the Court itself (*a*) to determine the existence of an arbitrable dispute between the parties, if this is contested by one of them; (*b*) to interpret or revise the award on the request of either party, if for any

[46] Ivanov, *loc.cit.*, p. 75.

[47] For the text see *Report of the International Law Commission Covering the Work of its Fourth Session*, GAOR, 7th Session, Supp. no. 9 (A/2163) pp. 3-10, or UNYB, 1952, pp. 792-795.

reason the original tribunal cannot be referred to for these purposes; and (*c*) to decide, on the application of either party, upon the validity of the award. The Soviet Government opposes such external intervention at any point in the proceedings and insists upon the unabated discretion of the parties to continue or arrest the process of arbitral settlement.

Ivanov's critique is a replica of the position taken by the representatives of the USSR, Byelorussia, and the Ukraine in the discussion of the draft on arbitral procedure by the Sixth Committee at the eighth and tenth Sessions of the General Assembly.[48] This position compares negatively with the attitudes of the United Kingdom and the United States as stated in their comments on the text sent to the governments for their observations. The United Kingdom strongly supports the draft in all but the articles empowering the International Court of Justice to decide, on application by either party, upon the validity of the award. Here the British Government would have welcomed greater firmness. It finds the grounds set out in Article 30 for challenging the award "dangerously wide," observing, on the basis of long experience, that the plea of excess of powers "will enable any decision of the tribunal as to its competence or jurisdiction to be automatically reopened." "Generally speaking," says the comment, "it is highly desirable that an award once given should be final, and should not be open to revision or annulment even on the part of the International Court of Justice."[49]

The United States has not committed itself so far as Britain. It nevertheless declares that the Commission's work is "an effort in the progressive development of international law," and adds, "Because of the history and practice in the field of international arbitration, there may be wide reluctance on the part of States at this time to enter into a convention along the lines of the one drafted by the International Law

[48] GAOR, *8th Session, 6th Com., 388th meeting,* pp. 135-136; 10th Session, the same, 462nd meeting, p. 90, and 464th meeting, pp. 101-102.

[49] General Assembly: 8th Session, Supp. no. 9 (A/2456) pp. 37-38.

Commission, intended to cover all types of cases. However, in any event the work of the International Law Commission will have positive value as a statement of desired goals."[50] There may be a warning here that the American Senate will find difficulty in approving ratification. The record reviewed in this chapter reveals a strong tendency on the part of the United States Government to maintain in practice a control over each step in the arbitral process hardly less decisive than that now demanded by the Soviet Government. The actively constructive part taken by Washington in the recent development of international agencies for the collective resolution of common problems and the peaceful settlement of disputes may encourage the belief that this tendency will be less manifest in future. But if the reservations attached to acceptance of the compulsory jurisdiction of the International Court of Justice in the declaration made by the United States on August 14, 1946, be any guide, the omens hardly support this belief. It has often been observed that the reservation withholding from the Court's jurisdiction disputes touching matters essentially within the domestic jurisdiction of the declarant as determined by the declarant—a reservation in which France, Mexico, Pakistan, Liberia, India, and South Africa have followed the example set by the United States—means that a completely uncontrollable statement by the declarant can in any specific case render the declaration nugatory. Less attention has been paid to the control which the reservation gives even after an initial submission. For if the proceedings touch even incidentally at any point upon matters which a declarant says are essentially within his domestic jurisdiction, the process of adjudication can be arrested.

The negative position taken by the Government of the USSR on the proposed convention on arbitral procedure is probably not unconnected with an incident in the diplomacy of what Soviet literature calls "the peoples' democracies." In the 1947 treaties of peace, Hungary, Romania, and Bul-

[50] *ibid.*

garia undertook to secure to all persons under their jurisdiction certain specified human rights.[51] The same treaties[52] provided for the submission of disputes as to their interpretation or execution to Commissions "composed of one representative of each party and a third member selected by mutual agreement of the two parties from nationals of a third country." Failing an agreement upon the third member within one month, either party might request the Secretary-General of the United Nations to make this appointment.

By 1949 the Governments of the United States, Great Britain, Canada, Australia, and New Zealand were joining in protests to the three ex-enemy countries against flagrant violations of human rights, and demanding that the procedures prescribed in the treaties should be resorted to for an impartial examination of their charges. The accused governments, with vigorous support from the Soviet Union, denied the charges and refused to join in setting up the Commissions. The matter was brought before the General Assembly of the United Nations, where the Soviet delegation joined in the defense that the charges were groundless, the measures complained of having been taken as necessary steps in the suppression of plots to overthrow established governments, that these measures were moreover a matter of domestic jurisdiction, that the treaty procedures were not applicable, and that the General Assembly had no competence in the premises. A resolution was then proposed by the delegations of Bolivia, the United States, and Canada asking the opinion of the International Court of Justice. This was adopted by a vote of 47 to 5 with 7 abstentions, the Soviet Union, Byelorussia, and the Ukraine providing three of the nays.[53]

The questions put to the Court for its advisory opinion were as follows:

[51] Article 2 in the treaties with Hungary and Bulgaria, Article 3 in the treaty with Romania.

[52] In Articles 40, 36, and 38 respectively.

[53] An account of the dispute up to this point will be found in *U. S. and U. N.*, 1949, pp. 58-63.

I

Do the diplomatic exchanges between Bulgaria, Hungary and Romania, on the one hand, and certain Allied and Associated Powers signatories to the Treaties of Peace on the other, concerning the implementation of Article 2 of the Treaties with Bulgaria and Hungary and Article 3 of the Treaty with Romania, disclose disputes subject to the provisions for the settlement of disputes contained in Article 36 of the Treaty of Peace with Bulgaria, Article 40 of the Treaty of Peace with Hungary, and Article 38 of the Treaty of Peace with Romania?

II

In the event of an affirmative answer to Question I: Are the governments of Bulgaria, Hungary and Romania obligated to carry out the provisions of the Articles referred to in Question I, including the provisions for the appointment of their representatives to the Treaty Commissions?

III

In the event of an affirmative answer to Question II and if within thirty days from the date when the Court delivers its opinion, the Governments concerned have not notified the Secretary-General that they have appointed their representatives to the Treaty Commissions, and the Secretary-General has so advised the International Court of Justice:

If one party fails to appoint a representative to a Treaty Commission under the Treaties of Peace with Bulgaria, Hungary and Romania where that party is obligated to appoint a representative to the Treaty Commission, is the Secretary-General of the United Nations authorized to appoint the third member of the Commission upon the request of the other party to a dispute according to the provisions of the respective Treaties?

IV

In the event of an affirmative reply to Question III: Would a Treaty Commission composed of a representative of one party and a third member appointed by the Secretary-General of the United Nations constitute a Commission, within the meaning of the relevant Treaty articles, competent to make a definitive and binding decision in settlement of a dispute?

To the first two questions the Court gave an affirmative answer. The vote on the bench was eleven to three, the dissenting judges being those from the Soviet Union, Poland, and Yugoslavia. This ended the first phase of the proceedings.[54]

Thirty days having elapsed without notification that the appointments had been made, the Court addressed itself to Question III. Clinging to the strict literal meaning of the term "third member," the judges, by a majority of eleven to two, held that the Secretary-General had authority to appoint only if the parties, having appointed their representatives, failed to agree upon a third member. Thus they admitted that the treaty arrangement for settlement could be defeated by the refusal of one party to name a representative to a Commission, notwithstanding their finding that such refusal would violate the treaty obligation. Having answered Question III in the negative, the Court did not take up Question IV.[55]

In his comment upon this opinion, Professor Manley Hudson, formerly a judge of the Permanent Court of International Justice, regrets that "the issues arose with reference to provisions in the Peace Treaties which are cast in such terms as to throw doubt upon the seriousness with which the parties sought an effective system of arbitral procedure."[56] Expanding the same theme, Professor Charles De Visscher, formerly a judge of the International Court of Justice, traces the inadequacy of these provisions to the will of the parties not to commit themselves beyond a certain point. The political tensions existing when the treaties were drafted in 1946 were such that the treaty-makers would not undertake to submit future disputes about interpretation or execution to an ironclad arrangement for impartial settlement. The defects in the mechanism were not oversights; they were consciously designed to keep a loophole open. In 1950, the same tensions were there, augmented by others. The Soviet Government actively as-

[54] ICJ Reports, 1950, pp. 67-68, 77-78.
[55] ICJ Reports, 1950, p. 230.
[56] AJIL, vol. 45, January, 1951, p. 10.

sisted their client governments in keeping within their own hands the implementation of the treaty clauses on human rights. It was the Court's duty to interpret, not to revise, the treaties.[57] This of course reduces the written verbal undertaking to nothing more than an agreement to arbitrate provided both parties consider the circumstances of the moment auspicious. As such it is a somewhat more than usually conspicuous instance of the general frailty of treaties.

The United States has been able to reap some modest advantage from the virtual certainty that the Soviet Government and its allies will refuse to join in the submission of any question in which they are concerned to the International Court of Justice. On February 16, 1954, the Government addressed to the Court applications against the Governments of Hungary and the Soviet Union in pursuance of claims arising out of the seizure of an American aircraft over Hungary and the detention of its crew. In March and June, 1955, it filed similar applications against Czechoslovakia and the Soviet Union, claiming damages for the shooting down of aircraft in the United States zone of Germany and in the sea off Japan. In these communications the United States Government acknowledged that the Court had no jurisdiction, but suggested that an appropriate declaration by the other government in each case would give it the power to hear and decide the dispute. In no case was the necessary declaration forthcoming. This negative result must have been fully expected; but in the war of propaganda, the demonstration of American willingness to submit to adjudication, and the stubborn refusal of Moscow, Prague, and Budapest to go to court, may perhaps have counted as a minor gain.[58]

[57] *Théories et Réalités en Droit International Public*, 2nd edn., Paris, 1955, pp. 314-315, 413-414 (Corbett translation, pp. 250-251, 333-334).

[58] ICJ Yearbook, 1953-54, pp. 92-93; 1954-55, pp. 70-73. A similar challenge to Bulgaria in 1957 was joined in by Israel and Great Britain. This arose out of the shooting down of an Israeli aircraft on July 27, 1955, by Bulgarian units, and the resulting death of Israeli, British, and United States nationals. Here, however, the application invoked a Bulgarian declaration of 1921 accepting the compulsory jurisdiction of the PCIJ and may

British view on limits of arbitration

The limit beyond which even the best-disposed government will not go in submission to international adjudication is authoritatively stated in a British memorandum of 1928 to the Committee on Arbitration and Security of the Preparatory Commission on Disarmament. The relevant passage runs as follows:

> It is because it is so generally felt that there are some questions—justiciable in their nature—which no country could safely submit to arbitration that it has been usual to make reservations limiting the extent of the obligation to arbitrate. These limitations may vary in form, but their existence indicates the consciousness on the part of Governments that there is a point beyond which they cannot count on their peoples giving effect to the obligations of the treaty.[59]

It is to be especially noted that this limit is explicitly stated to exist in relation to justiciable disputes. As a matter of course, it applies to those commonly described as "nonjusticiable" or "political." Indeed, the classification of a dispute as "political" often means nothing more than that it is one which a party is unwilling to submit to impartial settlement. That the statement embraces the kind of adjudication practiced in the International Court of Justice as well as the less stably organized type of arbitration is indicated by the reference in the same passage to the League Covenant:

> That there are limits beyond which a State cannot go in accepting binding obligations to arbitrate justiciable questions in all cases is recognized in Article 13 of the Covenant of the League of Nations. By that provision the members of the League accept *in principle* but not definitely the obligation to arbitrate justiciable disputes. The framers of the Covenant realised that it was not feasible to embody in the Covenant a definite and comprehensive obligation to arbitrate all justiciable disputes.

---

perhaps hope for more substantial results. ICJ, *Communiqués*, 57/41, 57/43, 57/45.

[59] LNOJ, May, 1928, p. 696.

The assertion of this commodious loophole in what looks like the very comprehensive language of Article 13 is a lesson in treaty-interpretation.

Paragraph 1 of Article 13 reads thus:

> The Members of the League agree that, whenever any dispute shall arise between them which they recognize to be suitable for submission to arbitration or judicial settlement, and which can not be satisfactorily settled by diplomacy, they will submit the whole subject-matter to arbitration or judicial settlement.

The full power of selection is of course retained here by the uncontrollable "which they recognize to be suitable." But does the next paragraph not remove this discretion? It incorporates the description of legal or justiciable dispute afterwards adopted in Article 36 of the Statutes of the Permanent Court and the International Court of Justice:

> Disputes as to the interpretation of a treaty, as to any question of international law, as to the existence of any fact which, if established, would constitute a breach of any international obligation, or as to the extent and nature of the reparation to be made for any such breach, are declared to be among those which are generally suitable for submission to arbitration or judicial settlement.

Here the line of escape is kept open by the word "generally." Whether any specific dispute is suitable and therefore subject to submission must again be determined by a decision of the party summoned.

The Buraimi Oasis arbitration

So much for the limits to initial submission. A recent case in which Great Britain was concerned indicates that, even after proceedings have begun, a point may be reached beyond which it becomes "impossible," that is to say, highly inexpedient in the opinion of Her Majesty's Government, to continue.

On July 28, 1954, Mr. Anthony Eden, then Secretary of State for Foreign Affairs, reported in the House of Commons that an agreement had been reached to submit to arbitration a long-standing dispute with Saudi Arabia over sovereignty in the Buraimi Oasis. Britain was acting for the Rulers of Abu Dhabi and Muscat, who claimed parts of the oasis and its zone while Saudi Arabia claimed the whole. Oil prospects had made it urgently important to settle this question and to define the boundary between Saudi Arabia and Abu Dhabi.

The agreement provided for a tribunal composed of one British and one Saudi member, two neutral members, and a neutral President. Arrangements were made to maintain law and order and to prevent either side taking action that would prejudice the position pending the award. Professor Charles De Visscher of Belgium agreed to act as President.[60]

Hearings were held at Geneva between January and September 1955. The British complained that Saudi Arabia had violated the arbitration agreement by bribery and other forms of pressure designed to win over the local population and its sheiks and ensure control of the territory in dispute. On September 16 the proceedings were suspended by the resignation of the British member of the tribunal on the ground that the Saudi member was maintaining relations with persons on the Saudi side of the case that disqualified him as an arbiter. A week later the President of the Tribunal resigned, an example shortly followed by one of the neutral arbiters.[61]

On October 26, 1955, Sir Anthony Eden, Prime Minister, reported to the House of Commons the total breakdown of the arbitration. He said:

> Bribery and intimidation on a wide scale have taken place in the disputed areas, with the result that it is no longer possible, I regret to say, to estimate where the loyalties of the inhabitants lay before Turki's invasion. . . . A fair and impartial arbitration is not possible in such circumstances.
>
> These facts, combined with the conduct of the Saudi Government in relation to the Tribunal itself, have led Her Majesty's

[60] *Parliamentary Debates, House of Commons*, 1953-54, July 26 to October 29, pp. 467-469. Appointment of the Tribunal, *London Times*, December 30, 1954, 6f.

[61] *London Times*, September 17, 1955, 6e, and September 24, 5d.

Government to conclude that the Saudi Arabian Government are no more willing now to reach an equitable solution by arbitration than they were previously by negotiation. Their actions and conduct amount to a repudiation of the Arbitration Agreement, and have made a continuation of the arbitration impossible.

Her Majesty's Government have, therefore, felt obliged, in the exercise of their duty to protect the legitimate interests of the Ruler of Abu Dhabi and the Sultan of Muscat, to advise them that the attempt to reach a just compromise by means of arbitration has failed. The forces of those Rulers, supported by the Trucial Oman levies, have accordingly this morning taken steps to resume their previous control of the Buraimi Oasis, and areas to the west of it.[62]

An assessment of the rights and wrongs of this case would be probably impossible and certainly irrelevant here. Literally, of course, it would have been quite possible to appoint fresh members of the Tribunal and proceed to an award. It will be sufficient for our purposes to emphasize the degree of control retained by the British Government after proceedings had begun, and to underline parts of the Prime Minister's speech in which that Government's notion of the role and nature of arbitration in this case is indicated. This was an "attempt to reach a just compromise by means of arbitration," and the British Government had concluded that "the Saudi Arabian Government are no more willing now to reach an equitable solution by arbitration than they were previously by negotiation." The language reflects the earlier concept of arbitration, which did not distinguish it from conciliation, and associates the proceedings more closely with negotiation than with decision by the application of legal norms.

The Buraimi case has some importance as an indication that the course of development in international adjudication via arbitral tribunals is not a straight upward line. Its sequel in relation to the same development via the International Court of Justice is at least equally interesting.

[62] *Parliamentary Debates, House of Commons*, 1955-56, October 25 to November 11, pp. 198-201.

Professor C. H. M. Waldock was of British counsel in this case. In an article under the title "Decline of the Optional Clause"[63] he indicates the connection between the Buraimi dispute and the latest revised form of the United Kingdom's declaration accepting the compulsory jurisdiction of the International Court of Justice. On June 2, 1955, the British Government had replaced an earlier declaration with one listing six classes of excepted disputes and subject to termination on notice. On October 31, 1955, five days after the speech by the Prime Minister quoted above, it replaced the declaration of June 2 with one in the same terms except for the addition of a seventh class of excepted disputes. The new exception was worded as follows:

> Disputes in respect of which arbitral or judicial proceedings are taking, or have taken place, with any state which, at the date of the commencement of the proceedings, had not itself accepted the compulsory jurisdiction of the International Court of Justice.

Professor Waldock explains this addition as a move specifically designed to prevent any future reference of the Buraimi dispute to the Court. He attributes the breakdown of arbitration to "the wholesale bribery of potential witnesses by the Saudi Arabian Government," and declares that the "United Kingdom had the best of reasons for acting as it did." This is not entirely clear. It is part of the normal business of Courts to discount bribed evidence. The determination to keep this dispute out of the hands of the International Court of Justice suggests either a lack of confidence in that tribunal or some doubt as to the justice of the British case. Or had Her Majesty's Government discovered in midstream that this was one of the cases, referred to in the memorandum of 1928, "which no country could safely submit to arbitration?" In any event, few will dispute Professor Waldock's conclusion that the action taken was "a striking illustration of how a declaration terminable on notice may be terminated *ad hoc* for the purpose of declining jurisdiction in a current dispute."

[63] BYBIL, 1955-56, p. 268.

The optional clause

The reservations, exceptions, and time limitations which are now commonly attached to declarations under Article 36 of the Court Statute have turned this route to generalized compulsory jurisdiction into something of a blind alley. In some cases the "optional clause" has served less to expand the Court's authority than to emphasize the obstacles to international adjudication in a period of mounting political tensions. Happily the International Court of Justice has other sources of jurisdiction. Its Yearbooks show more than a hundred agreements and declarations, apart from those made under Article 36, that refer to it problems of interpretation and the adjudication of disputes between specified parties on specified matters. These arrangements are of course subject to all the weaknesses that beset contracts in a milieu that has no built-in machinery of enforcement. They nonetheless exhibit the Court in the role of an accepted institution facilitating inter-State business as a standing referee in unforeseen differences.

Compulsory jurisdiction

The majority of the governments concerned in the transition from League to United Nations were in favor of making general compulsory jurisdiction part of the Statute of the International Court of Justice. The proposal was defeated by the opposition of the Soviet Union and the United States.[64] The hope that it might succeed had been based upon an erroneous calculation of the probable postwar attitude of the governments and peoples of the two super-Powers. General compulsory jurisdiction would have been out of line with the great-Power veto in the Security Council and with the other reservations of sovereignty in the Charter. Even if it could have been formally accepted as part of an organization which did not unmistakably subordinate the State to supranational

[64] UNCIO, *Documents*, vol. 13, pp. 224-227, 246-255; vol. 14, pp. 146-166.

authority, it must soon have been abandoned in practice, given the absence of community and the general hostility between the two divisions into which the wartime coalition so speedily fell. There is nothing in history to suggest that a paper commitment to the adjudication of legal disputes could have arrested this disintegration.

The General Act for Pacific Settlement

The history of the General Act for the Pacific Settlement of International Disputes, concluded at Geneva on September 26, 1928, and revised by resolution of the United Nations General Assembly on April 28, 1949, tends to confirm the conclusion stated above. The General Act binds the parties to the peaceful settlement of all kinds of disputes, whether "legal" or "political." Where direct negotiation ("diplomacy"), or any special procedure prearranged by the parties, fails to achieve a settlement, the Act prescribed conciliation, arbitration, or reference to the Permanent Court of International Justice. By 1946 twenty-two States, including Great Britain and France but neither the United States nor the USSR, were parties to this instrument, and one other, Spain, had acceded and then withdrawn.

The General Act relied at various points on machinery of the League of Nations and the Permanent Court of International Justice. To be fully operative, it therefore needed revision to accord with the replacement of this machinery by that of the United Nations. The Belgian Government proposed that the Act should be revised, and this proposal, adopted by the Interim Committee of the General Assembly in 1948, was acted upon by the General Assembly in a Resolution of April 28, 1949.

In the Interim Committee, the *Ad Hoc* Political Committee, and the plenary meetings of the General Assembly, the Soviet bloc never relaxed its opposition to this restoration of the General Act. Its objections were wholly in line with the position taken by the Soviet Government since the early twenties in regard to arbitration. Representatives from the Soviet Union, Czechoslovakia, Poland, Byelorussia, and the Ukraine made the most of the small number of States that had acceded to the General Act, and of the failure even of those States to make use of it. The sole purpose, they said, in attempting to restore its "efficacy," was to "show a way of circumventing the principle of unanimity of the permanent members of the Security Council and of removing the investigation and settlement of international disputes from the scope of the Security Council's activities." Litvinov, Korovin, and Zadorozhny reappear in the charge that "in appointing the judges of the court of arbitration, the President of the International Court of Justice would be unable to find genuinely impartial persons; the court of arbitration would certainly serve as a political tool for States in a position to command the majority of votes in the court."

No one could do much by way of rebutting the Soviet contention that the General Act was a "useless document." All that Mr. van Langenhoven of Belgium could say in defense was that "even if the Act were used in only a few cases, the General Assembly would still be able to congratulate itself on having contributed to such a result, as it would have facilitated the drawing up of an important treaty."[65]

The amended General Act came into force on September 20, 1950, ninety days after the second accession, which was that of Sweden. Belgium had already acceded. The Secretary-General's annual report to the General Assembly, covering June 16, 1955-June 15, 1956,[66] shows that only Norway and Denmark had in the intervening six years joined Belgium and Sweden as parties to the amended instrument. The amend-

[65] *Reports of the Interim Committee*, General Assembly, 3rd Session, Supp. no. 10. Soviet opposition, and Mr. van Langenhoven's reply, General Assembly, 3rd Session, Part 1, *Ad Hoc* Political Committee, Summary Records of Meetings, 1948, p. 314; General Assembly, 3rd Session, 1949, Plenary Meetings, vol. 2, pp. 176-177, 195-200. Cf. Yuen-Li Liang, "Legal Notes," AJIL, vol. 43 (1949), pp. 706-709.

[66] P. 98.

ments apply only as between States acceding to the amended Act. The Resolution adopted by the General Assembly on April 28, 1949, made it clear that the changes do "not affect the rights of such States, parties to the Act as established on 26 September, 1928, as should claim to invoke it in so far as it might still be operative."[67] Minus some of its operative machinery, the original text retains a ghostly binding power upon those parties that have not followed the provisions for denunciation.[68] In the Interim Committee the United Kingdom's representative, perhaps indulging the national habit of understatement, had observed that "while his Government was a party to the General Act, it had acceded with reservations and now had doubts concerning the value of some of its provisions."[69] I have seen no record of its being invoked. Non-use, and the failure of all but four of the parties to keep the plan in operative repair, are some measure of the practical utility of this laboriously contrived document. It is not any lack of blueprints that prevents the pacific settlement of international disputes.

[67] General Assembly, Documents, A/809.

[68] Article 45.

[69] See General Assembly, Third Session, Supp. no. 10, p. 28.

CHAPTER VI

INTERNATIONAL ORGANIZATION

INTERNATIONAL organization is a form of diplomacy in which set rules and procedures play a particularly prominent part. In some cases there is the special inducement to comply, in the form of a substantial sanction, which is characteristic of the legal rule in national systems. These constitute the nearest approach to effective law in the international sphere. International organization falls into three main types.[1]

The first and earliest type, which began to proliferate after the middle of the nineteenth century, is established for the collective administration of specific interests such as postal and telegraphic communication, health, meteorological observation and information, international aviation. It is in this type, where questions of national power and security are least directly involved, and where mutual advantage from collective management is concrete and calculable, that the most effective sanctions are to be found. These organizations have been traditionally described as administrative or technical unions; but the broadening scope and implications of their functions have made this terminology inadequate, and the common appellation now is "specialized agencies."

The second type is the regional association. In these organizations States in more or less distinct geographical areas join for purposes specified in the articles of association. The most common purpose is defense; but the tendency now is to include the improvement of living standards and development of material resources which are closely allied to defense. Most

[1] I am concerned here with associations of States planned and established by international treaties that define purposes and methods, not with such historical growths as the British Commonwealth of Nations, in which an Empire evolves into a grouping of independent nations linked by varied and flexible understandings.

of the existing regional organizations are improved models of the traditional defense alliance, the new and distinguishing feature being standing consultative and secretarial organs and, in the case of NATO, joint military forces under unified command. As in the older and simpler type of alliance, reliance for cohesion is mainly on the added security achieved by association, sanctions are not usually specified, and there is usually no provision for majority decision. There is of course nothing in the nature of regional association to prevent a wide range of purpose or provision for majority decision and sanctions. From a modest beginning in 1889, and after many years of consultative activity distinguished more by oratory, florid resolutions, and unratified conventions than by practical results, the Organization of American States has developed an ambitious program of political, social, economic, scientific, and cultural collaboration, pacific settlement of disputes, and joint defense, and has provided for majority decision, to be enforced if need be by vigorous sanctions. In Europe, a growing complex of interlocking unions, "communities," and councils is administering collective interests still more substantial than those with which the Organization of American States is charged, and is moving towards a greater measure of formally centralized authority.

The third type of international organization is distinguished by its unlimited geographical scope and by the great range of interests that it is designed to serve. These characteristics place it in a category which merits the description "general." It is a recent phenomenon in world politics, the earliest exemplar being the League of Nations founded in 1919 and replaced in 1945 by the United Nations.

At least two very active organizations fail to fit neatly into this specialized-regional-general classification. They are the International Labor Organization and the United Nations Educational, Scientific and Cultural Organization. Brought into relationship with the United Nations and classified there as "specialized agencies," they can hardly be described as technical or administrative. Their specialization is an expansive one, and they are as comprehensive in their geographical scope as the United Nations.

These associations of States, whatever their classification, are designed to make and to secure the observation of rules for their members. Each of them, in regard to the subject matter assigned to it and within any geographical boundaries set in its constituent agreement, aims to create a domain of law. This is the instrumental objective sought by all as the common means of achieving their ultimate purposes of efficient service, welfare, security, or peace. The degree in which they realize instrumental or ultimate objectives differs greatly from one organization to another. The two general organizations have found progress most difficult. The League of Nations broke down in war, and its successor has realized few of the stated hopes of its founders. On the other hand, many of the specialized agencies have rendered services which have now come to be regarded as indispensable and which ensure their indefinite life. Reasons for these differences will be sought in this study. It may be that so long as States insist on formal sovereignty, this advance in international technical services will be the only progress towards an effective legal system. The content of sovereignty is gradually reduced by the continuing assignment of narrowly defined areas of competence to specialized international agencies. But the retained political sovereignty may erupt at any time and suspend this advance, even retaking surrendered competences. We cannot therefore be confident that the present tendency to pool large technical services is leading to a general legal system. In what follows, we limit ourselves to the conflict of law and power exhibited in such general international organizations as the League of Nations and the United Nations.

It seems reasonably clear that none of the various plans elaborated during the war of 1914-1918 to establish an organization to keep the world's peace would have survived the bitter struggles of the Peace Conference if it had not been for the unyielding insistence of President Wilson, expressing, it was believed at the time, the firm purpose of the American people. How that purpose was dissipated in the ruthless strategy of a personal and party feud is a familiar story constituting one of the least creditable chapters in the history of the United States Senate. The League, minus the Power whose continued leadership had everywhere been taken for granted, led a crippled existence for twenty years, the absence of the United States figuring frequently as the principal reason, or most popular excuse, for its failures. These failures strengthened the revulsion in American sentiment which Wilson's enemies had been able to stimulate and exploit, and it took a second world war to replace the resulting suspicious isolationism with a new drive for general international organization.

For the purposes of this study, the interest of the experience lies in the relationship between the law as set out in the Covenant and what was actually done under it. The record reveals many antecedents of that *de facto* adaptation of constitution to contingencies that can be observed in the United Nations of today. We shall study this adaptation as a phenomenon common to both general organizations, selecting episodes in the history of each that show it in the clearest light.

In the drafting of the Covenant, the Governments of Britain and the United States had been at one in rejecting French pleas for a standing military organization to enforce the law of the League. London and Washington wanted universal peace, order, and justice, but would have no super-State and saw no inconsistency between their desires and their reservations. The political leaderships of the United States and the British Commonwealth ostensibly believed that the world's good sense, alive now as never before to the horrors of war, could be relied upon to impose the pacific settlement of disputes. Supported by this enlightened opinion, the good faith and rational calculation of the civilized governments would ensure adequate collective action as required. Council or Assembly would deliberate, the covenant-breaker would be unmasked, the members' pledges to uphold each other's territorial integrity and political independence would come into effective play, and justice would be done. So the Covenant made substantive decisions in Council and Assembly dependent on unanimity, made no provision for a League army or general staff, and, as practice swiftly showed, left participation in any collective measures of constraint to the discretion of each member. Thus, the fourth of the nineteen Resolutions concerning the Economic Weapon adopted by the Assembly on October 4, 1921, began with the statement: "It is the duty of each member to decide for itself whether a breach of the Covenant has been committed." As for military measures, the same dependence upon the individual member's judgment is abundantly clear in such declarations as that in the Collective Note to Germany appended to the Final Protocol of the Locarno Conference. This was signed by representatives of Belgium, France, Great Britain, Italy, Czechoslovakia, and Poland, and it records the meaning attached by their respective governments to the military clauses of Article 16, namely that "each State Member of the League is bound to co-operate loyally and effectively in support of the Covenant and in resistance to any act of aggression *to an extent which is compatible with its military situation and takes its geographical position into account*."[2] Yet the essentially optional character so often emphasized in this way did not prevent the opposition in the United States Senate from finding in sanctions a device for sending "our boys" to fight the wars of foreign despots—some indication of the reception that would have awaited any more imperative provisions for coercion.

Vilna

Faith in a new era when world law could rely on a voluntary hue and cry for any needed enforcement was speedily put to a harsh test. The Covenant had hardly come into effect

[2] *League of Nations Treaty Series*, 54, p. 301. My italics.

when the League of Nations was called upon to grapple with the Polish-Lithuanian dispute over Vilna. The contestants were weak States, just restored to independence after long division and absorption by powerful neighbors. The Council of the League, on the other hand, which was seized of the dispute, counted as permanent members Britain, France, Italy, and Japan. It secured the formal agreement of the disputants to a provisional line of demarcation and named a Commission of five officers to supervise a truce. But that was about all that this body of victorious great Powers contrived to do. It was unable to prevent or terminate the immediate Polish occupation of the city by a move blandly attributed to the patriotic and disobedient zeal of one General Zeligowski but in fact planned and carried out by the government in violent breach of its promises to Lithuania and the League. No moral compunction and no fear of world opinion restrained Marshal Pilsudski in his determination to win and hold Vilna, or induced France to check the trickery of her Polish protégé.

The situation was one of a type that has become familiar in the United Nations. France was building up alliances to take the place of the guarantees which she had not succeeded in getting into the structure of the League and which it now seemed she would not obtain independently of that structure from Britain and the United States. Poland was to have a leading role in the reinsurance system. To curb the nationalistic fervor of the Poles and defeat their designs of expansion would not advance the interests of France as the French Government saw them.

True, Léon Bourgeois (most devoted of French champions of the League and at the time President of its Council) conveyed that body's protest against the seizure of Vilna in defiance of the demarcation agreement.[8] The Polish Government was politely apologetic about its inability to dislodge a national hero whose invasion had been welcomed by the captive city. At the same time, counting upon the strong favor

[8] LNOJ, special supp. no. 4, p. 71.

of the French Government and the division of serious purpose that this brought into the Council, it asserted the political impossibility of allowing any other authority to turn him out.[4]

There was just strength enough in the Council to insist that the allegiance of Vilna and its territory must be decided by plebiscite. On the basis of population and culture, Poland had a case at least as strong as Lithuania's, and might well have won the popular decision even before the occupation. During the occupation, if Lithuanian allegations were anywhere near the truth, anti-Polish elements had been effectively weakened by direct methods on the part of General Zeligowski and his patriots. Warsaw therefore agreed that the reputedly immovable general should be withdrawn with his troops, and that a League contingent should enter Vilna to keep the peace and ensure a free vote. Lithuania asked for time to repair some of the intimidating effects of the occupation; but preparations for the plebiscite were under way when an unexpected complication intervened. The Soviet Government interposed a *de facto* veto.

Viewed from Moscow at this time, the League of Nations was simply another conspiracy of those capitalist-imperialist States which had aimed to defeat the revolution by armed intervention. Of course the League was to send less than two thousand men, and Vilna was now far to the west of the Russian frontier. But this could be the thin edge of another wedge. In 1920, the Soviet Government had recognized Lithuania as sovereign of the city and province. It now took the preposterous line that it was for the militarily weak government at Kovno to clear the Poles out without foreign assistance, and warned against admitting the international contingent.

The Council, taking the Soviet threat perhaps more seriously than it deserved, feared that a small force so far from any allied base might become involved in difficulties that

[4] Cf. T. P. Conwell-Evans, *The League Council in Action*, London, 1929, pp. 89-100.

would force the League, failing a most improbable intervention in strength, to accept conspicuous defeat. The plebiscite was abandoned in favor of negotiation between the parties under League auspices. In January 1922, these were given up in despair.[5] In the following year the Conference of Ambassadors, irritated by Lithuania's seizure of Memel, recognized Poland's title to Vilna. That city had been the Lithuanian capital in the days of the nation's ancient greatness, and the original design of the Allied Powers had been to make it that again. Not until 1927 did the Lithuanian Government agree to end what it considered its state of war with Poland, accepting, though to that extent only, the *fait accompli*.[6]

The final result here might well have been the same if the procedure defined by the League had been allowed to take its course. What is important for our purposes is that the procedure was violently and with impunity interfered with by one party to the conflict and finally abandoned because political calculations outweighed legal considerations.

The failure was of course explained as that of a new and inexperienced organization of States afflicted with unexpected weaknesses and confronted with forces that might have yielded to nothing less than a major military effort. The ambiguous posture of France was comprehensible enough in the light of her constant fear of German recovery and her disappointment in the matter of automatic and massive guarantees of her security. This fear and disappointment were to blunt the edge of collective action throughout the twenty years of the League.

Explanation in terms of the political factors bearing on this case is relatively easy. The question that remains to be adequately examined is whether the kind of paralysis of law that occurred is not a normal incident of any plan to control the conduct of governments without destroying the sovereignty of the State. Whatever may be done to hedge it about with limi-

[5] LNOJ, September 1921, no. 764-785; February 1922, pp. 99-100.

[6] Cf. F. P. Walters, *A History of the League of Nations*, Oxford, 1952, vol. 1, pp. 105-109, 140-143, 398-400.

tations in theory, sovereignty is interpreted in practice as giving to the government of the moment the final decision on the needs of the State and the choice of means to satisfy them. It is doubtful whether any discretion less than this would be tolerated by the forces that sustain government even in the democratic States. As for the Communist governments, no doubt is left by their statements or by their policy that this is the meaning of the sovereignty which they insist upon as an essential mark of statehood. The history of the League and of the United Nations is full of demonstrations of the prevalence of this doctrine in democratic as in totalitarian regimes. It also abounds in instances where even weak States, exploiting the differences of purpose which are a normal feature of the relations of great Powers, have made good the claim to sovereignty in this sense.

Corfu

The League had barely demonstrated its inability to settle a dispute between two minor States where great-Power interests were indirectly involved, when one of its lesser members applied for protection against one of the great Powers permanently represented in the Council.

As after the Napoleonic wars, a Conference of Ambassadors had been established in Paris to be the organ through which the Principal Allied Powers would supervise the execution of treaties of peace. It consisted of representatives of Great Britain, France, Italy, and Japan. One of its myriad tasks was to settle the frontiers of Albania, and it had appointed a Delimitation Commission of three persons for the purpose, one British, one French, and one Italian. The Italian, General Tellini, was chairman of the Commission. On August 27, 1923, he was killed by persons unknown at Janina, some forty miles inside the Greek boundary. Three other Italians were assassinated with him.

By August 31 the Conference of Ambassadors had delivered a note in Athens demanding a prompt investigation, punishment of the guilty, and compensation to the bereaved families. In reply the Greek Government invited the Conference to send its own investigators, and promised to abide by any resulting decision.

Mussolini, however, far from leaving the tragedy in the hands of the Conference, of which the Delimitation Commission was an agency, saw in it an opportunity for an heroic display of Fascist resolution. His brutal ultimatum to Athens was issued on August 29. The total responsibility of Greece was assumed. There must be a solemn funeral service and military honors for the victims, and a formal apology with a humiliating naval salute to Italy. An enquiry to be carried out with the assistance of the Italian military attaché must be completed in five days and followed by sentence of death for the guilty. Fifty million lire must be handed over as immediate penalty.

The Greek Government agreed to apologize and to hold an enquiry. It rejected the demand that the Italian attaché be present during the investigations and, though willing to compensate the families if proved responsible, refused to pay unheard. If Mussolini was not satisfied, the whole matter could be submitted to the League of Nations, whose Council was now in session at Geneva and whose Assembly would be meeting there in a few days. The dictator's answer was to bombard and occupy Corfu. The attack with its casualties was not, he proclaimed, an act of war. It was merely the Fascist way, for which he could cite democratic precedents, of upholding the dignity of Italy and removing any doubt about the intention to exact satisfaction.

The Greek Government now appealed to the Council of the League under Articles 12 and 15 of the Covenant, which bound the members to submit to that body "any dispute likely to lead to a rupture, which is not submitted to arbitration."

Mussolini, noisily declaring Italy's right and will to vindicate her honor and avenge the murder of her nationals in her own way, proclaimed that if the Council presumed to take up the case he would remain in Corfu and withdraw from the League. But having satisfied the demands of melodrama and electrified the Fascist multitude with this defiance, he now found it expedient to bend under the mounting weight of international disapproval to the extent of accepting the jurisdiction of the Conference of Ambassadors. Of the four members of the Conference, only Britain was likely to be troublesome. Japan took little part in such purely European matters and France was the one member of the League Council that had not been outspoken in its opposition to the Italian attitude. As in the Vilna affair, the French Government had other fish to fry. It wanted Italian support for its occupation of the Ruhr to compel payment of German reparations.

The League Council consisted at this time of representatives of the British Empire, France, Italy, Japan, Spain, Belgium, China, Sweden, Brazil, and Uruguay. Except for the Italian and French representatives, all had made plain their conviction that the case was manifestly one with which the Council was intended to deal. They could not, however, deny the right of the Conference of Ambassadors to establish responsibilities for the murder of those engaged in its business. Greece had already admitted this right, and Mussolini's concession pointed at least to a peaceful solution, whereas to insist that the League's jurisdiction should be exercised might well prolong and embitter the conflict. Yet to turn the case over unreservedly to the Conference would look like acquiescing in the Fascist repudiation of League competence. So, by way of asserting a continuing part in the "work of pacification," Cecil of Britain persuaded the Council to convey to the Ambassadors a verbatim report of a meeting in which a statement of appropriate lines of settlement had been approved. These differed from the Italian ultimatum in three principal respects—(*1*) apology and salutes were to be addressed not to Italy alone, but to the three Powers represented on the Delimitation Commission, and representatives of the same three were to participate in the enquiry to be held by the Greek Government; (2) the question and amount of indemnity were to be determined by the Permanent Court of International Justice; and (3) the fifty million lire were not to be paid as an immediate penalty, but merely deposited as security for any compensation the Court might order. In substance these became the terms proposed by the Conference to Greece and Italy. They were accepted by Greece, and, it was thought, by Italy. The Council of the League congratulated itself on pointing the way to a just decision.[7]

The congratulations were premature. Mussolini had decided that he was surrendering more than he need. By reinforcing rather than withdrawing the troops occupying Corfu and some neighboring isles, he induced the Conference, concerned lest he proceed to an annexation that would disturb the European balance of power, to buy him off. This was done by abandoning any reference to the Permanent Court and ordering immediate payment of the fifty million lire. The Duce was thus spared any smirch of defeat or softness. Greece, without trial, was guilty because he said so.[8]

The decision, bitterly accepted by Greece, was received with dismayed indignation at Geneva. Even before this it had been widely felt that something must be done to avert permanent damage to the potentialities of the League Council. The attempt at repair was now pushed with some determination. The step taken recalls the device adopted by the London Conference of 1871 when, after accepting the *fait accompli* of Russia's deneutralization of the Black Sea in violation of the Treaty of Paris, 1856, it saved face and principle by declaring unaltered the law that a treaty may not be unilaterally abrogated. A Special Commission of Jurists was set up and asked to answer five questions concerning the competence of the Council, the consistency with the Covenant of acts of

[7] LNOJ, November 1923, pp. 1294-1310.

[8] Good accounts of the episode as a whole are to be found in the Royal Institute of International Affairs *Survey*, 1920-1923, pp. 348-356, and F. P. Walters, *op.cit.*, vol. 1, pp. 244-255.

coercion not intended as acts of war, and the responsibility of a State for political crime in its territory.

The answers to the questions put on the first point were accepted by the Council as satisfactory reaffirmations of its powers of enquiry. On the third point also, it was agreed that the Commission of Jurists had done good service in rebutting the assumption, upon which the Conference of Ambassadors had ostensibly proceeded, that a State is always responsible for a political crime committed within its borders. The answer upheld the orthodox view that the State is responsible only if it "has neglected to take all reasonable measures for the prevention of the crime and the pursuit, arrest and bringing to justice of the criminal." It added the ill-expressed but reasonable rider that "the recognized public character of a foreigner and the circumstances in which he is present in its territory entail upon the State a corresponding duty of special vigilance on his behalf."

The answer on the second point was an elaborate Yes and No. It drew criticism for its subtlety or vagueness from the representatives of Czechoslovakia (which had now succeeded China on the Council), Sweden, and Uruguay, but not enough to prevent them from joining in the general approval. "Coercive measures," it ran, "which are not intended to constitute acts of war may or may not be consistent with the provisions of Articles 12 to 15 of the Covenant, and it is for the Council, when the dispute has been submitted to it, to decide immediately, having due regard to all the circumstances of the case and to the nature of the measures adopted, whether it should recommend the maintenance or the withdrawal of such measures."[9]

The Commission, being a group of jurists, was not to be blamed for failing to find in the words of the Covenant any prohibition of force not labeled as war. Even without this signpost pointing to a unilateral resort to violence that could still be defended as legal, Italy had known what to do, as

[9] LNOJ, April 1924, pp. 523-527.

Japan, eight years later, would probably have known. But the Council's complacent approval lent countenance to tricks of aggression that were eventually to shatter the League. The lesson was not lost when the time came to draft the Charter of the United Nations. There, everything that words can do is done to outlaw aggressive force, whether or not it calls itself war.

In the Vilna dispute, the League of Nations had seemed on the point of resolving the conflict in a way that promised to satisfy the great-Power interest of France without compelling the French Government entirely to override the devotion of such Frenchmen as Bourgeois to the League ideals. The factors favoring continued legal proceedings there had been outweighed by the unexpected political counter of vaguely threatening Soviet opposition. In the case of Corfu, legal proceedings had been blocked from the beginning by the defiance of a newly established great-Power dictator who knew that legal decision would mean humiliating retreat. But the record in this period was by no means one of uniform failure. The League was, after all, an alternative mechanism of settlement which the great Powers could on occasion work with success and with no greater violence to equity than would have accompanied other means at their disposal. Examples were the division of Upper Silesia, the settlement of the Mosul boundary and—grand classic of League method—the handling of the Greek assault on Bulgaria in 1925.

Upper Silesia

The League Council was still engaged in its unsuccessful attempt to dispose of Vilna by direct Polish-Lithuanian negotiations when the Supreme Council of the Allied Powers dumped in its lap the thorny problem of Upper Silesia. This was in August 1921, and the Supreme Council, consisting of representatives of France, Britain, Italy, and Japan, had not yet delegated its liquidating functions to the Conference of

Ambassadors. France was actively supporting Polish claims to Upper Silesia, while Britain and Italy held that Germany should have the thickly populated Industrial Triangle, where an indivisible complex of industries had been developed under German rule. A plebiscite held in March 1921, had yielded a vote sixty-percent in favor of Germany for the whole area in dispute, and the German ratio was still higher in the Triangle. The French Government, intent as it was on weakening Germany and strengthening Poland, urged that, in addition to the entire Triangle, more than half the remaining area should be awarded to its protégé. The British and Italian members of the Supreme Council were at one in their opposition to so flagrant a disregard of the plebiscite. The Allied Forces still occupying the area were mostly French, and the command was French. British and Italian officers agreed with the Germans that the French command was doing what it could to strengthen Poland's grip on the territory. In May 1921, the Polish General Korfanty had attempted to repeat Zeligowski's Vilna coup and had been defeated only after serious fighting, with civilian and military casualties. By August the Supreme Council admitted a complete impasse. Neither side showed the least disposition to yield enough to make an agreed settlement possible. Yet so little impression had the Council of the League made in world politics that the decision of Briand and Lloyd George to let that body try its hand at a solution was greeted with incredulous surprise.

There was here no possibility of drawing a line that would divide predominantly Polish from predominantly German communes. Compromise was essential, and the compromise finally adopted by the League Council undoubtedly gave more to Poland than it would have received without a championship from France that had nothing to do with the historic, cultural, economic, or ethnic merits of the contending claims. The dividing line ran through the Industrial Triangle, cutting factories off from their supplies of material or labor, fractioning communications and transport systems under different sovereignties, and generally bringing into the economic organization of the area a conflict of allegiances that evoked confident predictions of swift disaster. The prophets attached little weight to the Geneva Convention which, extending to more than six hundred articles, made elaborate provision to prevent the political division from fatally disrupting economic and social activity in Upper Silesia. The division was made conditional upon acceptance of this instrument by Poland and Germany; and acceptance followed within two months, Germany acquiescing with protestations of another unforgivable injustice, while Poland and France complained of unwarranted restrictions on Polish sovereignty.

The results were of a sort to confound the pessimists. Under the shrewd and sympathetic supervision and adjudication of the Mixed Commission and Mixed Tribunal set up in accordance with the Convention, the complex plan drawn up by the League experts actually worked. Mines and factories resumed their prosperous operation, and though an unbroken succession of complaints from racial minorities on both sides plagued the League, the prescribed procedures kept these troubles short of general violence. There was reason to hope that, if the external stimulation of grievances could be stopped, permanently tolerable arrangements would evolve in the territory. The chief obstacle was Berlin's determination not to let this happen. Official irredentism, which was neither unnatural nor unusual, hardened as the Nazis gained power, and when the Geneva Convention ran out in 1937 there was no question of renewing it. The entire arrangement was swallowed up in the second world war, and today Upper Silesia lies wholly within the Yalta boundaries of Poland.[10]

Mosul

It had been the intention of the victorious allies to take the province of Mosul from Turkey and incorporate it in the new State of Iraq, which they were carving out of the Turk-

[10] For facts and documents see Georges Kaeckenbeeck, *The International Experiment of Upper Silesia*, London, 1942.

ish Empire and assigning to Britain as a Class A mandate.[11] This intention found expression in Articles 27 (3) and 94 of the draft Treaty of Sevres. The swift resurgence of Turkish power under Kemal Pasha having relegated this document to the vast limbo of unratified acts, sovereignty over Mosul was again in question when the treaty of peace with Turkey was finally worked out at Lausanne in 1923. Unable to agree, the negotiating Powers made provision in Article 3 that the boundary between Turkey and Iraq should be amicably determined by Great Britain and Turkey or, failing such determination within nine months, should be referred to the Council of the League. Nothing having resulted from the Anglo-Turkish negotiations within the set time, the British Government applied to the Council on August 6, 1924, for a decision.

Turkey was not a member of the League, but accepted the Council's invitation to appear before it on the same footing as Great Britain. Both sides repeated the undertaking in the Treaty of Lausanne not to alter the *status quo* pending decision, and the Turkish delegate eventually followed the British in the promise to accept whatever finding the Council might reach. They disagreed, however, on the dividing line which this undertaking bound them to observe, and there were frontier incidents with casualties. The Turkish Government, faced with a British ultimatum to withdraw its troops on pain of military measures, applied to the Council to fix a provisional line. This was done, and a neutral three-man Commission of Enquiry was then sent to the area to confer with the Turkish, British, and Iraqi authorities and enquire into the preferences of the people in the frontier area. The Commission found that the Kurds, who were the largest and most closely knit part of the population, really desired to be independent of both Turkey and Iraq; but it reported a rather vague majority preference for union with Iraq if the choice must be limited to incorporation in one or the other, and pro-

[11] See statement by Prime Minister Lloyd George, April 29, 1920, *Parliamentary Debates, House of Commons*, 1920, vol. 128, pp. 1469-1470.

vided the mandate were continued for twenty-five years. As between Turkey on the one hand and an entirely independent Iraq on the other, the local choice would apparently have been definitely in favor of Turkey. The Commission accordingly recommended that the province should be assigned to Iraq on the condition specified but that, if Britain and Iraq refused to extend the mandate from its actual four-year term to twenty-five years, almost the whole area should be returned to Turkey.

With reluctance, and on condition that the mandate would be terminated if Iraq won admission to the League before the stipulated term, the British and Iraqi Governments agreed to accept the Commission's verdict. But the Turkish delegate to the Council now revived a legal objection which had been raised early in the proceedings, but which the other representatives had thought to be disposed of by agreement to accept the Council's finding. It was to the effect that the Council was acting under Article 15 of the Covenant, and that, if it failed to bring the contestants into agreement on a settlement, all that it could do was to issue a report with recommendations with which the parties might or might not comply. The British view was that the Treaty of Lausanne gave the Council power to make a binding decision irrespective of the consent of the parties; but the Turkish arguments raised such doubt in a body sensitively anxious not to exceed its authority that an advisory opinion was requested from the Permanent Court of International Justice.

The questions put were as follows:

> What is the character of the decision to be taken by the Council in virtue of Article 3, paragraph 2 of the Treaty of Lausanne? Is it, for example, an arbitral award, a recommendation, or a simple mediation?
>
> Must the decision be unanimous, or may it be taken by a majority? May the representatives of the interested parties take part in the vote?

The tribunal handed down a unanimous opinion to the effect that what had been intended in the Treaty of Lausanne had been a definitive and binding decision by the Council and that such decision demanded unanimity, but that, while the parties were entitled to vote, their votes need not, in conformity with the principle of Article 15 of the Covenant, be counted to constitute unanimity.[12]

In protest, Turkey withdrew from the proceedings. The Council nevertheless endorsed the recommendations of the Commission of Enquiry, adding special guarantees by Great Britain as mandatory in favor of the Kurds. Within six months the Turkish Government came to the conclusion that a decision confirming the will of the great Powers, approved by the Council as a whole, and reinforced by the Permanent Court's assertion of the Council's authority, could not profitably be resisted. On June 5, 1926, it joined with Iraq and Great Britain in a treaty which accepted the Council's line as the permanent boundary between Turkey and Iraq. Its continuing resentment was expressed in a five-year delay in applying for membership in the League.

The particular features of this case made it relatively easy for Great Britain to accept the jurisdiction of the Council. Despite the current belief that the province had large oil reserves, the British Government and people did not regard it as a vital interest to retain formal control. They were more than willing to limit their mandate to four years, and would probably have preferred to see Turkey in possession rather than accept an unconditional extension to twenty-five years. For the same reason, they would in all likelihood have cheerfully carried out their repeated pledge to abide by any decision of the Council in what seemed the unlikely event that that body, dominated as it was by the allied great Powers, reversed a previous decision of those Powers. Altogether, this was one of those conflicts in which the moral profits of submission to collective authority outweighed any substantive risks.

[12] PCIJ, series B, no. 12, pp. 6-7, 33.

Greece and Bulgaria, 1925

In a skirmish on the Greco-Bulgarian frontier in October 1925, a Greek officer carrying a flag of truce had been killed. Greek forces then invaded Bulgaria to the accompaniment of artillery fire and bombing from the air. Bulgaria telegraphed her appeal to the League Council, which was immediately summoned by the Secretary-General. Pending the Council's meeting, its President, Aristide Briand, telegraphed to the Greek and Bulgarian Governments urging an immediate cease-fire and withdrawal of troops. This was not literally obeyed; but the Greek advance stopped, and while some skirmishing continued, a major engagement was countermanded in the nick of time.

The Council met in Paris on October 26, three days after the Secretary-General's summons. It at once turned Briand's telegraphed request into an order, backed by unofficial threats of sanctions. Bulgaria, the invaded party, was entirely willing to comply with the Council's directions; but it took the combined firmness of Britain and France, acting here in a unison unimpaired by any contrary interest, to prevail upon Greece. It was an occasion when the representative of Italy could also appear with the angels, though memories of the Corfu business were still fresh enough in the Council to make this virtue a trifle self-conscious. At the Council's request, military attachés of all three Powers were sent to the front to report on compliance with the order of cease-fire and withdrawal. This display of great-Power purpose was too much for General Pangalos, the newly established dictator of Greece, who had neither the resources nor the happy conjuncture of circumstances to repeat the 1923 performance of his Italian model. The prompt and efficient action of the Council had prevented a frontier incident from developing into a serious Balkan war. In addition, a Commission of Enquiry was able to reach an agreed estimate of responsibilities and injuries, leading to the modest award of roughly two hundred thousand dollars damages in favor of Bulgaria. Between two small States, neither of which had a great-Power champion, the law of the Covenant had been enforced.[18]

The year 1925, which witnessed this success of the League of Nations, witnessed what was hailed at the time as a far greater triumph of peacemaking. The Locarno Conference, with its packet of treaties, seemed to remove in one flashing stroke the greatest obstacle to the political health of Europe and the general advancement of collective security. The habitual frightened tension between France and Germany gave way to a period of almost cordial cooperation. Sharp misgivings were voiced by representatives of some humbler States as the "Locarno Powers" took over the making of decisions vested by the Covenant in the League Council or Assembly. Spain and Brazil withdrew from the world organization in the course of manipulations that brought Germany in with a permanent seat in the Council. But the dominant note was one of confidence that the way had at last been cleared for effective implementation of the universal law of the Covenant. Any suggestion that Locarno was to prove the beginning of a general retreat from universalism to regional and particular security arrangements, with their inevitable diversion of attention and influence from the League, was drowned in hosannas to the newly discovered "spirit of Geneva."

Systematic steps now began to be taken towards the negotiation of the general reduction of armaments stipulated in Article 8 of the Covenant. At the same time, preliminary studies were inaugurated in preparation for a World Economic Conference to be held at Geneva in 1927. A simultaneous attack was thus being organized upon the competitive accumulation of armaments and the restrictive practices of economic nationalism, which were more and more widely regarded as not merely symptoms but also as related causes of international

[18] LNOJ, November 1925, pp. 1696-1717.

conflict. In 1928 the Briand-Kellogg Pact restated and extended to such non-League Powers as the United States and Russia the Covenant's renunciation of aggressive war. The Economic Conference, when it came, was a meeting of experts appointed by the governments of fifty countries, many of them public servants but speaking for themselves. Their deliberations ended in a unanimous report condemning the autarkic policies which since the end of the war had stifled international trade. This was accompanied by a draft program of reform. Report and recommendations were given the enthusiastic reception with which governments had for years greeted statements of orthodox economic principles while continuing to violate them. They even had some practical results in the form of tariff reductions by bilateral treaty; and before the year was out there followed an official conference aiming at the removal of import and export restrictions and prohibitions. This produced a draft convention signed by 29 States and ratified, mostly on condition of ratification by specified other States, by twenty. What seemed a promising movement towards the economic pacification that the world so much needed had in two years lost its impetus. By 1930 only seven States continued to be parties.[14] The Convention foundered finally in the tidal wave of the great depression.

The League's period of rising prestige and promise lasted about six years. By 1930 world-wide economic calamity had begun to revive old enmities and to engender new ones. The physical and moral miseries of unemployment and destitution following on a precipitate decline of trade stimulated the resurgence of German nationalism in its most brutish form and facilitated the conquest of civilian authority by military force in Japan. The long-planned Disarmament Conference opened at Geneva on February 2, 1932, with the participation of sixty governments including those of the United States and the Soviet Union. But already the world political outlook was dark enough to prompt suggestions of postponement to

[14] *League of Nations Treaty Series*, no. 97, p. 397.

a more propitious time, and, when these were dismissed, to produce widespread pessimism as to any substantial results. The Conference, long drawn out as one reef after another changed its course, and embarrassed from the first by the unrelenting aggression of Japan in China, ground agonizingly to a stop in the irreconcilable conflict of French insistence upon security and German demands for equality, of treaty revision and the *status quo*.

Japan in Manchuria

If the Corfu affair left some shreds of the fallacy that a body of abstract rules, however broadly and solemnly accepted, could be relied upon to rally spontaneously any pressures needed for their enforcement, these should have been finally destroyed by Japan's conquest of Manchuria. Here the Covenant was reinforced by the Nine-Power Treaty of 1922 and the Briand-Kellogg Pact of 1928, and moral exhortation from Washington amplified the voice of the League. Here, as the Council faltered, the Assembly was called in to broaden the impact of world opinion upon the offending nation and upon the great Powers that had the means to enforce the Covenant. And possibly, if the world had had no other major problems pressing upon it, these measures might have prevailed. But one of the vital lessons of this resounding defeat for "collective security" is the complex interaction of the plurality of major problems with which our world is constantly faced.[15]

Why were the sanctions of Article 16 never seriously considered? Was it because the Japanese Government, following the precedent set by Mussolini in 1923, insisted that the exploits of the army in Manchuria were not war, but measures of peaceful coercion; not a campaign to appropriate territory, but "police operations" against bandits whom the Chinese

[15] For the facts underlying the dispute, see League of Nations, *Appeal by the Chinese Government, Report of the Commission of Enquiry* (The "Lytton Report"), C. 663, M. 320, 1932, VII, pp. 37-111.

authorities were unable to suppress? This formal and transparent pretext, so incongruous with the gravity of the issue, was employed even in the far-famed Lytton Report and in the Assembly's final utterance on the whole catastrophe.[16] An embarrassing obligation to act could be reduced to nothing by emphasis upon one technically legal interpretation of a phrase. The systematic occupation of territory by a foreign army using all the contemporary weapons, with the resultant slaughter and destruction, could with legal respectability be classified as something other than Article 16's "resort to war in disregard of covenants." Law here enabled the social organization to avoid an admission of impotence in a primary function—the protection of the weak against the violence of the strong.

This was a case where the victim himself did not ask for collective action in the form that the Covenant seemed to provide. He did not do so because he knew that the Powers that must take the lead in such action had neither individually the will nor collectively the unity of purpose that effective action would demand, and knew further that half-measures would merely goad the aggressor into greater violence. Given will and unity, there would have been no difficulty in overriding the argument that because no one had declared war there was no breach of covenant. Everyone knew that in all but the most artificial sense the Japanese Government was violating its pledges. Obviously it was imposing its will by violence upon another member of the League, and the argument that this was being done throughout in self-defense and without violating the undertaking to "respect and preserve . . . the territorial integrity and existing political independence" of that member was too thin to withstand any serious intent to implement the guarantees of the Covenant.

There was no such intent. The Government of Great Britain, in the throes of a desperate struggle to avert commercial and financial collapse, would not consider "severance of all

[16] *ibid.*, p. 126-127.

trade or financial relations" with the covenant-breaker. Japan's naval strength in the Pacific since the Washington Treaties of 1922 and Britain's weakness there robbed possible military sanctions of all attraction. France, warily watching Germany and Italy, was loath to alienate a nation that could be a valuable ally or a formidable enemy. Stimson's assurances of American moral support could not outweigh Congressional opposition to involvement or silence the doubt whether good will would in any circumstances be translated into either economic or military action. World Organization—the League of Nations and all the minor elements—had failed to engender the sense of community and accumulate the cohesive strength that would have compelled and enabled it to check the developments converging into this situation or to cope now with their consequences.

The conquest of Ethiopia

On October 8, 1935, the Council of the League unanimously adopted a report to the effect that Italy's invasion of Ethiopia was a resort to war in violation of its covenants. There had been no declaration of war, and what the Fascist Government was doing differed in no essential from what the Japanese army had done in Manchuria four years earlier. Yet in this instance the Council found no difficulty in classifying the aggression as war. The Assembly enthusiastically supported the Council's stand, and no less than fifty of the fifty-four members participating in the meeting joined in a "Coordinating Committee" to plan and direct the sanctions which they intended to apply under Article 16 of the Covenant. The impression spread about the world that a determined effort was at last being launched to rehabilitate and use the crumbled structure of "collective security."

Yet from the first there was a stultifying division and confusion of counsel in the governments ostensibly leading this enterprise. It is not hard to understand the reluctance of contemporary political leaders to embark on a policy that might reverse Mussolini's tendency to resist the expansive designs of Adolf Hitler. Nor is it surprising that the Fascist regime should have been regarded in some quarters as a precious bulwark against the Communist threat—something not to be destroyed by a defeat administered for the minor object of preserving a "semi-barbarous" African State. What is almost literally incredible, much as we may try to discount the advantage of hindsight as we look back upon the steady build-up of Italian forces on the Ethiopian borders and the halting procedures of the League, is that the British and French Governments should continue to see any prospect of halting the conquest by sanctions which they were from the first determined should never be so effective as to goad the Fascists into military retaliation or to forfeit their ultimate support against the rising Nazi menace. Mussolini was fully aware of this determination, and accordingly knew that a little added bluster would arrest any decisive move against him. The apparent assumption that his vaunted plan to build a new Roman Empire could be frustrated by pressures that would not mortally offend a posturing autocrat now seems so gratuitous that we cannot but doubt whether the dominant motive in London and Paris was really to preserve a fellow member and the League itself or merely to placate by an imposing gesture the pro-League sentiment which, at least in Great Britain, had recently become a substantial political factor. There was in the British and French Governments of the period some genuine devotion to the League and its methods. This was almost neutralized at the beginning, and quite outweighed in the end, by the opposing view that the Covenant represented a costly indulgence in other-worldly idealism. The result was a hybrid policy which, when it broke down for want of definition and decision, brought an end for all practical purposes to the League as a mode of combating aggression.

The story of this one resort to sanctions under the Covenant has been told often enough.[17] What follows is an attempt to

[17] See for example Walters, *op.cit.*, vol. 2, pp. 623-691; Royal Institute of International Affairs, *International Sanctions*, Oxford, 1938.

extract its lessons touching the developing of law for a supranational community.

There was here an even more impressive accumulation of so-called law against the aggressor than faced Japan in Manchuria. The Anglo-French-Italian Treaty of 1906 was not only a delimitation of spheres of influence but an agreement to "maintain intact the integrity of Abyssinia." In 1923, largely under the sponsorship of Italy, Ethiopia had become a member of the League, and Italian Governments were thus under something more than the normal obligation of Article 10 to respect and preserve her territorial integrity and political independence. Both countries were parties to the Briand-Kellogg Pact of 1928, and in that same year had concluded their own Treaty of Friendship, Conciliation and Arbitration, undertaking (Art. 5) to submit to "a procedure of conciliation and arbitration" disputes that they could not settle "by ordinary diplomatic methods."

It might seem more difficult and hazardous to violate four treaties than one. In fact, this lamentable episode shows how the multiplication of agreements of guarantee and peaceful settlement may help to defeat the ostensible purpose of such arrangements. The Fascist Government was repeatedly able to use one agreement to stall off action under another. Machiavelli himself could not have guided a more adept exhibition of exploiting the letter to defeat the spirit of law.

When Emperor Haile Selassie first appealed to the Council, Baron Aloisi, the Italian representative, declared that his Government stood ready to settle the dispute over the frontier affray at Walwal in accordance with Article 5 of the Italo-Ethiopian Treaty of 1928. The Emperor asked nothing better. The Council therefore postponed any discussion of his application under the Covenant. For two months then, while its military preparations went on apace, the Italian Government refused to proceed to the appointment of arbiters. Did not Article 5 of the Treaty call for arbitration only if and when ordinary diplomatic negotiation failed? Seeing through the Italian tactics, Haile Selassie now asked the Council to take action under Article 15 of the Covenant. Pressed by the Council, Aloisi informed the members that his Government was now prepared to arbitrate, and that Article 15, which referred solely to disputes not submitted to arbitration, was therefore irrelevant. The Ethiopian request was postponed to the next session. When that convened, it learned that arbitration had not got under way because the Italian Government would not admit that the Emperor might appoint foreigners instead of Ethiopians as his two members of the arbitral committee. Haile Selassie's first communication to the Council was dated December 15, 1934. The end of May was now near. The Italians had gained five months by playing off the Treaty of 1928 against the Covenant.

When the arbitral committee finally met, further time was gained by denying its competence to enquire whether Walwal was in Italian or Ethiopian territory. In harmony with the practice of conceding every arguable point to the Italians, it was then instructed to confine itself strictly to responsibility for the fracas of December 5, 1934. Its unanimous verdict that neither side had been proved culpable was reported to the Council in September 1935. Fully prepared to have the Walwal pretext for military action swept from under his feet, Aloisi brushed the verdict aside with a voluminous printed statement of Ethiopian aggressions and barbarities, and declared that his Government, in the cause of civilization and in defense of its own interests, would henceforth take such measures as it saw fit.

The Treaty of 1906 was hardly less useful. Italy's partners in that imperial dispensation of Ethiopia's fortunes were great Powers with whom the Duce could negotiate without loss of dignity. In that company he was not before the League's bar of public opinion or confronted as an equal by his despised African opponent. Discussion there gave him unfettered liberty to play upon the fears and sympathies of Laval and his French colleagues—fears and sympathies shared by strong elements in the British Government. Best of all—without risking anything, it confused and delayed action under the Covenant. Again and again both Council and Coordinating Committee were held up pending reports from these fruitless tripartite negotiations. The Hoare-Laval plan, which would have ceded roughly sixty thousand square miles of Ethiopia to Italy and placed the Italians in administration of half the remainder under the nominal auspices of the League, was but the most abject of the Anglo-French efforts to reach a settlement outside the League. Instantly refused by the long-suffering Haile Selassie, it was spurned by the insatiable Mussolini, and received with such public shame in England that Hoare had to resign as Secretary of State for Foreign Affairs. But it won for Italy further precious delay in the movement to step up sanctions.

Where a member of the League was found to have resorted to war in disregard of its covenants, Article 16 called for an immediate severance of all trade and financial relations, and of all personal intercourse with the covenant-breakers. The general obligation was to prevent not merely the nationals of members but those of all other States as well from having any dealings with the delinquent State. At a very early stage it had been widely felt that such a total embargo, particularly in the absence of the United States and Russia, was a practical impossibility. The Assembly had therefore in 1921 voted amendments to substitute sanctions developing gradually and regulated in accordance with the particular circumstances of each case. The French refusal to ratify these draft amendments, on the ground that they still further weakened the already defective guarantees of the Covenant, prevented them from coming formally into effect. The Assembly had, however, recommended that the Council be guided by them pending ratification; and in fact, by one of those informal adaptations to contingencies that occur under most constitutions, they were accepted as defining the obligations of Article 16. Thus the Coordinating Committee set up in the Ethiopian affair never attempted cutting off relations between Italy and States not members of the League. Confining itself to the business of the participating members with Italy, it began with an embargo on arms shipments, followed this with a prohibition of loans or credits, and then went on to deal with imports and exports. The proposal to stop imports from Italy was adopted, but exports to Italy presented a more difficult problem. Here only a very partial advance was possible. This began with a prohibition of exports of a list of raw materials necessary for carrying on war and the supply of which could be effectively controlled by the sanctioning members. As regards commodities that could be supplied by nonmembers, the Committee never got beyond study and discussion.

In the category last mentioned, the proposal to consider adding oil, coal, iron, and steel to the list of prohibited commodities was first made by the Canadian delegate to the Coordinating Committee. After some Italian intimations of consequences, his initiative was repudiated by the newly returned Liberal Government of Mr. MacKenzie King. But discussion of an oil embargo continued at Geneva, and on February 12, 1936, a committee of experts reported that it should within four months so reduce Italy's supplies as to make continuation of her mechanized war in Ethiopia impossible. But the Hoare-Laval plan had cast contempt and suspicion on the leadership of Great Britain and France, the general international situation was deteriorating, and the impetus had gone out of the enterprise in sanctions.

By March, Italian arms, decisively aided by the use of gas in violation of the Washington Protocol of 1922, were well on the way to complete victory over the gallant but uncivilized levies of Haile Selassie. On the seventh of the month Hitler's march into the Rhineland administered what was really the *coup de grâce* to a halfhearted adventure in the enforcement of law against an aggressive dictator. On May 9 Mussolini had the sublime pleasure of announcing that the King of Italy was now also Emperor of Ethiopia. By July 15 the Coordinating Committee had bowed to the *fait accompli* by calling off all sanctions.

In March 1932, the League Assembly, on the motion of Sir John Simon, Foreign Secretary of Great Britain, and following the promptings of Secretary of State Stimson, had adopted the famous resolution that "it is incumbent upon the Members of the League not to recognize any situation or agreement which may be brought about by means contrary to the Covenant of the League or to the Pact of Paris." This palliating by-product of defeat in Manchuria had in the meantime come to be regarded as an established principle. It did not deter Britain or France in 1938 from recognizing the *de jure* sovereignty of Italy in Ethiopia. This recognition was the crowning point of the Duce's second triumph over the law of the Covenant. This time the legal debacle was absolute, the surrender unconditional. In the struggle following the Janina murders, there had been good reason to recognize the special competence of the Conference of Ambassadors and to accept its proceedings as an alternative to those laid down in the Covenant. True, its handling of the issue had been characterized more by politics than by law; but, following in part lines suggested by the Council of the League, it had secured the evacuation of the occupied islands and some mitigation of Italian demands. In the Ethiopian tragedy no such honors were scored by great-Power devices outside the League. Mussolini had grown both in military stature and in finesse of maneuver to the point where Anglo-French diplomacy was as powerless against him as League law.

With all its weaknesses, this was the League's most substantial essay in law enforcement. As such, it exhibited in a particular case what was then and is now the general official attitude towards international organization. This is the attitude which precludes moving far enough in the direction of centralized formal authority and substantive power to ensure a reasonable chance of success in the major tasks ostensibly assigned to the agencies of collective action. Even at the creative moments following wars that expose the worst defects of the State-system, silent or declared reservations are made in the name of national sovereignty, which remains the dominant principle of the policies of governments. As the enthusiasm for international curbs on the national use of force fades in the relaxations of peace, these reservations are revealed and emphasized. They are sometimes said to be in conflict with the wills of the peoples whose governments insist upon them. But, though polls of popular opinion may elicit overwhelming support for abstract propositions supporting this hypothesis, the acid test of concrete situations and specific interests refutes it. The sum of the evidence is that governments, in their slow and intermittent advance towards the establishment and implementation of world law, have not been lagging behind their peoples.

This being so, actual attempts to arrest the lawbreaking enterprise of a powerful government are very likely to afford some grounds for the charge that unhampered diplomacy of the old style would have succeeded where newfangled international organization has failed. The supporting arguments are necessarily speculative, and the history of diplomacy, old-style, is full of its own failures. In the national field the development of efficient political structures has been a slow and piecemeal process, in which advance and retreat, suspension, temporary defeat and half-success are normal incidents. It is not yet proved that any other way of substantial progress lies open in the international sphere. Certainly the two major essays in the construction by blueprint of political association on a world scale have thus far failed to demonstrate that the process of trial, error, and slow *de facto* adaptation can be avoided by any swiftly drawn plan. The best that we can hope is that intelligent planning, taking into account the wide diversity of interest and the limited range of conscious community among nations, and guided always by the unprejudiced assessment of experience, may shorten the process.

After the recognition of Italy's imperial sovereignty over

Ethiopia, little was to be expected in the way of protection from the League of Nations. Governments of small States that had been among its warmest advocates now became convinced that the full obligations of membership involved risks that were out of all proportion to any probable advantages, and began to issue public declarations limiting their future participation in action under the Covenant. One febrile gesture of "collective security" was still to be made. That was the expulsion of the USSR in December 1939, for its invasion of Finland.[18]

The Soviet Union and the League

The Russian part in the attempts made by the League to arrest aggression can be briefly told. In the Vilna dispute, as we have seen, Soviet obstruction was the final blow to the plan to hold a plebiscite under protection of an international military force. Throughout the Manchurian episode, Moscow was an aloof and contemptuous spectator. When Italy attacked Ethiopia, the Soviet Union, being at last a member of the League, joined in imposing sanctions, and its representative, Litvinov, became one of the clearest expositors of League principles. His performance did not, however, mean that the Kremlin was trying to stimulate more decisive action. Like the French and the British, the Russians wished to avoid throwing Mussolini into the arms of Hitler. To do so would be to reinforce the obvious Nazi threat to Russia. It was this threat that cast the Soviet Government in its final role in the League of Nations, that of convicted criminal.

In their plan to secure the defenses of Leningrad against possible Nazi attack through Finland, Stalin and Molotov used all the devices of traditional diplomacy. Knowing that their demands could not be sustained before an international forum, they never considered seeking an arrangement with their small

[18] In AJIL, vol. 39, 1945, pp. 35-44, Professor Leo Gross casts doubt upon the legal validity of this act.

neighbor through the League. As Finland proved obdurate against ceding territory and bases, they resorted to force. Following the Japanese and Italian precedents, they abstained from any declaration and denied that they were at war with Finland, asserting indeed the most cordial relations with the real government of that country, which, they insisted with a fine contempt for facts, was that of their puppet Kuusinen and his handful of followers. In the circumstances, the verdict of Assembly and Council was as easy as it was fruitless.

The United Nations

> The Charter of the United Nations came into force as a fundamental law for the peoples of the world on October 24, 1945.[19]

The governments represented in the United Nations Conference on International Organization at San Francisco in 1945 gave the impression of intending to create a structure with powers of collective action less restricted than those of the League. But they wrote into the Charter reservations that were quite adequate, on their face, to save the sovereignty of the greatest States and, in practice, to provide serviceable defenses for that of their smaller associates.

Article 2 begins with the assurance that "the Organization is based on the principle of the sovereign equality of all its Members." Whether "sovereign equality" means, as it presumably does, sovereignty and equality or, conceivably, that equality is sovereign, it suffers implicit contradiction in the provisions concerning the composition, powers, and voting of the Security Council. These provisions formally give the Council authority to call for action by members of the United Nations Organization, but make decisions to do this conditional upon the concurring vote of each of the five Powers permanently represented in the Council. The collective will, that is

[19] President Truman, *U. S. and U. N.*, 1946, Letter of Transmittal, p. VIII, February 5, 1947.

to say, can theoretically be imposed upon members of the Organization other than these five, but not upon any of the five. All members other than the five thus formally surrender a measure of sovereignty that is retained by the five. The difference amounts to a constitutional inequality. But, as practice since 1945 has demonstrated, the great-Power veto must in most cases be expected to be at the *de facto* service of the lesser members as well, since, in the tightly interwoven complex of contemporary world politics, the small State need rarely lack a patron among the five privileged members.

A similar inequality exists under Article 108 on amendments. Each permanent member of the Security Council can prevent any amendment, but the other States belonging to the Organization are bound by amendments if these are ratified by two-thirds of the membership, including all the permanent members of the Security Council. There has been no practice to show whether the lesser States-members may in such cases count upon the veto of a friendly great Power. They have, however, the final and formally complete safeguard of sovereignty in the right of withdrawal. This was not written into the Charter, but consigned to a supplementary statement which, having served as a general condition of entry, must be taken even legally as one of the articles of association. It can be used not only to avoid an undesired amendment, but to escape any obligation which a member considers too onerous to be balanced by the advantages of membership.

There are other safeguards of sovereignty in the Charter even for States not prepared to take the drastic step of withdrawal. One is the uncontrollable reservation in Article 2, paragraph 7, of matters "essentially within the domestic jurisdiction of any State." Another is the rule in Article 43 which makes obligatory participation in military sanctions conditional upon special agreements between each member-State and the Security Council.[20] Since none of these agreements

[20] Cf. Statement of U. S. Representative in the Security Council on June 4, *U. S. and U. N.*, 1947, p. 106: "Until these agreements have been con-

has ever been made, contribution to the military measures taken in Korea was not commanded by the Security Council but merely requested or recommended. Compliance was thus optional. When, to avoid the Soviet veto, the collective supervision of this enterprise was transferred to the General Assembly, its voluntary quality was still further emphasized, since that body has no authority in such matters to issue anything stronger than recommendations.

The veto

What has paralyzed the Security Council as an agency of international law enforcement is, however, the great-Power veto. By a very dubious constitutional interpretation it was evaded at the outset of the war in Korea, the rule of Article 27 requiring the "concurring votes of the permanent members" not being allowed to invalidate resolutions adopted in the absence of Soviet representation. Needless to say, these acts have always been condemned as unconstitutional by the Soviet Government. The return of its representative made necessary the shift to the General Assembly already mentioned. Since that time the Kremlin has taken care to be represented when any question of applying restraints has been on the agenda, and its *Nyet* has long been one of the characteristic sounds of the Security Council's deliberations.

Iran

The beginning had not been inauspicious. The Charter came into effect on October 24, 1945, and the first Session of the General Assembly opened in London on January 10, 1946. No provision like that in Article 4 of the League Covenant having been made in the Charter for the interim composition

cluded and put into force, the Security Council will be unable to fulfill its responsibilities as the enforcement agency of the United Nations. Chapter VII of the Charter, in so far as it relates to military enforcement measures, will remain inoperative."

of the Security Council pending General Assembly election of the nonpermanent members, one of the earliest acts of the Session was to create the Council by electing the States which, with the United States, Great Britain, France, China, and the USSR, were to make it up. Barely had it been created, when the Government of Iran complained to it of Soviet interference in Iranian internal affairs. The subsequent proceedings, halting and indecisive at each stage, nevertheless helped to produce results that could be hailed as a success by the champions of international organization, though their opponents called them the prelude to disaster.

How Great Britain and the Soviet Union combined in August 1941, to take control of Iran's territory, depose the Shah who had shown himself too amenable to German persuasion, and place his better-disposed son on the throne has been unforgettably told by Churchill. It was a case, as that statesman without mock penitence observes, where law had to cede to military requirements.[21] The position was legitimized in the Anglo-Soviet-Iranian Treaty of January 29, 1942, which promised withdrawal of British and Russian troops within six months after the cessation of hostilities with Germany and her associates.

After victory in the West, the Soviet Government began high-pressure negotiations in Teheran for exclusive oil concessions in the northern provinces where its troops were, accompanying them with the alarmingly benevolent offer to assist in administering the area. The stubborn resistance of the Iranian Government and Majlis prompted less direct methods. Soviet agents fostered the revolt that led to proclamation of the Autonomous Republic of Azerbaijan and the Soviet forces there prevented the deployment of Iranian troops to restore the central authority.

These developments were discussed at Yalta in February 1945, at Potsdam in July, and again at the Council of Foreign Ministers in London in September. The British and United

[21] *The Second World War*, vol. 3, *The Grand Alliance*, p. 482.

States Governments urged that the competition for oil rights should be suspended until withdrawal of the allied forces and that this evacuation should proceed without waiting for the date set by the Treaty. The Russians saw no reason why negotiations for concessions should not go on and stood upon the treaty rights which, in view of the date of the Japanese armistice, gave them until March 2, 1946, to bring their forces out. By way of explaining their reluctance to evacuate the country, they pointed to its proximity to Baku and unconvincingly suggested danger of Iranian sabotage in the oil fields there.[22]

From November 1945 on, the Iranian Government kept lodging protests at Moscow, London, and Washington over Soviet activities in the country. Renewed pressure from Britain and the United States had no visible effect on the Russian ally, and the Iranian Government, despite British and American misgivings about the conflict that might ensue in the newborn organization, took literally the first opportunity to seize the Security Council of its grievance.

The situation was an ominous one. The Security Council depended for effective action upon unanimity among its permanent members, and the very first substantive business to come before it found them at loggerheads. Worse than that, it was a charge against one of themselves. Was the whole frailty of the assumption of unanimity to be exposed at once?

The Council's response was commendably cautious. The United States representative moved and the Council agreed that no action should be taken at this stage other than commending the parties to further direct negotiation. By way of demonstrating the concern of the United Nations, the complaint would be kept on the agenda.

Two months later the Iranian Government found it expedient to complain again of Soviet intervention. This time, it added the charge that Russian troops were being kept in

[22] James F. Byrnes, *Speaking Frankly*, New York, 1947, p. 119; R. W. Van Wagenen, *The Iranian Case*, 1946. Carnegie Endowment for International Peace, 1952, p. 27.

its territory beyond the treaty term. The Soviet representative moved that consideration be postponed. On the ground that it could not do this without hearing a representative of Iran on the question of postponement, the Council rejected this proposal, whereupon the Soviet representative staged the first of those walkouts that were to supplement the veto as the Russian mode of paralyzing the Security Council. He was absent for the next three meetings.

Nevertheless, the vein of unexpected firmness encountered in the Council was producing its effect. The opposition had reached the point where its disadvantages outweighed the attractions of rapid advance towards an objective that could wait. A momentary retreat was indicated. The Security Council, provisionally accepting Soviet assurances that unconditional withdrawal was proceeding, deferred discussion pending further report. On April 14, 1946, a telegram from Teheran, expressing "complete confidence in the word and pledge of the USSR Government," withdrew the complaint. Thereupon Mr. Gromyko, who had returned to the Council, resumed the Soviet effort to remove the "so-called Iranian question" from the agenda. He had previously argued, like the Italians in the Ethiopian case before the League, that, since no dispute and no situation likely to endanger peace existed, the Security Council was acting unconstitutionally in dealing with the Iranian complaint. It would be doubly illegal, he now contended, to retain on the agenda an application that had been dropped by the applicant. But the Council was far from satisfied that the Iranian Government was acting as a free agent. The majority of its membership was already exhibiting a distrust of Soviet policy which, matched as it is by Soviet distrust of the West, has ever since that time undermined the most serious work of the United Nations. Overriding a legal opinion submitted by the Secretary-General, a Committee of Experts appointed by the Security Council returned a majority report that only a Council decision could free its agenda of an item once admitted to it. No such decision was taken, though France joined Poland in supporting the Soviet position.

Events during the summer by no means removed the Security Council's doubts. True, the evacuation of uniformed Soviet troops from Iran was completed in May. But evidence of subversionist activities, particularly in support of the Tudeh, Iran's Communist party, continued to accumulate. Even before the end of May, Hussein Ala, the Iranian Ambassador in Washington, was trying to persuade the Security Council that the telegram of April 14 had withdrawn only that part of the complaint that had reference to the continued presence of Russian troops. In any event, the Council was easily satisfied that the case should not be dropped. By the autumn, Prime Minister Qavam, strengthened by this vigilance on the part of the United Nations, by the active diplomatic support of the United States in Teheran, and by vigorous British steps to suppress Tudeh activities in the southern provinces, was ready for a decisive test. On December 5 he informed the Security Council that the Iranian Government, having thus far been prevented by Soviet interference from re-establishing its authority in Azerbaijan province, was now despatching troops there as part of its military measures in all provinces to secure orderly elections to the Majlis. The action so diplomatically planned and described was taken despite warnings from the Soviet Ambassador in Teheran that "the movement of government forces into this part of Iran may result in disturbances within that province and on the Persian borders adjacent to Russia." In fact it resulted, after some desultory skirmishing, in the easy suppression of the artificially stimulated separatist movement and the restoration of central authority. Though the "so-called Iranian Question" remained quiescently on the agenda of the Security Council, it required no further attention. By October 1947, the new Majlis felt sufficiently fortified against Soviet pressure to refuse by a vote of 102 to 2 ratification of the Soviet-Iranian oil agreement signed by the Government at a weaker moment.[23]

Hussein Ala had said at one point in the proceedings,[24] "Iran has received assurances and positive results through the United Nations which it could not have achieved by itself." This assistance to a small State against a great Power occupying a position of the highest authority in the Organization was, he thought, something of permanent and general significance—"the foundation upon which the hopes of the future must rest." We can agree that the vindication of Iran's independence could not have been achieved without external aid; but we cannot conclude that such aid would not have been forthcoming in the absence of a United Nations Organization. It may nevertheless be worth observing that the ancient temptation to settle at the expense of the weak country, for example by some agreed division among the great Powers of the oil and mineral rights to which they all wanted access, was rendered less attractive in this case by the existence of the Charter and the public proceedings for which it called. Even this was of general significance. Something had been added to the traditional curbs on great-Power avidity, and repetitions of even this measure of success would have been significant indeed.

Nor is it clear, as some would have it, that the United Nations had to pay a disastrous price for the check administered to the Soviet Union. It may possibly be reckoned a misfortune that the first political business of the new organization should have arrayed it against one of its two most powerful members. Conceivably the USSR might but for this have been more cooperative in the early stages and assisted in the despatch of business in which it was less directly concerned. But,

[23] Van Wagenen, *op.cit.*, p. 88. For the Security Council's deliberations, and Soviet arguments, see SCOR, 1st Year; 1st series, especially no. 2, 27th and 32nd meetings.

[24] *ibid.*, 30th meeting, p. 98.

viewed from this distance in time, the record suggests that the almost universal diversity of interest and lack of solidarity among the lately allied nations, as revealed in business entirely outside the United Nations Organization, must speedily have manifested itself there as well. It was probably indeed because the Iranian matter was already only a minor case of friction between Russia and the West that it was so creditably disposed of.

How wide and deep were these conflicts of interest, and how pervasive their negative influence on United Nations proceedings, may be gathered from a survey of Western proposals blocked by Soviet opposition, especially by veto in the Security Council, and of Soviet proposals defeated by Western votes.

In the Iranian matter, any business transacted by the Council in the presence of the Soviet representative was kept on the procedural level where no veto is available. Even the Resolution of April 4, 1946, which was adopted in his absence, could be plausibly classified as essentially a postponement of proceedings, though it did contain a request for reports as well as some stand-by provisions.[25] The interesting result was that, although the Soviet Government began as early as February in this first year of operations to use the veto in other business, it did not do so in the case against itself.

Allied Forces in Greece, Syria, and Lebanon

The direct Soviet riposte to American-British resistance in Iran was the charge that British troops in Greece were an interference with internal affairs, creating tensions dangerous to peace. Unable to convince the Security Council on this point, the Russian delegation next attempted to exploit complaints from Syria and Lebanon about the protracted presence of French and British forces in their territories. Here was a chance to score morally by demanding stern treatment of a

[25] SCOR, 1st Year, 1st series, no. 2, 30th meeting, pp. 88-89.

violation of the sovereignty guaranteed by the Charter. From this point of view the Resolution moved by the United States representative, to express the Council's confidence that negotiations would begin immediately and lead to the earliest possible withdrawal, was culpably mild. The Soviet veto prevented its adoption; but the French and British representatives announced their governments' intention of observing its terms, and by May both complainants reported satisfactory progress. The United Nations had again proved useful in asserting the rights of small members against the great.

Spain

Similar motives probably explain the Soviet veto of a Resolution by which the Council would have requested the Assembly to recommend severance of diplomatic relations with Spain unless the Franco regime was superseded and political freedom assured. This was a modification of action asked by the Polish representative on April 10, 1946. The Resolution proposed by him would have been a direct call upon members of the United Nations to sever diplomatic relations on the ground that the Franco Government was a danger to international peace. The reference to the General Assembly, having been vetoed in the form of a Council Resolution, was effected by the procedural device of dropping the matter from the agenda, thus leaving the Assembly free under Article 12 of the Charter to deal with it. In the 1946 and 1947 Sessions of the Assembly the Soviet bloc continued to press for breaking off relations and even adding economic sanctions, while the United States Government, doubting the legitimacy and efficacy of such direct efforts to change the domestic regime of a sovereign State, headed a group favoring more moderate action including an appeal to the Spanish people. The result was a Resolution recommending (*a*) immediate recall of ambassadors and ministers plenipotentiary from Madrid; (*b*) exclusion of Spain from the United Nations and its agencies pending establishment of a democratic government; and (*c*) failing such establishment within a reasonable time, consideration by the Security Council of appropriate measures. The response of the membership to this Resolution of December 12, 1946, was anything but wholehearted[26] and at subsequent Sessions of both Assembly and Council delegations from the Soviet bloc tried to have it reaffirmed and strengthened. These attempts were defeated, and by 1950 the wind was so much in the other direction that despite Soviet resistance the clauses recommending the recall of ambassadors and ministers and the exclusion of Spain from the specialized agencies (the bar to membership in the United Nations being left standing) were repealed by the General Assembly.[27] Spain's strategic attractions in the defense of western Europe against a possible Soviet invasion now outweighed our distaste for its political institutions, admissions to the specialized agencies set in immediately, and in 1955 Spain became a member of the United Nations as part of that year's great "package deal."

Admission of new members

The clash of views over Spain in 1947 and 1948 was softened by the fact that the regime there was only less unpopular in the Western than in the Soviet group, and turned largely on the most effective way of remedying a situation that was generally deplored. The ideological rift was more clearly defined in the treatment of applications for membership. Here it speedily became obvious that the considerations determining votes were far from identical with the conditions of membership laid down in Article 4 of the Charter. In 1946 only four of nine applicants were admitted. The opposition of the United States to Albania and Outer Mongolia could

[26] According to the Secretary-General's 1947 *Report on the Work of the Organization*, p. 3, three States recalled their senior diplomatic representatives, nineteen had no ambassadors or ministers plenipotentiary in Spain, and thirty had no diplomatic relations with the Franco regime.

[27] UNYB, 1950, p. 344.

perhaps be accounted for by doubts of their "peace-loving" character or will and ability to carry out the obligations of the Charter, though its offer to waive these doubts in return for Soviet acceptance of Portugal, Eire, and Jordan suggests that it sprang at least partly from Soviet and Communist influence in the two countries. In any event, it seems obvious to us, though possibly not to the Russians, that Portugal, Eire, and Jordan could not all be regarded as either inimical to peace or incapable of meeting the obligations of membership.

The United States has never yet had to resort to its veto to stop an undesired candidate; it has always had with it enough other members of the Security Council to prevent a count of seven votes in favor of admission. In 1946, the Soviet Government also found the actual veto unnecessary in this context; the threat was enough. By the end of 1949, however, it had vetoed no less than seventeen applications. Membership in the United Nations had become a counter in the general conflict between Russia and the West. In November 1947, a large majority being already convinced that States fully qualified for membership were being rejected, the General Assembly had requested an advisory opinion of the International Court of Justice on two questions. The first was whether a member was legally entitled to make its consent to admissions dependent on conditions other than those provided in Article 4; the second, whether, recognizing the applicant's possession of the qualifications required by that article, a member might make its affirmative vote conditional upon the simultaneous admission of other States. The Court's negative answer to both questions has had no visible effect on the political haggling over membership. In 1950 the General Assembly, seeking a more drastic remedy, asked for an advisory opinion as to whether the Security Council's failure to recommend a candidate need prevent admission by the Assembly vote. The opinion was to the effect that the Security Council's recommendation could not be dispensed with.[28]

[28] ICJ, *Reports*, 1947-48, p. 65; 1950, p. 10.

The Greek guerrillas

By 1947, then, the Soviet Government was taking the drastic step of the veto to register dissatisfaction over the inadequate vigor and severity of decisions moving in the general direction that it desired, and to prevent developments in membership likely to augment the formidable majorities now lining up against its policies. If the first use of this privileged power seemed to reflect a petulant resentment of Western resistance, it was also part of the build-up for the role of champion anti-imperialist and supporter of "popular" and "democratic" movements against "reactionary" governments. The most portentous and revealing of these early roadblocks were, however, the five 1947 vetoes on decisions concerning the aid rendered by the "northern neighbors" to the rebel guerrillas fighting the Government of Greece.

Though the reports of a United Nations Investigating Commission, confirming volumes of more casual evidence, established the fact and the detailed character of this assistance, the Soviet bloc persisted in the assertion that it was a capitalist myth. The civil war in Greece, it insisted, was a struggle of native democratic elements against a Fascist regime, and the sole external interference was the support furnished an oppressive monarchy by the British-American imperialist conspiracy. With a contumacy that was soon to be recognized as characteristic of the bloc, Yugoslavia, Bulgaria, and Albania, far from welcoming verification on the spot, refused to have anything to do with the General Assembly Special Committee on the Balkans to which Greece gave full cooperation. Even the defection of Yugoslavia from the northern group in 1949, following that country's ejection from the Cominform, failed to break down the arrogant denial of the obvious. More important to Moscow than any purpose of the United Nations was the object of maintaining Soviet predominance in the Balkans. The quarrel with Yugoslavia only made it more essential to shield remaining friends and to offer all possible resistance to measures by which the Western Powers might increase their influence in the peninsula. A characteristic specimen of such shielding was the veto in this same year 1947 of a Resolution moved by the United Kingdom, United States, and France that would have amounted to charging the Government of Albania with complicity in the laying of the minefield in the Corfu Channel.

But Soviet support of the Greek guerrillas was doomed to failure. The moral and material aid brought by the United Nations and the United States enabled Athens by 1950 to re-establish its authority throughout Greece. Another victory had been added to the score against the Soviet Union.

Korea, 1950

The pattern had been set. Far from an association through which the great Powers would work together to further the general interests of a world community, the United Nations was proving to be another battleground in the far-flung contest between Russia and the West. The San Francisco plan of peace and security seemed bankrupt. One symptom of its insolvency was the North Atlantic Treaty of 1949. But the whole irony of contrast between blueprint and performance struck home only with the war in Korea. Here, indeed, the United Nations was to be instrumental again in saving the independence of a small country. But in this instance it was to act, in a manner never planned by the founders, as the formal rallying-point for military force voluntarily contributed by part of the membership and used, soon without direction by the Security Council, to defeat the designs of a member whose consent the Charter had made a condition of enforcement action. Here the General Assembly was to replace the Security Council as the prime agency of collective action, bringing the international political organization back to the voluntary basis upon which the League of Nations had operated. The power of compulsion formally given to the

Council at San Francisco, it was now to be demonstrated for all to see, could not be exercised to control the main sources of international violence.

In the case of Greece, the Soviet Government was already lending moral and material support to a group of countries offering combined defiance to the will of the United Nations membership as expressed in large-majority votes. But this was a small affair, never carried to the point where it would call for mobilizing collective military force. The launching of North Korea's Soviet-trained and -supplied army against the United Nations-sponsored Republic of Korea on June 25, 1950, began a major probe into the Far-Eastern position of the United States and, at the same time, into the strength of the United Nations Organization as an obstacle to Soviet expansion.

The Soviet Union had consistently resisted the effort of the United Nations to unify Korea under one government freely elected by the whole Korean people. The Commission set up in 1947 to assist in the preparation for self-government and to ensure free elections throughout the peninsula was, characteristically, refused admission to the Soviet-controlled area north of the thirty-eighth parallel. When the General Assembly's Interim Committee decided to go ahead with the election in the southern zone and the General Assembly recognized the resulting government as that of the Republic of Korea[29] a Soviet veto in the Security Council prevented admission of this entity to the United Nations.[30] In the General Assembly on October 21, 1949, a Soviet Resolution calling for the recall and disbandment of the United Nations Commission on Korea as an "inadmissible foreign intervention" was defeated by 42 votes to 6.

The General Assembly Resolution of December 12, 1948, had recommended withdrawal of occupation forces from Ko-

[29] G. A. Resolution of December 12, 1948, GAOR, 3rd Session, part 1, *Resolutions*, p. 25.

[30] SCOR, 4th Year, no. 26, April 8, 1949, p. 15.

rea, and had instructed the Commission to observe this operation. The United States completed its withdrawal on June 29, 1949, under the Commission's observation. The Soviet Union had announced its intention to withdraw all its forces before the end of 1948, but would not so much as discuss verification by the Commission.

The withdrawal of American forces, and a description of the defense perimeter of the United States by Secretary of State Acheson on January 12, 1950,[31] that omitted Korea, may have supplied the cue for an accelerated plan of attack. They were at least some excuse for miscalculating the strength of Washington's intent to protect the independence of South Korea and to back the United Nations against a direct challenge to its work and authority.

As it turned out, the North Korean assault encountered a coincidence of American strategic interest with the persuasion of moral and political values in a reinvigorated United Nations that led to action almost as unexpected in the West as it was in Russia.

By 1950 the policy which had been based upon the conception of Japan as enemy No. 1 in the Pacific, and therefore called for disarmament and a debilitating control, had given way to the opposite program of building the country up militarily, economically, and politically as a major bastion against the advance of Russian and Chinese communism in the Far East. To permit Communist conquest of Korea would be a poor inauguration of this program, not only because the peninsula was at Japan's door, but because an unchecked invasion there would almost certainly be the signal for attacks elsewhere, as on Formosa and Indo-China. The fact that the invasion was also an assault upon the heart of the Charter provided real and complete justification for taking, under the flag of the United Nations, the measures necessary to avert a major blow to the new American policy. The conjuncture was not unlike that of 1935, when the shattered League of Nations

[31] DSB, January 23, 1950, pp. 111-118.

rallied to the defense of Ethiopia. Here was a chance not only to save the United Nations from final discredit, but to give it a bold new start by demonstrating its capacity to adjust itself effectively to the gravest kind of contingency. At the same time, any contributions of men, equipment, and supplies from other members should mean an economy in American lives and resources.

The arguments used to justify an apparent breach of the Charter in the action taken by the Security Council during the first days of the war in Korea are two. The first is a derivative of the usage described in the President's 1947 Report to Congress on United States participation in the United Nations.[32] Commenting upon the fact that until July 29 the Soviet vote in the Corfu Channel question had been the only resort to the veto in 1947, the President had this to say: "The chief reason for this improvement during the first seven months of 1947 was the development of the practice of voluntary abstention from voting by the permanent members of the Security Council in decisions which they could not favor, but where, for one or another reason and in a spirit of compromise, they were willing to forego the employment of the veto. It became the well-established practice of the Security Council that abstention by a permanent member did not have the effect of a negative vote and did not, therefore, defeat substantive decisions concurred in by seven members of the Security Council, including the other permanent members voting on the decision." The next step was to assume that absence was merely a form of abstention; and this was not unreasonable where the decision to be taken could fairly be presumed to be one "which they could not favor, but where . . . they were willing to forego the employment of the veto." But when Jacob Malik walked out of the Security Council at its first meeting in January 1950, after the Council had refused to unseat the representative of the Chinese National Government, he declared that subse-

[32] *U. S. and U. N.*, 1947, pp. 34-36.

quent acts of the Security Council would be invalid—[38]a statement that looks much like a general rebuttal of the kind of presumption just mentioned. Even if this was conveniently forgotten, it is difficult to believe that anyone acquainted with Soviet habits could in June 1956 regard it as a fair presumption that the Soviet Government would have waived its veto on resolutions condemning North Korean aggression and asking the aid of members to check it.

The second argument, though formally weak, makes a more substantial appeal. It was to the effect that since, under Article 28 of the Charter, the Security Council is to function continuously, the Soviet Government was violating the Charter in making it impossible for that organ to operate with the prescribed composition, and that a member in violation could not claim its Charter rights. The questionable conclusion was that it would be legal to proceed in a manner different from that laid down in the Charter. The substantial appeal is of course the equity of denying a contumacious member the benefit of his contumacy. If the Charter were regarded as a rough working instrument subject to informal adjustment to unforeseen circumstances, this position would be quite normal. But, like other treaties, it was worked out with care, and not merely the USSR but every other member can be expected, when a proposed application threatens national policy, to insist upon the letter of the document. The carefully detailed provisions for amendment prove the general intention to make the Organization proof against casual adjustments that would alter the position of the members.

The legality of the Council's action in June 1950 was never referred to the International Court of Justice. If it had been, the case against it would probably have relied heavily upon the Court's advisory opinion on the third question put to it concerning the arbitral provisions in the treaties of peace with Hungary, Romania, and Bulgaria. There, it will be remembered, the Court held that the refusal by one party to name

[38] *U. S. and U. N.*, 1950, pp. 8-9.

its representative in an arbitral commission, though the refusal was a violation of the treaty, made the provision for appointment of a third member inapplicable and so defeated the treaty arrangements for arbitration. This opinion has been defended as corresponding to the will of the parties when the treaty was concluded. They were unwilling, so the argument runs, to commit themselves to an inescapable obligation to arbitrate.[34] Would each of the proposed permanent members have been willing in 1945 to contemplate a Security Council that could operate in its absence?

From the beginning of hostilities in Korea until the armistice of 1953, the conduct of affairs in the name of the United Nations was less a matter of pre-established procedures applying law than the shifting, diplomatically improvised action of a *de facto* alliance. Even the common objective was redefined as fortunes waxed and waned. Again the experience of the League of Nations in the case of Ethiopia comes to mind. There is no reason to doubt the desire of the participants to give effect to the spirit of the Charter, but a rough approximation to application of its provisions and fulfillment of its obligations was all that they found possible in the circumstances. Again the complex ramifications of world politics made complete performance impossible, though the nominal aggressor in this case was a far less powerful entity than the Italy of 1935. It remains an important fact that the result was not a repetition of the League's climactic failure, but a substantial though partial victory for the kind of principles that the United Nations was designed to implement.

Suez and Hungary

In 1956 the United Nations won what some consider its most brilliant victory and suffered its most humiliating defeat. It brought about a cease-fire in the Anglo-French attack upon Suez, and sent an international armed force to ensure

[34] See above, pp. 176-177.

order in the troubled area. It failed utterly to arrest the Soviet Union's brutal intervention in Hungary.

The Suez affair was another case where a weak country was able, by playing off great-Power rivalries against one another, to hold out against the settlement of a problem of international concern on any terms but its own.

During the war with Israel, the Egyptian Government had stopped Israeli shipping and cargoes in the Suez Canal. Arguing that the armistice of 1948 had not put an end to the state of war, and that the 1888 Convention of Constantinople did not require it to keep the Canal open to a belligerent at war with Egypt, it refused to desist from this obstruction even when regular hostilities in the Israeli-Arab war had come to an end. Israel's appeal to the United Nations, and a Resolution of the Security Council calling upon Egypt to permit free transit,[35] went unheeded.

On July 26, 1956, President Nasser completed the long process of establishing exclusive Egyptian control of what successive treaties had declared an international waterway open to all the world. The Governments of France and Great Britain at once protested his nationalization of the Universal Suez Maritime Canal Company, whose shares were mostly in British and French hands. This act, they charged, was not only a violation of the Company's concession, but a grave threat to the security and general availability of the waterway as guaranteed by the Convention of Constantinople and the Anglo-Egyptian Agreement of 1954. Two London Conferences, which the United States joined Britain and France in convoking, failed to produce an arrangement that President Nasser would accept.

On September 23, the British and French Governments submitted the whole issue to the Security Council. There the certainty of Soviet veto prevented direct action; but four days of private negotiation between the British, French, and Egyptian representatives brought agreement upon six principles of

[35] SCOR, 6th Year, 558th meeting, September 1, 1951, pp. 2-3.

settlement which the Council endorsed. The principles were admirably calculated to safeguard the international interest in adequate maintenance, universal freedom of transit, and fair charges, while at the same time paying generous respect to Egypt's sovereignty.

On October 30, 1956, nothing having yet been done to implement the six principles, the Israeli army invaded the Sinai Peninsula for the stated purpose of ending once and for all the threat of attack from irregular Egyptian forces organizing there. The Security Council at once met, and the United States proposed a resolution summoning Israel to desist from this violation of the 1948 armistice and to withdraw its forces immediately. All members of the United Nations were at the same time urged to abstain from force in the conflict. The resolution was defeated by the vote of France and the United Kingdom.[36]

Ever since the nationalization of the Canal Company, Britain and France had been preparing for the ultimate use of force to compel the Egyptian Government to accept an effective international arrangement for the waterway. The United States, on the contrary, had made it clear that it would have no part in any plan to "shoot a way" through the Canal. This difference among the three Western Powers, and encouragement from Russia, had been major factors in Nasser's obdurate resistance to international settlement.[37]

London and Paris at once followed the Israeli attack with an ultimatum. Unless fighting ceased and both sides withdrew ten miles from the Canal, French and British forces would invade and occupy the Canal zone to protect the waterway against the hazards of war in the area. On October 31, the Egyptian Government having rejected the ultimatum, the Mediterranean forces of Britain and France launched an at-

[36] For a general account see United Nations, *Annual Report of the Secretary-General on the Work of the Organization*, June 16, 1956-June 15, 1957, pp. 4-25.

[37] Cf. Percy E. Corbett, "Law and Power at Suez," Canadian Institute of International Affairs, *International Journal*, Winter 1956-57, pp. 1-12.

tack which failed to achieve its objectives in the set time and brought about at once what it had been ostensibly designed to prevent—namely the effective blockage of the Canal.

The Anglo-French invasion was a badly bungled attempt to gain by swiftly effective force a position from which it would be possible not only to prevent immediate closure of the Canal but to force acceptance of a permanent settlement which successive efforts at peaceful persuasion had failed to achieve. As alternative or subsidiary justifications, the two governments also argued that their recourse to violence was calculated to prevent the Israeli attack from developing into a general war, or, short of that, to check the growth of Soviet influence in an area on which western Europe depended for its vital oil supply.

The General Assembly of the United Nations left no doubt that the great majority of its members regarded the Anglo-French attack as a violation of the Charter. Resolutions with overwhelming support demanded an immediate cease-fire and set up an international force "to secure and supervise the cessation of hostilities."[38] The United States Government, obeying what it regarded as the clear law of the Charter, assumed a leading role in this action against its two chief allies. Beside it stood the Soviet Government, rejoicing in a perfect opportunity to exploit a rift in the North Atlantic Alliance. To its enthusiastic support of the Assembly's cease-fire Resolution, Moscow added less formal threats to meet force by force. By their precipitate action, taken without consultation with their partners in the North Atlantic Treaty Organization, Britain and France had put themselves in the position of wrongdoers unredeemed by success and open to righteous condemnation by governments that on their own occasions had systematically flouted the Charter and would do so again. They had also suffered economic damage which only the help

[38] GAOR, First Emergency Special Session, Plenary Meetings 562 (November 1, 1956), pp. 34-35, and 563, p. 71.

of the United States, offended and offending, but still in its own compelling interest an ally, could repair.

Neither for Britain nor for France was this the first case of conflict with majority sentiment in the United Nations. British delegations have consistently opposed moves in the General Assembly to take up the question of race relations in the Union of South Africa, a sister member of the Commonwealth. France has walked out of Assembly discussion of the conflict in Algeria. Both took the formal position that the issue was essentially domestic and therefore, under Article 2, paragraph 7 of the Charter, proof against United Nations intervention.

This time the matter was incalculably more serious and the indictment overwhelming. A leading part in the move to stop the invasion was taken by Canada, chief, after the United Kingdom, of the Commonwealth nations. The two governments speedily surrendered to United Nations pressure, reinforced as it was by independent Soviet threats of force.

Hungary, 1956

Very different was the result of the Hungarian appeal. There too a great majority declared its unequivocal condemnation of the Soviet repression of the Hungarian revolt and demanded immediate withdrawal of Russian troops and the admission of United Nations observers who would report to the Secretary-General on the state of affairs.[39] But a neutralist group, headed by India, appeared to take seriously the Russian defense that the massive and destructive military intervention had been undertaken at the request of the Hungarian people to put down a rising inspired by the capitalist-imperialist conspiracy. There was not the same approach to unanimity as in the Suez affair. Nor was there any prospect of force to implement the General Assembly's decision. The Soviet Government met it with total disregard.[40]

[39] GAOR, 2nd Emergency Session, meeting 564, p. 20.
[40] *Secretary-General's Report*, June 16, 1956-June 15, 1957, pp. 31-45.

The Soviet Union and military sanctions

How little the policies of a great Power may be swayed by the most massive expressions of collective will through the channels of world organization has been demonstrated by the Soviet Union in many ways. Walkouts from the Security Council, and multiplied vetoes while in attendance, have been only the more dramatic manifestations of the Russian determination to pursue its own course. No less important in its paralyzing effect on United Nations action has been the obstruction to otherwise unanimous plans for placing military power at the permanent disposal of the Security Council and for eliminating nuclear weapons from national armaments.

Article 43 was designed to give the Security Council the striking power which was to be at once a major deterrent of international aggression and the last-resort means of law enforcement. Soviet opposition has kept it a dead letter and has thus held open for any member wishing to use it a way of escape from the intended duty to join at the Council's bidding in military sanctions. For, though the members assume in Article 2, paragraph 5, the general obligation to "give the United Nations every assistance in any action it may take in accordance with the present Charter," the Security Council would seem to have no authority to command military assistance in the absence of the agreements called for in Article 43.[41]

The Charter provided in Articles 45-47 for a Military Staff Committee, consisting of the Chiefs of Staff of the permanent members of the Security Council, or their representatives, to advise and assist in all plans for the application of armed force. The Council lost no time in instructing this Committee to prepare and submit recommendations; but the report submitted in April 1947 showed differences so profound between the positions of the Soviet Union on the one side and the United States, Great Britain, France, and China on the other

[41] Cf. the Statement by the United States representative in the Security Council, quoted above, pp. 221-222.

that they have never yet been reconciled and that none of the stipulated special agreements has ever been concluded. The Soviet Union has remained immovably in a minority of one.

The Soviet Government would have no part in any plan that did not make the contributions of armed units by the permanent members of the Security Council identical in type and equal in strength. The units must be quartered in the territory of the contributing member and must, save by special decision of the Council, return there within ninety days after completing any mission. No bases were to be included in the "facilities" that members must make available to the Council under Article 43. There were many other points of difference, but these are sufficient to suggest the Soviet Union's determination, while appearing to negotiate, to prevent any progress towards placing armed forces at the disposal of an organization in which it was constantly and overwhelmingly outvoted. If forces were once made available, the veto might not be enough to ensure that they would not be turned against the Soviet Union or its protégés. Tricks evading the veto might be devised.

The Soviet Union and nuclear disarmament

Equally obstructive, for similar reasons, has been the Soviet attitude in regard to the proposals approved by the great majority in the United Nations for eliminating nuclear weapons from national armaments. In 1946, at the first session of the General Assembly, the USSR joined the United States, the United Kingdom, France, China, and Canada in sponsoring a Resolution setting up the United Nations Atomic Energy Commission. This body is manned by the members of the Security Council, plus Canada when that country is not in the Council.[42] In three reports to the Security Council between 1946 and 1948, the Atomic Energy Commission presented a

[42] Canada's permanent representation on the Commission alongside the great Powers is due to its part in the creation of atomic weapons and its importance as a source of the necessary raw materials.

plan of control acceptable to all its members except those representing countries of the Soviet bloc, and at the same time recorded its inability "to secure the agreement of the USSR to even those elements of effective control considered essential from the technical point of view. . . ."[43] In 1948, forty members of the General Assembly voted approval of the plan as "the necessary basis for establishing an effective system of international control of atomic energy to ensure its use only for peaceful purposes."[44] The six votes of the Soviet bloc constituted the only opposition. The Soviet Government had already, against the favoring vote of nine of the eleven members, vetoed approval in the Security Council.[45]

The international convention proposed with the agreement of all but the Soviet bloc would have had the following main features:

a) An international control agency owning and controlling all source materials, and exclusively authorized to carry on dangerous research and development and to license nondangerous research and development by national agencies.

b) Powers of comprehensive inspection, extending to the whole territory of each party and to unreported as well as reported activities, to be lodged in the international authority.

c) Elimination of atomic weapons from national armaments when the control system had reached a point of development offering security to all parties.

d) Punishment of detected violations, no party having a veto at any stage of the proceedings.

The Soviet bloc would not agree to international ownership or to the prohibition of national research and development in the dangerous field. It rejected comprehensive inspection and opposed any surrender of the veto. It demanded immediate destruction of existing atomic weapons and prohibition of

[43] United Nations Atomic Energy Commission, *Third Report to the Security Council*, May 17, 1948, p. 5.

[44] GAOR, 3rd Session, 1948, Plenary Meetings, vol. 1, p. 470 and supps., vol. 2, *Resolutions*, pp. 16-17.

[45] SCOR, 3rd Year, 325th meeting, p. 12.

further manufacture. Initially it insisted that the convention to this effect must precede any arrangements for inspection and enforcement. Later it conceded that the separate conventions on abolition and safeguards might be concluded simultaneously. Even then its proposals limited international inspection to activities reported by the governments and permitted governments to specify areas in which international inspection would be excluded. Essentially, that is to say, its plan relied upon the unaided good faith of governments.

The general conviction of the inadequacy of the Soviet proposals and their overwhelming rejection in the Atomic Energy Commission, Security Council, and General Assembly were of course due to lack of confidence that the Soviet Union and its allies would abide by any agreement guaranteed by nothing more than the good faith of the parties. The apparent willingness of the Soviet Government to rely upon such security was indeed taken as evidence that its proposals were merely a propagandist counter to the Western plan. The offer to join in an immediate total prohibition was regarded with the same scepticism as greeted Litvinov's challenge to general disarmament at the Conference of 1933. The lack of confidence persists to this day and is easily explained. True, there is some reason to question whether the Soviet attitude towards treaties is quite as cynical as many on the Western side appear to believe. If it were, why should not Moscow accept the majority proposals, join in the suggested convention, then obstruct progress towards effective control and proceed with clandestine research and development? It might thus avoid some of the odium of outright rejection of a plan so much desired by so many nations. Conceding this, however, the Soviet record in treaty-observance is not one to inspire a degree of confidence which, considering the interests at stake, would have been remarkable between opponents at any stage in international history.

With a slight effort to look at the problem from the other point of view, the Soviet distrust of our proposals ceases to be wholly incomprehensible. Revolutionary Russia had long been the great pariah of world politics. The question whether it merited this distinction is irrelevant here. The relevant fact is that pariahs do not easily imbibe confidence, even when they acquire power and friends that make it desirable for society, of course on terms, to reinstate them. In the specific instance, while the United States was still the sole possessor of atomic weapons, the Soviet Union was being asked to forego even achieving the capacity to manufacture this type of armament, under an arrangement that left the United States holding its stock of bombs until such time as it became satisfied that they were no longer needed. At the final stage of control, moreover, any atomic weapons in the world were to be in the hands of a United Nations agency, operating by majority vote, in which the Soviet Union seemed doomed to be in a permanent and small minority. This, said Soviet propaganda, would be the final step to American world dominance.

Thus it was that humanity, partitioned off into competing power blocs, failed to check a development that even at this early stage threatened the destruction of entire nations. As the Atomic Energy Commission observed in its Third Report, "Agreement on effective measures for the control of atomic energy is itself dependent on cooperation in broader fields of policy." This admirably colorless statement records the fact that, dire as it was, the prospect was not sufficiently terrifying to bring the governments into an agreement which, recognizing interests transcending national sovereignties, would have made effective provision for their protection.

Since 1948, when the Third Report was approved by the General Assembly, the destructive power of nuclear weapons has been multiplied. The hydrogen bomb, with its radioactive fall-out, threatens the survival of the race. Yet the governments on each side of the line now dividing the world still prefer the risks inherent in the present accumulation and distribution of power to those that they profess to see in any arrangement for nuclear disarmament acceptable to the other side. Even to avert total extermination, mankind is not able or not willing to devise and submit to one effectively enforced system of law which, even if it were formally limited to the control of armaments, would render obsolete the conception of the State and its sovereignty upon which governments still operate. The haggling still goes on, each side clinging to a position that is essentially the same as it was in 1948.

The Soviet Union continues to insist upon immediate abolition; the Western Powers, upon disarmament proceeding by stages in step with reliable arrangements for inspection and enforcement. Recent negotiation has focused upon stopping nuclear-weapon tests—an activity apparently essential to further progress in the art of destruction. Here again the opposing attitudes are characteristic. Moscow demands immediate and unconditional prohibition of tests; the United States and its allies offer a prohibition conditional upon arrangements for efficient inspection.

One of the excuses available to the Soviet Union in 1948 has become obsolete. Since 1949, Russia has been manufacturing and testing nuclear weapons and, though it is not believed to have reached general parity with the United States, it is credited with sufficient stocks to make a general nuclear war roughly equivalent to the annihilation of the American people. This is the "stalemate" that has to do service for the unattained system of effective law. But, since the Soviet Union appears to have forged ahead in intercontinental missiles, the stalemate is itself in peril.

What, now, of the reputed Soviet fear that any international agency in which it had no veto would be made an instrument of American world empire? In the General Assembly of the United Nations, an influx of small States and the growth of groups that are either neutral or pro-Soviet have reduced the dominance of the United States. But in any agency where the great Powers would have a determining role, as would probably now be the case in relation to disarmament, the Western bloc would still outvote the USSR.

Substitution of the Chinese People's Republic for the Nationalist Government in the councils of the United Nations would go some way towards balance; but the American Government and people have yet to be convinced that this would improve the prospect of disarmament with security.

In the matter of disarmament, as in that of placing military force at the disposition of the United Nations, the Soviet Government has hitherto set its face stubbornly against effective international control. Its voluble and incessant propaganda has insisted that international control means capitalist control and the destruction of that national sovereignty in which it professes to see the best guarantee of the advance to communism. With Communist China in its camp, pro-Soviet or anti-Western movements spreading in Asia and Africa, and now a boasted weapon-superiority over the United States and its allies, it obviously looks forward to a time when the over-all balance of power will have swung decisively to its side. If and as that moment approaches, its opposition to world government may conceivably diminish. It will expect to play the dominant role in the essential agencies of control. But as any such shift proceeds, the United States and its allies can be expected to see new disadvantages in the transfer of substantial powers to supranational agencies. Their present apparent willingness to move in that direction may not outlast their prospect of a determining voice in decisions. The recent cooling of Western enthusiasm for the United Nations in general, as the Afro-Asian group gains strength, suggests the pattern.

The problem of controlling atomic energy provides the acid test of the potentialities of international organization. If international organization is to count as a way of human salvation, it must soon show substantial progress in this area. Some comfort may be taken from the establishment in 1956 of an International Atomic Energy Agency. This is limited to cooperative advancement in the use of the new sources of energy for peaceful purposes. Essentially it is a device for accelerating progress by the sharing of materials and technical knowledge, and for making the benefits of progress available to all the peoples of the world rather than a monopoly of those that are rich and powerful. It is a new and promising recruit to those agencies that are bringing an ever broadening range of human activity under international direction and so expanding and strengthening the substantial basis of world community. Given time, the accumulation of these agencies might go far to weld mankind into one society in which the State would be a diminishing mechanism of local administration. But the great question posed by nuclear fission and fusion is whether there will be time for such evolution. This being so, the focus of international work on the problem must continue to be on ways and means of preventing nuclear war. The formidable difficulty of the task lies in the fact that, instead of a gradual and more or less involuntary merger, it demands the voluntary and immediate subordination of proudly independent entities to one authority.

CHAPTER VII

HUMAN RIGHTS AND WORLD COMMUNITY

There will be no international community so long as the political ends of the State overshadow the human ends of power.[1]

THE great shift in the last decades of the nineteenth century and in the early years of the twentieth from *laisser faire* to public responsibility for individual welfare found limited reflection in the Peace Treaties of 1919-1920 and the international organizations set up under their terms. Proceeding on the thesis that "injustice, hardship and privation" imperil "the peace and harmony of the world," Part XIII of the Treaty of Versailles stated the principles and blueprinted the international machinery for the sustained and progressive improvement of labor conditions. Articles 23 and 25 of the Covenant of the League of Nations, which formed Part I of the same treaty, pledged the States-members of the League to cooperate in the effort "to secure and maintain fair and humane conditions of labor for men, women and children," to "secure just treatment of the native inhabitants of territories under their control," to check the traffic in women and children, and to promote Red Cross organizations dedicated to "the improvement of health, the prevention of disease, and the mitigation of suffering throughout the world."

At the same time, special attention was given to ethnic, linguistic, and religious minorities in countries which the Peace Treaties made independent. These groups were to be freed from the multiple discriminations from which they had suffered in the past and assisted in maintaining and developing their cultural heritage. The League members who assumed mandates under Article 22 of the Covenant subscribed to "the

[1] Charles De Visscher, *Théories et Réalités en Droit International Public*, Corbett translation, p. 93.

principle that the well-being and development" of the inhabitants "form a sacred trust of civilization." Freedom of conscience and religion was to be guaranteed in the mandated territories, and the trade in slaves, arms, and liquor prohibited.

The relationship between living standards, opportunity for self-development, and peace, cited as justification for this preoccupation with individual welfare in societies ranging in social, economic, and political development all the way from the primitive tribe to the modern industrialized nation, was oversimplified. So too was the calculation that a doctrine of collective trust, replacing the old raw competition for colonies, would greatly reduce the inducements to war. Experience since 1920 provides fresh evidence that rising prosperity and new independence may stimulate aggressive ambition, while the drive for living space is easily diverted from "uncivilized" areas to the territory of weak neighbors. Yet the emphasis upon welfare that can be measured only in terms of the individual, far from being reduced, has been multiplied in the international organization following the second world war.

The reason is to be sought in another order of ideas, already discernible in the international organization of the twenties, but operating with new clarity and power in all the institutions of the United Nations. The conviction that the value of all human organization is ultimately measurable in the addition it makes to the welfare of the individual has become widespread, vocal, and influential. While not yet a constantly dominant factor in their foreign policy, this view of institutions demands increasing attention from democratic governments. The new dimensions in State-administered social security within nations have brought a quickened general awareness of the interdependence of national welfares and of the incapacity of purely national organization to render services now thought indispensable. There is a louder and more insistent call for authority and power to which man can repair even against his own State. The law of the State is to be subject to supranational scrutiny, evaluation, and, ideally, correction, to ensure that its treatment of the individual measures up to supranationally determined standards. This is the most direct and sustained demand in history for a universal community of men under a legal system of which the individual is the primary subject. The achievement to date has been admirably summed up as "the common law of mankind in an early phase of its development."[2] Because that is so, it is scarcely to be wondered at that the bright intent of 1945 has been dimmed by accumulating resistances.

The Government and people of the United States took the initiative in making the promotion of human rights a major purpose of the United Nations Organization. President Roosevelt's "four freedoms" message to Congress on January 6, 1941, inspired the statements of economic and social war aims in the Atlantic Charter of August 14, 1941, the Declaration by the United Nations on January 1, 1942, and the Teheran Declaration of December 1, 1943. Representatives of American associations flocked to San Francisco in 1945 to correct the reticence of the Dumbarton Oaks Proposals on this subject. That preliminary sketch of the United Nations Charter had relegated human rights to a sentence strongly reminiscent of the philosophy of 1919. "Stability and well-being" and "respect for human rights and fundamental freedoms" were to be made an object of international effort, not, apparently, for their own sake, but because they "are necessary for peaceful and friendly relations among nations."

American and other private organizations urged the San Francisco Conference to adopt a bill or declaration of human rights, and were supported in this by a number of the official delegations. In the light of subsequent experience, it is instructive to recall that the South African delegation was one of these. Since 1946, the treatment of the native population and of Indian settlers in South Africa has kept the Government of the Union almost continuously at odds with the United Nations. Every attempt of the General Assembly to explore

[2] C. W. Jenks in BYBIL, vol. XXXI, 1954, p. 2.

and correct the trouble has broken down against the immovable defence that the matter is essentially one of domestic jurisdiction in which any action by the United Nations would be an intervention violating Article 2, paragraph 7, of the Charter. But Field Marshal Smuts, Chief Delegate of the Union of South Africa at San Francisco, was one of those who urged that a bill of rights be incorporated in the Charter.[3] Chile and Panama submitted drafts,[4] concrete expression of a zeal for formulation that has characterized Latin-American participation in the human-rights program from that day to this.

This wave of enthusiasm, a natural reaction to the mass horrors perpetrated by the Nazis and their allies, failed to sweep the Conference. There were statesmen present with some apprehension of the obstacles likely to confront a drive for supranational institutions which, if they were to be effective, must limit the sovereignty of States over their own nationals. In any event, it was not too difficult to convince even the enthusiasts that much more time for deliberation would be needed than the Conference could spare. They had to be content with seeing the promotion of human rights listed as third purpose of the United Nations[5] and third "basic objective" of the trusteeship system[6] together with three somewhat more specific provisions for carrying out these aims. Of these provisions one, Article 55, is a repetition with additional detail of the Dumbarton Oaks sentence, while the other two, Articles 62 and 68, lay the foundation for a Commission on Human Rights to be set up by and to operate under the Economic and Social Council. Article 55 preserves the conception of human-rights promotion as means to the end of "peaceful and friendly relations among nations." The Conference was not ready for an explicit recognition that satisfying the needs and developing the capabilities of the indi-

[3] UNCIO, *Documents*, vol. 1, p. 425.
[4] *ibid.*, pp. 495, 499-502.
[5] Article 1, para. 3. [6] Article 76, c.

vidual are ends in themselves and, indeed, the supreme object of human organization.

It has been argued that these Charter provisions already impose a legal obligation to respect "human rights and fundamental freedoms." In particular, the clause in Article 55 calling for an attack upon discriminations connected with race, sex, language, or religion, has been presented as in itself establishing the right not to be discriminated against. But the opinion upon which governments act is that these clauses merely define the objectives of collective effort in this field and the way in which the effort is to be conducted.[7] If there is a legal obligation at this stage it is the essentially vague one of cooperating in a program of promotion.[8] Any legal obligation to give effect to specific human rights must await each State's ratification of a covenant or convention stipulating them, and it is quite clear that governments regard themselves as entirely free to ratify or reject. The United States Government has indeed already asserted its intention not to become a party to any covenant of human rights elaborated by the United Nations.[9]

As instructed by Article 68 of the Charter, the Economic and Social Council set up its Commission on Human Rights in 1946, the first year of the United Nations Organization. From that time until 1954 the Commission zealously drafted texts purporting to endow the individual everywhere with a battery of liberties and rights that would guarantee him against arbitrary interference, and ensure his sustenance, welfare, and development "from the cradle to the grave." In 1955 its final report on this phase of its activities, accompanied by two draft covenants, was submitted to the General

[7] Cf. Percy E. Corbett, *The Individual and World Society*, Center for Research on World Political Institutions, Princeton, 1953, p. 36, note 21.

[8] Cf. Memorandum of Legal Adviser of the Department of State to the Attorney General of the United States, November 4, 1947, quoted in Hersh Lauterpacht, *International Law and Human Rights*, New York, 1950, p. 149n.

[9] See below, p. 265.

Assembly and an article-by-article discussion of the Covenants began in the Third Committee. This was continued in the two following years, and the Twelfth Session of the Assembly (1957) reserved a place on the agenda of the Thirteenth Session for the Third Committee's final report.

The starting point of this concerted official drive towards international definition and protection of human rights had been a set of optimistic assumptions of decisive common interest born of the victorious joint struggle against three of the world's oppressive totalitarian governments. The tedious and increasingly anemic enterprise of giving flesh and bone to the abstract design has exposed the gratuitousness of those assumptions as nothing else could have done. This is a costly, negative but useful by-product of a program that had sprung from and inspired excited hopes of positive achievement. Another by-product is the discovery of the extreme tenacity of age-old preconceptions of the virtues and material advantages of final national jurisdiction over the individual's lot.

If the enterprise has revealed irreconcilable differences, it has also thrown together some strange bedfellows. The combination of democratic and totalitarian opposition to proposals that would involve any substantial international control in this domain has been one of the rare manifestations of postwar solidarity between the Soviet bloc and the great Powers of the West.

The initial enthusiasm was still strong in 1948. On December 10 of that year the General Assembly adopted the Universal Declaration of Human Rights that had been drafted by the Commission and redrafted by the Assembly's Third Committee. No one voted against adoption, and there were forty-eight yeas. Saudi Arabia and South Africa joined the entire Soviet bloc in abstaining—an expression of disapproval, indeed, but of disapproval not strong enough to warrant the odium of active opposition to what looked like a promise of unqualified well-being to the world at large.

For anyone not committed to the doctrine of hardship as

the best stimulant of creative effort, the Universal Declaration may stand as an excellent statement of ideal conditions for man's life in society, including an ideal relationship between the individual and public authority. Both for its own sake and because it set the scope of the Commission's work for the next six years, it merits a rapid survey here.

As befitted a mere declaration not incorporated in a treaty to be ratified by States, the text did not pretend to be a law. It proclaimed itself, rather, "a common standard of achievement for all peoples." It could therefore be drafted without regard to the remoteness of its principles from actual conditions and immediate possibilities. Its authors made the most of this freedom from practical limitations.

Article 1 asserts that "all human beings are born free and equal in dignity and rights." Subsequent articles proclaim the right to life, liberty, personal security, property, nationality, marriage, and family, fair trial with presumption of innocence, freedom of movement and expatriation, freedom of opinion, expression, religion, assembly, association, and direct or indirect participation in government. Slavery, discrimination, cruel or degrading punishment, arbitrary arrest, arbitrary detention, arbitrary exile, arbitrary deprivation of property, and arbitrary interference with privacy, home, or correspondence are prohibited. Thus far we are not much beyond the explicit aims of democratic government, though not all even of the most democratic countries have been able to realize these aims in the perfection of detail specified by the Declaration.

It is when we come to the economic and cultural position of the individual that we enter another dimension of utopia. Here we find the picture of a supremely paternal society in which all but the most intimate needs of the individual become a responsibility of the State. Article 22 sets the general objective as social security giving to any member of society "the economic, social, and cultural rights indispensable for his dignity and the free development of his personality." These are spelled out in subsequent articles as work under just and favorable conditions, free choice of employment, protection against unemployment, equal pay for equal work, remuneration sufficient to secure for worker and family "an existence worthy of human dignity," the right to form and join trade unions, rest and leisure, a standard of living adequate for the health and well-being of worker and family, free and compulsory elementary education, available technical and professional education, higher education accessible to all on a merit basis, participation in the cultural life of the community, and protection of "the moral and material interests resulting from any scientific, literary, or artistic production."

This eloquent statement of a standard to which all men might repair was in 1948 regarded generally as merely a first step. The next would be to transform the principles of the Declaration into treaty law. In view of the position that was to be taken by the Government of the United States in 1953, it is interesting to recall that Mr. John Foster Dulles, being in Paris as a representative of the United States for the Third Session of the General Assembly, delivered a lecture there in which the following passage occurred: "I hope and believe this Assembly will endorse this Declaration. But we must not stop there. We must go on with the drafting of a Covenant which will seek to translate human rights into law."[10]

The Commission on Human Rights was in fact already engaged in this task, using, among other materials, a draft submitted by Great Britain.[11] With the Universal Declaration magnificently launched, it was able to give undivided attention to this more difficult phase of its assignment. Its labors were directed first to a covenant limited to civil and political rights, to be followed later by an economic, social, and cultural covenant; then, at the General Assembly's behest, to a single text embracing both; and finally back again (largely in deference to the United States, whose delegates feared that the Senate would not accept a treaty on economic, social, and cul-

[10] *International Conciliation*, no. 445, November 1948, pp. 584-585.
[11] Cf. UNYB, *1946-47*, p. 525.

tural rights) to separate covenants. These changes, together with special difficulties in regard to articles of implementation, kept the drafts shuttling back and forth between Commission and Assembly—a mode of deferment not unwelcome to some governments, including those of the United States and Great Britain, which had begun to grasp the full scope and embarrassing implications of an enterprise now somewhat out of hand.

The story will not be retold in any detail here.[12] What is most significant for our purposes is the assortment of differences and agreements that developed between the Soviet Union, the United States, and Great Britain, and the final abandonment of the Draft Covenants by the Government of the United States.

From the beginning the United States and Britain have been cool to the project of a covenant on social, economic, and cultural rights, while the Soviet Union has vigorously supported the majority, consisting largely of the less developed nations, that desire such a code. At the same time the delegates from the Communist bloc have tried to attach to the liberties of religion and expression limitations which the majority has refused to accept. These differences were perhaps to be expected between States which, like Great Britain and the United States, still favor relatively wide scope for private enterprise, and those which, like the Soviet Union and its allies, make governments the dispensers of such welfare as the individual enjoys and carefully control details of activity which the democracies leave to the discretion of the individual. But the tone of Soviet criticism of the British and American positions on these matters reveals another motive in the divergence.

[12] For a summary up to 1952, see my *The Individual and World Society*, pp. 35-46. The Brookings Institution, *The United Nations and Promotion of the General Welfare*, Washington, 1957, chaps. XV-XVIII by James Frederick Green, gives an excellent general account up to 1955, and reproduces in Appendices F and G the Draft Covenants with amendments made by the Third Committee of the General Assembly in 1955 and 1956.

Delegates from the Soviet bloc have sought to win favor with the peoples demanding social, economic, and cultural rights by assailing what they call the indifference of the capitalist-imperialist ruling circles to the welfare and advancement of the masses. Similar opportunities were seen and exploited when representatives of Britain and other colonial Powers unsuccessfully opposed insertion of the ill-assorted national right of self-determination in a covenant originally designed wholly for the benefit of the individual, and the automatic extension of the covenant to dependent territories;[13] when the United States delegation demanded an article releasing federal States from obligations that can be implemented only by their member-units; and, finally, when rising internal opposition induced the United States Government to announce that it would not be a party to the proposed covenants.[14] At the same time the Communists deride the civil, political, and religious liberties championed by British and United States delegations as cover for the alleged capitalist monopolies of information, opportunity, and power. They can vote for texts setting standards of material and spiritual welfare far beyond anything approached in their countries without fear of embarrassing investigation, since they have made it clear that their governments will have nothing to do with measures of international supervision or control.

In a word, the Russians have carried the "cold war" into the Commission on Human Rights. What some governments regarded, at least in the beginning, as a cooperative effort designed to make the status and treatment of the individual a

[13] Articles 1 and 53 of the Draft Covenant on Civil and Political Rights and 1 and 28 of that on Economic, Social and Cultural Rights.

[14] See GAOR, 5th Session, 1950, Plenary, vol. 1, pp. 553-563; GAOR, 5th Session, 3rd Com., meetings 292, 294, 295, and 299; GAOR, 6th Session, Plenary, February 5, 1952, and Resolution 545 (VI) of same date. The United States representative said that her government desired to have self-determination affirmed in the covenant on human rights, but considered that its insertion should be left to the Commission. The vote of the United States was against Assembly Resolution 545 (VI), February 5, 1952.

matter of effective universal law has become another sector of the general conflict.

If this has been the plan of the Soviet leaders, it must have been something of a disappointment to find themselves, though for ostensibly different reasons, on the same side as the United States and United Kingdom in the matter of implementation. True, Washington at one time, like London, contemplated an arrangement whereby *ad hoc* committees would investigate complaints, not from individuals, but from governments party to a human-rights covenant. A measure of collective moral suasion was as far as the leaders of the Western world were prepared to go towards the remote goal of effective international action. Moscow was immovably opposed even to *ad hoc* reporting committees as a device for imperialist intervention in the domestic affairs of other States. When it came to petitions, however, the three Powers were together.

The defeat by the great Powers of proposals to include in the covenant of civil and political rights a right of petition to international authority by individuals and private associations comes very close to a *reductio ad absurdum* of this whole essay in international legislation. Nothing more than an elementary sense of humor should have been necessary to expose the anomaly of endowing the individual with so magnificent a panoply of liberties and rights and refusing him the one effective means of making them good. The final production resembles an elaborate but transparent hoax. A cripple is armed for battle.

The Soviet Government's opposition was consistent with its invariable rejection of plans purporting to endow any international agency with substantial power. It pays all the usual lip-service to international law; but international law must for it remain sanctionless. Good faith—that commodity with which the opponents in the contemporary world struggle least credit one another—is to be the sole guarantee of observance. Sovereignty is to continue inviolate regardless of the State's performance in terms of human welfare. Before it can wither away, the State must indeed attain new heights of power. The climax is not to be retarded by international restraints.

Compared with this iron-bound position, the Anglo-American objections to petitions look flimsy. The international authority would be flooded with frivolous complaints, and the task of answering such charges would add an intolerable burden to governments already overextended. They would be diverted from their legitimate business. The argument would have carried more conviction if it had been advanced against the proposal to proceed from mere declaration to a binding treaty. The whole plan to make international law of the declared principles assumes that individual welfare is, if not the primary purpose of governments, at least a major part of their legitimate business, and that operative international machinery is needed to ensure the general performance of this function. Otherwise why aim at anything more than the moral influence of the Universal Declaration? Obviously there must be screening devices to stop frivolous cases at an early stage. If a government seeking to make political capital out of unjustified charges can exploit a petitions procedure, it can also exploit the arrangement, which Britain and the United States at one time jointly supported, for investigating complaints lodged by States parties to a covenant.

The true explanation lies deeper than the nuisance of captious summons to justify legislative or administrative conduct. Essentially the British, American, and Soviet governments' rejection of private petition springs from the same source. It is an insistence upon State sovereignty in the relations between government and citizen, and a refusal to join in creating an institution that would recognize and implement international personality in the individual. There is much to be said for the view that international community has not reached a stage of development where it can safely or usefully be given so vigorous a constitution. But this again is an objection to the whole attempt to give legal force now to the standards defined in the Declaration.

In any event, the arrangement ultimately adopted by majority vote in the Commission on Human Rights as Articles 27-48 of the Draft Covenant on Civil and Political Rights, which has been before the General Assembly ever since 1955, seems poorly calculated either for substantial protection to the individual or for insurance against perversion to frivolous or alien ends. It substitutes for the *ad hoc* committees of the Anglo-American proposal a permanent Human Rights Committee; but, like that proposal, it is limited to investigation and report and relies upon States to initiate proceedings. It follows, in other words, the old principle of refusing private persons and groups a *locus standi* before international agencies and requiring that their complaints be presented, if at all, by the government of a State. Deplorable delay and confusion result from this principle when individuals suffer denial of justice in a foreign country and must depend for redress upon adoption of their claims by their own governments.[15] Here the problem is complicated by the fact that the person or group will have to obtain the intervention of a foreign government. The plan will afford only erratic purchase to the individual, for no government will act in his behalf when its political interests might be jeopardized by doing so. On the other hand, governments on the lookout for victories in propaganda can easily suborn complaints. To be most successful, then, persons deprived of the covenanted rights will have to detect and exploit antagonisms between governments, and the persons in a position to do this are not likely to be those most in need of special international protection.

As between the Soviet Union on the one hand and the United States and United Kingdom on the other, there is no doubt in most Western minds where the greater solicitude for the liberties and opportunities of the individual resides.

[15] Cf. Corbett, *Law and Society in the Relations of States*, pp. 178-188.

But the acid test of serious intent to make the protection of human rights a matter of effective universal law is in the direct means of recourse to supranational authority given to the individual. It is important that American citizens and subjects of the United Kingdom should not forget that here their governments are at one with that of the Soviet Union.

On the surface, indeed, the posture of the United States in this international legislative venture is now more negative than that of the Soviet Union. In 1951 Senator Bricker of Ohio began the crusade which led to the proposed "Bricker Amendment" and to the statement made by Secretary of State Dulles on April 6, 1953, before the Senate Committee on the Judiciary. The first move in what subsequently broadened into an attempt to place explicit limits on the federal treaty-making power was an attack upon the human-rights covenant in the drafting of which United States representatives were then participating under the auspices of the United Nations. On the imaginative pretext that the covenant, if ratified by the United States, would endanger the constitutional rights of American citizens, Senator Bricker introduced a resolution by which the Senate would have asked the President to inform the United Nations that the United States would not be a party to the covenant and to withdraw from negotiations on it. His real concern would seem to have been not the rights of American citizens, but the powers of the several states in that domain. This resolution never came to a vote; but by the time the Republican administration came into power in 1953, the "Bricker Amendment" had assumed a form and rallied support that required decisive opposition if the treaty-making power was to be preserved intact.[16]

The statement by Secretary Dulles before the Judiciary Committee indicates that objections to the proposed international legislation on human rights were still at the heart of the formidable support for the "Bricker Amendment."

[16] See Whitton and Fowler, "The Bricker Amendment—Fallacies and Dangers," AJIL, vol. 48, January 1954, pp. 23-56.

"The present administration," said the Secretary of State, "intends to encourage the promotion everywhere of human rights and individual freedoms, but to favor methods of persuasion, education and example rather than formal undertakings which commit one part of the world to impose its particular social and moral standards upon another part of the world community, which has different standards. . . . We therefore do not intend to become a party to any such covenant or present it as a treaty for consideration by the Senate."[17]

The Secretary's language, in approved political style, attributed to lofty general principle a decision usually explained by less elevated considerations. A delicate reluctance to impose alien standards on other parts of the world is not generally supposed to have been the determining motive for the shift in the United States position on human-rights conventions. A more obvious reason was the accumulating congressional opposition to prospective treaties that would vest in the federal government powers normally exercised by the states. Underlying this was the objection to a plan that would authorize an international agency to probe, however gently, into explosive situations within the United States.

In the particular case, nothing was gained by this language. No one was convinced of the noble disinterestedness that it suggested. It did nothing to defeat foreign charges that the United States had been hypocritically fostering a program that would tie other hands while leaving its own quite free.

Individual liberties and welfare in the United States set what is in many respects a world standard. The nation has formidable problems of discrimination and exploitation which it is slowly and painfully on the way to solving, and there is more than a little ground for the belief that external intervention would delay rather than hasten solution. If not in 1945, then at least in 1948, it should have been clear that internal political conditions would prevent the United States from becoming a party to any treaty transforming such prin-

[17] DSB, April 20, 1953, p. 592.

ciples as those of the Universal Declaration of Human Rights into compulsory international rules. A frank statement to this effect in 1949, coupled with such proposals of another mode of operation as were to be submitted to the Commission on Human Rights by the United States delegate in 1953, might have prevented the tangled and costly confusion into which this United Nations enterprise has since fallen.

This is not to say that there was any more reason in 1953 than in 1945 to doubt the desire of the United States Government to make a substantial contribution to the world-wide promotion of human rights. The nation is convinced that it has material as well as moral interests in the advancement of liberty and welfare everywhere. The plan of action which the government now finds best adapted to its own capabilities would have been best from the beginning for all concerned. For a program designed to effect by swift legislation a transformation of society the like of which has hitherto required slow evolution, it substitutes one of piecemeal and gradual improvement. Promotion takes the form, not of an attempt to establish general legal obligations, but of assistance adapted to carefully studied local conditions and aspirations.[18]

It is difficult to understand why, with this wholesome proposal of an approach better adapted to the magnitude and complex difficulties of the task, the United States Government should not have desisted from any further part in the drafting of the covenants on human rights. The continued participation in this work by a government that has publicly announced its determination to have no part in the result places it in a posture of ambiguous irresponsibility that adds nothing to its influence. It is moreover abetting a kind of activity which long since began to look like an evasion of the Charter obligation to promote human rights.

So long as the approach to this task could be kept on the artificial plane of abstract formulation, with recurrent conflicts over content between members of the Commission, and

[18] DSB, June 15, 1953, pp. 842-847.

between the Commission and General Assembly, to be followed perhaps by submission to governments for problematic ratification, the embarrassment of complaint, investigation, and report was postponed. Time without visible limits could be spent in *preparing to promote* human rights. Fighting off investigation in sensitive areas was already proving troublesome enough in a General Assembly that periodically reminded its members of their duty under the Charter, the Universal Declaration, and various agreements and treaties, to prevent discrimination and foster democratic liberties for all within their gates.

It is therefore not surprising that the American proposals were not greeted with anything approaching general enthusiasm. In contrast with the prospect of indefinite delay connected with the draft covenants, they called for an immediate beginning on the actual work of promotion. All members of the United Nations were to be asked to make periodic reports on developments in the field of human rights. Services of research and technical assistance were to furnish informed guidance and material aid to governments willing to be helped in the advance towards the standards defined in the Universal Declaration.[19]

The Soviet Government did not miss the opportunity offered by these proposals for an attack on United States intentions. The Communist delegations greeted them with charges of concealment and evasion. The United States was described as opposing all effective promotion of human rights and its so-called action program condemned as a blind for active sabotage of the draft conventions. This initial opposition gave way, however, to grudging and critical acceptance when successive amendments extended the program of reports and studies to dependent territories and to the progress of self-determination. With these additions the United States resolutions of-

[19] For the text of the U. S. resolutions as submitted to the 10th Session of the Human Rights Commission, see Documents E/CN 4/L. 266/Rev. 3; E/CN 4/L 268/Rev. 1; and E/CN 4/L 267/Rev. 2 (April 13, 1954).

fered new occasions for baiting the colonial powers. In the end, the Soviet Government and its allies supported the plan in the form that it reached in 1956, leaving Great Britain in the small opposing minority.[20]

From the beginning, the British Government took a dim view of the American proposals. Alluding to the political maneuvering that had characterized the deliberations of the Commission on Human Rights, the British representative expressed the fear that reports, studies, and technical assistance would open new doors to incriminating propaganda against States making the most serious efforts to promote the liberty and welfare of the individual. The governments exploiting these openings would be precisely those whose social policies made the greatest mockery of human rights.[21] This reluctant British opposition to the American proposals had not been overcome when in 1956 they were adopted by the Human Rights Commission and confirmed by the Economic and Social Council.[22] The British Government thinks technical aid ill-adapted to the promotion of human rights and doubts whether special studies will earn their cost. Principally, however, it is the insistence upon self-determination, and the extension to dependent territories, that have put what is still perhaps the freest people in our world in this posture of opposition to the international promotion of human rights.

As the draft covenants and assorted resolutions have shuttled to and fro between Commission, Economic and Social Council, and General Assembly, so much of the rivalry, suspicion, and general tension of contemporary world politics has been brought into this enterprise that a feasible plan of operation must now surmount obstacles that would probably not have confronted it in 1949. At that time, however, a combina-

[20] Summary Record of 11th Session, Human Rights Commission, meetings 494, pp. 7-8; 496, pp. 6-8; 501, pp. 6-7; 506, pp. 11-12.

[21] GAOR, 8th Session, 3rd Com., 528th meeting, November 19, 1953, pp. 261-262.

[22] ESCOR, 22nd Session, supp. no. 3, p. 26 and supp. no. 1, p. 12; and Summary Record of the 525th meeting of the Human Rights Commission, pp. 5-7.

tion of zeal and imprudence demanded swift and spectacular achievements.

In 1955 the General Assembly authorized the establishment of "Advisory Services in the Field of Human Rights," and practical work under this Resolution, which provides for a modest system of technical assistance, has begun.[23] In addition, Resolutions of the Economic and Social Council call for reports from members at three-year intervals on developments in the promotion of human rights, and for special studies of specific rights, beginning with the right of freedom from arbitrary arrest, detention, and exile.

All of this is to proceed upon a voluntary basis. Neither the General Assembly nor the Economic and Social Council can impose legal obligations in this domain. Whether and what to report will remain optional with the members. And there will be no coercion to accept the advice or assistance made available. Yet the prospects are that more will be achieved along this path of assistance by request than by the ambitious covenants that still await serious action.

Meanwhile, the Declaration of 1948 has not remained a wholly dead letter. In *The Impact of the Universal Declaration of Human Rights*, now in a revised edition of 1953, the United Nations has given an optimistic account of the way in which that document has been invoked in resolutions of the General Assembly, in national constitutions and legislation, in international treaties, in courts of justice and in the work of unofficial organizations. On the results of such invocation in actual release from oppression, increased welfare, and broadened opportunities of self-improvement and self-expression, the record has little to say. The most substantial item under this head is the group of decisions in the Philippines Supreme Court where the Charter and Declaration appear to have had some influence in securing the release of deportable aliens from detention.[24] There are scores of countries whose written constitutions endow the individual with liberties and rights that

[23] GAOR, 10th Session, supp. no. 19, pp. 13-14.
[24] *op.cit.*, pp. 36-39.

he rarely experiences in fact. The total failure of the General Assembly of the United Nations to secure by repeated Resolutions greater respect for human rights in South Africa, Hungary, Romania, and Bulgaria demonstrates the gap that may exist between document and deed.

Yet, while it is easy to overrate the immediate importance of such citations of the international instruments declaring human rights, a long-term view of the undertaking will not count them negligible. They are, indeed, necessary first steps; and not all will remain without sequel. The setbacks that we are now witnessing may serve to remind us that this project upon which we so lightheartedly embarked in 1945 is nothing less than the perfection of world community.

On a more limited scale, some progress is being made in western Europe. Fifteen of the States-members of the Council of Europe signed a draft convention at Rome in 1950 which makes some approach to effective procedures for protecting basic civil liberties. By the end of 1955 fourteen States had ratified this instrument, and the Commission of Human Rights for which it provides has been competent since 1953 to receive and investigate complaints by one State party against another. Among seven parties, moreover (Sweden, Ireland, Denmark, Iceland, Belgium, the Federal Republic of Germany, and Norway), the right of petition by individuals has been in effect under Article 25 since December 1955. The organization is even gaining some practical experience. In 1957 a six-member commission was set up to investigate complaints by the Government of Greece that the British authorities were violating human rights in Cyprus, and this body has proceeded to the island for investigations on the spot. Success in this restricted group of States, besides being a major achievement in itself, would point the way to advance on a wider plane.[25]

[25] *United Nations Yearbook on Human Rights*, 1953, pp. 354-355, 1954, pp. 392-393, 1955, pp. 333-336; A. H. Robertson, *The Council of Europe*, New York, 1956, pp. 146-169; *New York Times*, Jan. 13, 1958, 48:5.

CHAPTER VIII

CONCLUSIONS

UNDER such headings as recognition; treaties; maritime jurisdiction; the immunities of sovereigns, their representatives and their property; arbitration; and international organization, we have in this book examined the use made of legal principles and procedures by three great Powers in their dealings with the governments and nationals of other States. To this we added a study of the respective positions taken by the same three Powers in the effort to reach a general agreement upon the liberties and rights due to the individual human being in all countries and upon means of securing their enjoyment. We have been concerned both with the citation and attempted application of rules said to be already established and with movements towards new rules and procedures.

Our study has shown no slackening in the tendency of governments to formulate their mutual relations in terms of law. It has shown considerable progress in the regulation of details involved in those relations and some advances towards acceptance and improvement of peaceful modes of settling disputes. Terrible as the crimes of belligerent governments and their armed forces continue to be, the sustained effort to mitigate the savagery of war by rule has not been a total loss. But these forward steps do not mean that we are within sight of an effective world community with its necessary general submission to law and collective monopoly of force. There continues to be grave danger—the accompaniment of complacent self-deception—in the kind of statement that represents these still distant consummations as just around the corner.

In so far as law operates among States, it is a law of excessive flexibility—a flexibility not mercifully administered by impartial authority in the general interest, but a flexibility at the service of the subjectively defined interest of each State. It is a truism of political discourse that governments will abide by no rule and defer to no external authority when the existence of the State is thought to be at stake. In this study we have concentrated upon three great Powers, and it would require similar investigation to establish the degree of difference, if any, between small and great in this respect. Along the way, however, we have from time to time seen governments of small States exhibiting the same insistence upon their own sovereign judgment of interests, rights, and duties, and this phenomenon is familiar to all who know the history of the League of Nations and the United Nations. Writers on international law have argued that this discretion does not constitute a real difference between the legal system of the State and that of the "community of States." Within the State, they point out, the individual also has the right of self-defense. But—and this is surely a profound difference—the national law determines the limits of this self-defense and imposes its penalty when they are exceeded. Article 51 of the United Nations Charter marks the first modest attempt to limit the discretion of governments in determining what is self-defense for the State; and the paralysis of the Security Council keeps this a dead letter.

Law thus fares rather badly in diplomacy. It seeks to correct human weaknesses: diplomacy accommodates them. Between the two there is an inevitable strain, and at a certain tension law breaks. This has been made especially plain by the pervasiveness and intensity of the current struggle for power between two main groups whose leaders believe power-superiority necessary to their way of life and justify their struggle to hold or gain it by a general philosophy about man in society.

It is a matter of common observation, confirmed by the episodes analyzed in the preceding chapters, that no institutions yet developed on the international plane have been able to perform the ordering and pacifying functions of the legal system in the national domain. The jurist's art finds active employment in the intercourse of States; but four centuries of jurisprudence have not sufficed to bring major national interests under legal regulation. The lawyer's craft can never supply the wanting social and political basis for an effective legal system. The literature of international law in the main took this basis as given, together with a legal superstructure that needed only steady juristic elaboration and occasional official adjustment to changing circumstances. Thus it ignored and even obscured the revolutionary changes in human attitudes and in the distribution of political power without which no legal order on a world scale can become a reality.

Innumerable writers have noted the more obvious differences between national systems of law and their asserted international system and have contrived to reconcile the differences with their notions of the specific characteristics of law. The absence in the international domain of objectively binding legislative or judicial authority, the inappropriateness of reprisals and war in the role of those sanctions that are a usual if not indispensable part of legal norms, the irreducible sovereignty of States, the freedom of governments to resort to violence and their reservation of an indefinable area of unfettered discretion—these and related contradictions, far from preventing the assertion of a legal order, provided the material for pleasing prodigies of juristic reasoning. These feats of intellect diverted attention from the deeper differences which, if noted at all, were usually dismissed as irrelevant to legal science.

It is not only or even mainly the mechanisms of compulsory interpretation, enforcement, and peaceful change that are missing among the props of an international legal order. Their absence is a symptom of more fundamental deficiencies. What is principally missing is the measure of agreement on supreme common values, the sense of community, loyalty, and mutual tolerance which within the State make compulsory institutions bearable. The reserved domain and the whole legal concept of sovereignty correspond to the fact that the State remains in the hearts and minds of men the highest center of human authority and chief guardian of the most treasured values. This habit of feeling and thought survives the mounting evidence of the State's inadequacy as an instrument of welfare or security. Piecemeal recognitions of that inadequacy are to be found in the accumulation of international agencies; but these are still thought of as exceptional and marginal. With the means of destruction now at their disposal, the continued existence of States independent of central authority means that mankind lives under the threat of imminent extinction. Yet the State continues to be for practical purposes the chief end of man. So long as this is so, whatever their covenants or declarations, governments will not assume in practice a position of general subjection to a law of nations.

These are the factors that explain the perpetual war between the actual conduct of governments in their international activities and the abstract, formalized image of that conduct reflected in the literature of international law. The contrast is so sharp that if the image were exclusively the work of juristic writers it must surely have been obliterated long since. That it is still current is due to another phenomenon—political rhetoric. With rare exceptions (when violation too flagrant for denial is excused as a necessity of self-preservation), governments assert the existence of an international legal order and the entire conformity of their official behavior with it. The attitude of the limited public that gives any thought to these matters is that there is of course a law of nations but that, while we observe it scrupulously, all our opponents and some of our allies ignore or shamelessly violate it. Like this public, international-law writers have accepted official utterances as true explanations of decision and reliable guides to policy. If they have concerned themselves with diplomacy, which is the actual conduct of business between governments, it has been mainly to pick out the explicit or tacit consents which make the treaty or customary rules of their assumed legal system.

The more systematic study of diplomacy casts no doubt upon the practice of invoking alleged legal rules. What it reveals is the intimate connection between the statement of the rule and the specific interest of the moment, and the resulting frequency of direct contradiction in the positions taken by the government of the same State. This is due to the fact that the primary purpose of the appeal to law is to make a respectable, "legitimate" case for action taken or proposed, or to justify a complaint against another government. There is always palpable advantage in gaining for any policy recognition as the application of a universally valid principle. Only in a very secondary manner, if at all, are governments concerned with building up, by their appeals to law, a binding system which would prove embarrassingly restrictive in another set of circumstances. In a milieu characterized by such liberty of subjective interpretation and differentiation, "rules" and "system" have little meaning. The premium still put upon this liberty is indicated by the paralyzing reservations with which compulsory jurisdiction, when it is not rejected, is hedged about.

Those temporary fixations of a pattern of behavior which are the object of treaty-making share the same fate as the so-called customary rules. Words like "forever," "eternal," "permanent," "perpetual" are perhaps less conspicuous in the texts than they once were, and the change may indicate some inclination to realism. Some nearer approach to law occurs when the treaty includes provision for the adjudication of disputes as to meaning and fulfillment. The approach is at best partial in the absence of any agency to compel submission to and compliance with judgment. Moreover, the rich wardrobe of *rebus sic stantibus* can always be relied upon to provide cover even for the refusal to submit.

If one approaches diplomacy not as the interaction of entities living in a society governed by law, but as the political interaction of groups denying subordination to any collective authority, yet fortifying their claims with legal argument, one has the advantage of seeing temporary patterns grow, recognizing their scope, observing their strength and weakness under strain, and witnessing their demise. Seen from this uncommitted point of view, they take on the appearance less of the stabilized institutions of a legal order than of highly adjustable *modi vivendi.*

Even law must of course be adjustable to new circumstances. Within the State this adjustment takes place mainly by legislative process which reflects the interests of the ruling element. In every society law is thus liable to change as the balance of power shifts. But the change is regulated in a way to preserve a tolerable balance between the need for stability and the need for adjustment. In the aggregate of States the *modi vivendi* are subject to immediate unilateral abandonment without reference to collective interest. Some champions of international law speak of this as a process of legislation by violation. The violation being acquiesced in by the generality of States, a new norm is substituted for the old. The so-called laws of contraband and blockade provide luminous examples. Belligerents in each successive war ignore the limits to interference with neutral trade accepted in the preceding conflict. Each war produces its own "law" defining relations between belligerents and neutrals. But the analogy with the practice by which customary law is formed and changed is vitiated by the omission of the elements of duration and of reasonableness in terms of community interest. What happens in blockade and contraband is a swift and forcible adjustment of previous limitations to the current demands of powerful belligerents. The difference in the degree of stability normally characterizing the institutions of legal orders and the *modi vivendi* of the aggregate of States is another consequence of the absence of collective authority regulating the use of power.

In a very general sense it can be said even of the strongest legal systems that their subjects bow to legal regulation only when they perceive a coincidence of interest and legality. In that context the prospect of coercion figures prominently in the calculation of interest, and this consideration is reinforced by all those sentiments of community, solidarity, and loyalty that make the collective interest a thing of substance. Since these deterrents and incentives are largely wanting in the aggregate of States, the balance between legality and interest is determined in a much more individualistic fashion. However eloquent and sincere their appeals to the general interest of the "family of nations," governments demonstrate in action the conviction that this individualism is their bounden duty to their people.[1]

There is no doubt about the utility of the body of usage that normally regulates the day-to-day business of governments with one another. Here the coincidence of interest and conformity is constant enough to be taken as a matter of course. Compliance with accepted patterns is secured against considerable strain by the ready availability of retaliation in kind. Any gain from violation is likely to be more than offset by inconvenience. But the boundary between routine and "vital" business is fluid. At any moment a minor detail, charged with accidental significance, may become the subject of political dispute that defies settlement by pre-established norm.

The modern expansion of intercourse between States has been accompanied by a corresponding increase in the volume of business smoothly transacted in modes that become traditional. Where many States are concerned, regulation is more and more effected by multilateral agreements setting up standing international agencies.

Some see in this accumulation of international agencies with their inroads upon the exclusive jurisdiction of States a process of evolution leading gradually but irresistibly to the point

[1] Cf. Charles De Visscher, *Théories et Réalités en Droit International Public*, 2nd edn., Paris, 1955, pp. 32, 171-172, 407-408; Corbett translation, pp. 17, 134-135, 328-329.

where even the most "vital" interests will be subject to effective world organization. The State will then be nothing more than a subordinate agency operating in the general human interest under one supranational authority. There could still be a wide diversity of cultures, including legal systems; but these would be the diversities permitted by the universal legal order. Such indeed are the essential conditions for an effective law for States; for law means government. The great obstacle to faith in such a culmination is the tenacity with which governments and peoples cling to the notion of majestic independence lodged in the State.

In a congeries of sovereign States, all that can be achieved is at best a rough approximation to a legal order. The approximation proceeds by piecemeal accretions to the area of international regulation. The work of the jurist in such a context should not be limited to the formulation of law appropriate to a perfected community. Much of the effort being made to widen the scope of substantial submission to international norms pays little heed to the conditions that foster or discourage such submission. There is a place for the legal techniques in the analysis of those conditions, and in the disciplined and economical direction of the several programs for the promotion of human rights and progressive development of international law that are proceeding under the auspices of the United Nations and a bevy of regional organizations.

INDEX

INDEX

The Library of Congress has cataloged this book as follows:

CORBETT, PERCY ELLWOOD, 1892— Law in diplomacy. Princeton, N.J., Princeton University Press, 1959. 290 p. 23 cm. 1. International relations. 2. Diplomacy. 3. International law. I. Title. JX1305.C6 (341) 59-5593 ‡ Library of Congress.

GPSR Authorized Representative: Easy Access System Europe - Mustamäe tee 50, 10621 Tallinn, Estonia, gpsr.requests@easproject.com

www.ingramcontent.com/pod-product-compliance
Lightning Source LLC
LaVergne TN
LVHW011748200926
848484LV00003B/649

* 9 7 8 0 6 9 1 6 5 2 6 5 8 *